I Can't Breathe!

ARPress
45 Dan Road Suite 5
Canton MA 02021

Hotline: 1(888) 821-0229
Fax: 1(508) 545-7580

Ordering Information:
Quantity sales. Special discounts are available on quantity purchases by corporations, associations, and others. For details, contact the publisher at the address above.

Printed in the United States of America.

ISBN-13:	Softcover	979-8-89330-775-7
	eBook	978-8-89330-776-4

Library of Congress Control Number: 2024903985

I Can't Breathe!

Baldip Kaur

ARPress

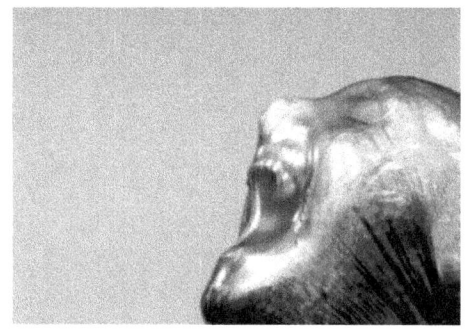

I Can't Breathe!

As George lay shackled on the floor

He looked up into the stony eyes of a policeman

Whose knee was on his throat

Crushing it

And as he gasped for air

He cried

I can't breathe!

whilst longing for the brutality to stop

he heard the murmur of death calling out to him

and his spirit arose and left his body

together with his dreams and hopes

his soul soared towards the heavens

to become a star in the skies

yet…the pain of injustice he had suffered whispered to him

to shape and awaken the people

for, they said, there was injustice and cruelty

surging powerfully across the world

and that once he had exposed its ruthlessness

he could be on his way.

Prologue

Khushboo was on her way to attend a rally to be held in the memory of George Floyd who, a year ago, had been arrested by the police outside a shop in Minneapolis, Minnesota.

However, ever since she had decided to attend the rally, she had been thinking about the video that had gone viral on the internet. The video was powerful and moving, as it showed the events that led to George's death, and she was disturbed, as many were, at the cruelty shown by a police officer in America who had first handcuffed George, thrown him on the floor, then knelt cruelly on his throat for more than nine minutes.'

George was breathless, gasping for air and repeatedly complaining that he could not breathe, to which the officer had replied cruelly, "Then stop talking and keep quiet, it takes heck a lot of oxygen to talk!"

When worried bystanders had noticed that Mr. Floyd was becoming un-responsive, they had urged the officers to check his pulse whilst another had phoned the police to report a crime taking place and that a police officer was ignoring his training of responsibility and duty of care by using unnecessary force.

When the policemen surrounding George finally decided to take his pulse, they could not find one, but the officer had still not taken his knee off George Floyd's neck, who was lying, face down still in handcuffs. And it was only at 20:27, that Mr. Chauvin had finally removed his knee from Mr. Floyd's neck; and a motionless George Floyd was rolled on to a gurney and taken to the County Medical Centre, where he was pronounced dead.

As she was early, Khushboo drove slowly, turning on the car radio for some quiet background music, which, she hoped, would help erase the heartrending images of the video from her mind.

She drove past houses with grounds and gardens that had trees that lined their driveway. As it was growing dark, lingering shadows of the evening were beginning to spread and wrap themselves lazily across the houses as if to protect them from the night.

The crowd that had gathered for George Floyd rally looked very emotional, and their show of unity suggested that their feelings were so intense that they were willing to disregard the threat of the corona virus to stand united against another common enemy – discrimination and injustice.

Khushboo looked at her watch, for at 6 p.m., the people who championed the movement of 'Black lives Matter' would gather in memory of George Floyd and would 'take the knee' by kneeling on one leg, one arm outstretched, the other across their chest, in silence and in his memory.

Khushboo had also heard the words, 'help, I cannot breathe' countless times, but in different situations, mainly by desperate women whom she represented, women who were trapped in suffocating relationships. In George's case, it had ended in death, but the women remained smothered in relationships in which they were exploited emotionally, financially, and physically, but was one's fate worse than the other? She felt that the women had a choice of escaping their dilemma, however difficult that was, whereas George had been given none.

Khushboo, was a lawyer who dealt with ethnic women and tried to provide them with a means of escape. For most of the women felt they could not express their feelings, as it was a long-standing tradition that they keep silent whilst the world ignored their feelings. But, as their emotions festered within them, they were left wondering why they were abandoned; slowly believing they were going insane. Over time, they began to doubt themselves and felt they were on the narrow verge of stability, one wrong move and she could plunge into insanity!

Khushboo braked as she came to a red light, and as she waited for it to turn green, rustled through her handbag for her phone and called her mother to let her know that she would be late. Having put the phone back, she sat back and took a sip of coffee from the paper cup.

As she waited, tapping her long fingers impatiently on the wheel, she wondered why it was that men did not realise the responsibility they held. She strongly believed that the well-being of society rested on the harmonious relationship between men and women, that would, she believed, eventually shape the character and future of children, then eventually of culture and tradition in a positive way, But why, she thought, irritably, should everything be a matter of power and control with men? Even her father Anil, made sure he controlled her mother!

Through her job in the legal system, Khushboo had found that black and minority ethnic women, especially victims of domestic violence suffered a double disadvantage. They did not receive help and support from the police, not only because they were victims of domestic violence, but also because of their ethnicity.

Although she was aware that racism was a global problem, she was surprised when one of her Russian friends told her that racism and sexism existed in Russia too, and was sending a woman, Olga, over to her as a refugee to London. Khristina told her that in Russia racism existed and strict measures were taken by some Russians toward people, who according to them, were not ethnically Russian. There, she said, sexism was not only tolerated, but was sustained by passing laws that protected men and ignored the plight of the women.

As soon as the light turned green, Khushboo took her foot off the brake, her mind returning to the events that had occurred after George's death and how people had reacted to the cruelty that led to his death by a figure of authority and trust. People had then, and were, even now, voicing their objection to the fact that whilst the system of justice had worked in favour of Chauvin and afforded him his freedom by granting him bail, George Floyd had been killed before he had a chance to be charged, arrested, and have a trial which would have proven his innocence.

But wasn't this how racism and bigotry worked? It thrived by operating with two faces. The straightforward public face, where all the right words are said, and the private face, where an ethnic family felt there was danger of being falsely accused, so their children are told, from a young age, to keep quiet, so as to not unintentionally provoke anyone, specially one in authority.

She had been touched to learn how, a year from the day that Floyd was killed, eight boys had taken part in a campaign in which they had written an open letter to the future. In the letter they detailed a world they hoped to live in when they grew up; and what needed to be done to accomplish that. They had felt the death of George so intensely that it was thought that by writing, the boys could thereby explore and process their feelings,

Incidents around racism were prevalent in London too, she had heard about the McPherson inquiry that was held after Stephen Lawrence, who had been killed by the police and who had arrived at the conclusion that the police were institutionally racist. However, that had always been the case, racism had always been prevalent, for racial clashes and battles between empires, religions, tribes, and clans was what really shaped the history of a country!

But one year on, had anything changed? Yes, people were more aware in all professions and in football especially, the players now 'took the knee' but here too racism was flourishing; and officers were also told that they could do so if they so wished. George's death had uncovered layers of racism and given people the confidence and passion to speak up against it.

A memorial service for George Floyd was held in Minneapolis and those gathered in tribute stood in silence for nine minutes 46 seconds, the time Mr. Floyd is alleged to have been pinned on the ground with the knee of a policeman on his neck! It was amazing how George Floyd was making his quiet and gentle presence felt from the shadows of the unknown by uniting people, thereby making them powerful enough to voice the injustice they had and were suffering from.

It was not only George and the women who could not breathe, however tragically it ended for George, it was mandatory in most countries to wear masks because of the spread of Covid-19, everyone finding it difficult to breathe when they wore them. Khushboo had heard on the news that the cries of the citizens of India too had resounded in the air as they gasped for breadth and pleaded for oxygen! Who was going to speak for the people who had died, been burnt en-masse, so unnecessarily and without dignity?

In the process of trying desperately to find a parking space in time, Khusboo managed to skilfully avoid some people who were crossing the road, for she had been deep in thought about a case she was currently dealing with. Most of her cases dealt with the political and legal status of women and it was her responsibility to find out how best to enhance their confidence, learning and skills that would improve their work opportunities should they escape from their stifling relationships.

Her present case was to do with a young Asian woman who had recently married and come to London to find that her husband not only had a mistress but who was also mentally, physically, and financially abusing her. As this was just one of the many similar cases she had to deal with, Khusboo suspected there might be a cultural pattern in the backdrop playing a role in creating such situations.

Finally, she saw a vacant space and quickly parked her car, hoping that the problems faced by those women were not too deeply rooted, otherwise, to help them, she would have to delve deep into their sociological psychological and even intellectual hurdles; barriers that were perhaps contributing towards nurturing the unfortunate situations they found themselves in.

However, she put the problem to one side as she walked towards the crowd, adjusting her mask over her face and ears.

It was cold as the sun had disappeared behind the clouds that had gathered and Khushboo's breadth misted around her face as she pulled the coat tightly about her and wrapped the matching scarf around her throat and ears.

She was a 26-year-old Indian woman, with a face that was heart shaped and mischievous brown eyes. She had a slim figure which was clad smartly and professionally in a trouser suit that hugged her slim figure, she looked around in alarm for it was nearly 6 p.m. but still some people were ardently talking amongst themselves, occasionally forgetting to adhere to social distancing that was so necessary to be followed at this time of the receding global pandemic, when she suddenly realised that the rules were now being relaxed as most of the people had been vaccinated.,

However, everybody was wearing masks, at precisely one minute to 6, everybody distanced themselves from each other and she joined them as they 'took the knee' knelt on one knee, one arm outstretched the other across their chest as they grieved for George Floyd.

In the rally that was held in London were protesters from diverse backgrounds, young and old, professional, and nonprofessional, all who had one thought in mind, to raise awareness and get justice not only for George Floyd, but for countless others who were voiceless and were undergoing discrimination at the hands of those in power. For power had become contaminated with prejudice and racism which had trickled its way down from the very top down to council, organisations, and corporations. And as the video showed, it had even found its way into the police force, an institution that was supposedly meant to protect everyone, irrespective of colour and creed.

However, the tragedy with George had ignited a fire in the people who felt that enough was enough and that it was time to claim their equal rights, to voice disapproval of recent events and demand to be heard. Floyd's death had awakened an anger and a widespread feeling of injustice, people who wanted and needed, at the very least, an acknowledgement of the harsh reality that people from ethnic groups still faced discrimination in all fields.

The cause thereafter had been taken up the group 'Black Lives Matter 'who had declared September 29, 2020, as **BREATHE Day.** A day the minorities would discuss issues that affected them. Khusboo, along with many, hoped that **BREATH Act** would hopefully #DefundthePolice and create a future for all to thrive equally and in peace. For too long, the minorities had been forced to hold their breath but now, the wait was over and the realisation and protests that were being held would be the beginning of peace and harmony and they could now breathe easy.

The line of discrimination had run like a thread throughout her life too and although she was born and lived in London, and considered herself to be British, others did not, so keeping in mind the misery she had endured at the hands of intolerant people., she was pleased to learn that The Black Lives Matter movement was focusing its attention on the many different institutions and services that treated people from ethnic minorities unfairly. Khusboo examined their objectives closely, glad that it was to transform and overcome prejudices hoping they would look at the education system, starting from schools to colleges maybe even prenursery? For she knew from experience that the attitude was rooted in institutions and teachers, who unfortunately brought their own attitudes and prejudices into the classroom.

Khushboo only stayed at the rally for 15 minutes before driving home impatiently, but her thoughts were still with the protesters who had reacted so strongly to George's untimely and cruel death. and she recollected an ongoing event which occurred often and upset her.

Khusboo worked in a large well-known firm for a couple of years however, she was always stopped by office's a security officer on duty, a man with ginger hair and beard and a round face in uniform, a ribbed wool sweater with name of their law company embroidered over his heart, However, he always presumed that she could only be either a defendant, or client who needed representation and the fact that she greeted him with a British accent and was a professional in the firm did not occur to him! But to be fair, as soon as he realised his mistake, he would abruptly turn away with a polite but baffled apologetic expression on his face.

Khushboo was a sensitive girl and thought his attitude it to be homophobic and narrow minded which always left her feeling; hurt, a feeling that she had become familiar with. However, she had a positive attitude to life, hoped that the trauma of facing racism from an early age had strengthened her in adulthood. Nonetheless, she had hope that the days of bullying and discrimination would remain a thing of the past, but the ugly head of bigotry would sometimes raise its head and awaken the old recognisable feeling that she would never be accepted.

After completing her degree, she had begun applying for jobs, keeping in mind that, in all probability, she would be rejected, for it was a well-known fact that applicants with Asian names were much less likely to receive a positive response than those with British names. Although unequal treatment of applicants by employers was considered to be illegal, therefore, she had been pleasantly surprised to get a job in a large law firm.

Chapter 1

As she arrived at her house, Khushboo parked her car in the garage and noticed that the leaves that had been blown in the wind from the trees had accumulated against a sewer in a wet mesh. Khushboo made her way gingerly around them and rustled in her bag for a tissue to wipe her face, making sure there were no signs of her tears.

She took off her coat as she entered, walked straight into the kitchen, and dropped it over the back of a chair.

She smiled as she saw her mother, Sameera, apron around her waist, busily bustling around the warm and cosy kitchen, her reading glasses, as always, dangling round her neck. She had her hair in a bun; however, a few strands fell across her face in the heat, but when she saw Khusboo she smiled and quickly pushed them over her ears,

"Mum did I tell you I love you? What have you cooked today?" Khushboo wrinkled her nose in anticipation as the aroma of her mother's cooking reached her nostrils.

She loved her mother Sameera, dearly but wished she would be confident and break away from what she had been taught from childhood, that after marriage, her status would be that of a dependant woman and stand up to her father who had no qualms in taking advantage of his wife's gentle and meek nature.

"Come sit, beti, (daughter) shall I lay out the dinner or shall I wait till you have changed?" Her mother asked as she smiled warmly and hugged her daughter. "I was worried for you are late today."

"Hang on Mum, I'll take off my coat, I won't change as I am starving, but will quickly wash my hands and will explain why I am late."

Khusboo said over her shoulder as she hung her coat in the cupboard then washed her hands before coming back to the kitchen.

As soon as Khushboo sat down at the table, her mother put a plate of spicy potatoes and tarka dal, (spicy lentils) her favourite, followed by a steaming hot bowl of basmati rice which her mother cooked to her liking; sometimes she seasoned the rice with spices like cardamon, cumin cloves and occasionally she added nuts and onions to boiled rice to give it flavour. Sameera had also made chutney, again alternating between making it with condiments and spreads, or for variety from mints tamarind and tomato which Khushboo loved to have with her food for it added a tangy taste to the delicious food.

"Yummy, Mum this looks delicious, as usual, but why only one plate? Have you been busy cooking for I noticed the kitchen and the house are not as clean as they usually are? Did Olga not come today? Mom you must tell me if she does not turn up because she needs to work regularly as well as attend her English classes!"

She was starving so quickly dished out the curry and rice on her plate as her mother joined her, looking at her tenderly.

"Calm down, she has been coming regularly and is a great help, though I prefer to do the work myself! Anyway, she rang to say that she was meeting her boyfriend and…Khusboo what is the matter? She is a young girl and…"

"Oh no mum you don't understand! She came to London to escape from him for he was violent to her and as there is no law in her country that protects women, her sister helped her get away…oh he must have followed her here. Mum do you have her phone number?" She pushed the plate aside.

Olga was a petite girl with blonde hair that was cut short and framed her expressive face. She had come as an Asylum seeker who had been sent by Khristina, a friend of Khushboo's who occasionally sent her women who needed to escape their violent relationships. She had explained Olga's dilemma and requested, once she was in London, to help her in finding a job, any light cleaning and Khusboo had immediately thought of her mother, who just that morning had complained that the housework was getting too much for her.

As Khusboo dialled Olga's number, she held her breadth, for she had become quite fond of the young Russian girl and let out her breadth in relief as Olga answered.

"Olga are you alright? Alexie, your ex-boyfriend, has not followed you here, has he? You told mum that you were meeting your boyfriend."

"No mam, he has not, thank god! It is somebody I met here, a nice decent man. I hope you didn't mind I did not come in today; it is just that today was the only time free as he is working most of the time. Don't worry, mam I will do extra hours and…" Olga reassured her.

"That is all right, Olga, I just wanted to find out if you were okay. Don't worry you just have a good evening!"

Khusboo closed her blackberry and turned her attention back to the dinner." Dad as usual is not home, so he will not be joining us for dinner?" she asked, then added sarcastically "I am sure he told you he is too busy working?"

"Yes, he did but you know your father does work late." Sameera remarked, however, Khusboo did not miss the tone of her mother's voice nor the way she firmly pressed her lips, which she knew was a sign of her disapproval which she only expressed on rare occasions. "Now tell me what was all that about, why are you so worried about Olga."

Khusboo briefly told her Olga's history and how it was that she came to be in London.

"Oh, that is terrible she is such a lovely young girl it would only be a monster who would treat her like that! "Sameera declared with disgust. "You see that is why I appreciate your father, even though he is not here, he provides for us and never has he been violent towards me." "Mum there are different types of abuse, mental, physical and financial also, for I deal with such cases every day!" however, she had sensed her mother's displeasure and how she tried to cover it with light-hearted conversation.

Her father Anil was hardly ever home, but her mother could not see any future for herself beyond that of being a mother and husband, for like her mother and other female relatives, she had been told that it was her duty to stay at home and be at her husband's beck and call. And that,

Khusboo thought, was her strength, for as her mother's expectations were not high and as she did not question her father, she was content; today being one of the rare times she had.

Khusboo did not remember him being with them whilst during her childhood, nor was he at any of her school functions, but her mother, like a typical Indian wife, had always found excuses for her father's absence. Therefore, she had been surprised when he turned up at her graduation, however briefly. And as she grew into a young woman, she often wondered that maybe her parents were really divorced or at the very least, separated but wanted to keep that knowledge from her?

"Mum, you know I have always felt that you are withholding something from me?" Khusboo thought she would confront her mother.

"What makes you say that Beti? (daughter)" However, Khusboo did not miss the fleeting look of alarm that had crossed her mother's face, however briefly. Had she hit a nerve?" And what is it that you think I am not telling you?" her mother smiled hastily.

"Maybe the fact that you and Dad are divorced or at the very least separated? When I left for school in the morning, he had already left, and I used to be asleep when he came in the evening. Nowadays it is the same, I go to work, and he has left before me, I come in the evening, and he comes late! He is not here in the weekends either, in fact it is so bad now that when we do meet, we find it difficult to have a conversation for it is like talking to a stranger. Come on, Mum, please don't pull the wool over my eyes, I am not a child!" However, what she did not say out aloud was that she suspected he might be having an affair.

Sameera looked at her first in astonishment than started laughing loudly.

Chapter 2

"It is not funny, Mum!" Khusboo said crossly

"Of course, it isn't Khushboo, no it is!" Sameera wiped the tears that were streaming from her eyes. "Anil your father, bless him, works very hard, and after what you told me about Olga and other Asian women, let me assure you we are happily married."

As Khusboo had finished eating, her mother stretched her arm to take her plate, but Khusboo held her wrist firmly.

"Mum, first I am sorry for what I said, I hope you are not offended, and you never let me help. You made delicious dinner the least I can do is to do the dishes. And then I will make tea which we shall have together! And gossip!" she grinned impishly

"Which I would love, I am fortunate to have a lovely daughter, I am dreading the emptiness I will feel after you get married, talking about which I think it is time that we got you..."

"Oh no, Mum, please don't go there, you suffocate me by repeating the same thing over and over! I know you mean well but you don't have to worry about my marriage!" Khusboo said indignantly.

She cleared the table angrily and after stalking the plates in the dishwasher put on the kettle, whilst her mother watched her thoughtfully for, she considered her daughter's independence to be unfeminine and felt strongly that the more dependant a woman was the more cherished and appreciated she would be by her husband.

"Khusboo, I won't talk about it if you don't want me to, however I feel, should you decide to, you would be a good wife, just remember that if you do meet someone you will tell me? We are not fussy as long as he is a good decent boy who would make you happy."

"No, Mum you are wrong, I won't make a good wife, Mum, I will not always obey my husband as you do, nor can I cook, at least not the way you do and those are the two main reasons important to an Indian man!"

"Now, now, those are not valid reasons to base your attitude towards marriage on, Khushboo, I only knew how to cook because, by the time I was 15, my mother made sure that I was helping her in cooking and looking after our house and one day in the week I had to do everything by myself! So, when the responsibility fell on me after marriage, it was quite straight forward. Aha! maybe that is what I should do; on weekends the responsibility of the kitchen will be yours and..."

"Oh no Mum please not that! And it is not because I don't want to help you, but I hate cooking and…" She shuddered at the thought.

"Okay okay, Khusboo, there are lots of women who actually learn after marriage and are very successful at it too!"

"Well, I don't intend to take on those duties! Anyway, that is not the only reason Mum, it is because I think men are selfish who think that women are born to serve them! They do not really care about their emotions, think she is of no value, has no contribution to make towards society, therefore, they feel justified in not caring or worrying about them!"

"All right, Khusboo, point taken, I was just joking anyway!" Sameera smiled "My, my I did not think you felt so strongly about it."

"I didn't want to start with, but when I see the way father treats you, how he shows, in a hundred different ways, what he thinks of you; that you are only capable of looking after the house! If he would remain long enough at home, I would make him see think that a woman has the potential to have the highest frame of mind as well as the lowest, if that makes any sense! Let me see if I can explain what I mean, I think that it is in her weaknesses that her power lies! And for a working woman, what with having to deal with discrimination, within her office and outdoors then having to deal and her husband's demands at home, why, it would be just too much for her to handle!"

"It seems that it is because of our marriage that you have become so bitter and cynical, Khusboo, I am so sorry you feel that way for your dad is actually a very decent man…" Sameera tried to justify her husband's behaviour, hoping that would change Khushboo's view on marriage.,

"And pigs can fly! Please don't feel guilty Mum, it is not only because of you that I feel this way, every day I deal with women who are put in those impossible situations by men and often worse. That is why I have concluded that by allowing a man to invade my independence he would only make demands, create arguments over trivial matters which, I am sure, would only lead to resentments on both sides. No thank you!" Khusboo declared.

"You do realise that is no way to live, Khusboo," Sameera said in alarm. "Why, you would become a recluse and however you try and justify your way of thinking, one needs a shoulder to cry on someone to laugh with, you know the saying, 'Sorrow shared is sorrow halved, joy shared is joy doubled.' Anyway, I am sure you will meet someone who will make you change your way of thinking, and when you do, just be sure to tell me for I would be delighted, unless you already have?"

"No Mum, I have not met anyone and of course I will tell you if I do," She carried over two steaming mugs of tea, "Now, can we please change the subject, we can either sit here or go into the lounge? I prefer the lounge, the armchairs there are so much more comfortable!"

"Okay Khusboo, and I agree the lounge seems the most comfortable!" Sameera got up from the table, undid her apron, hung it behind the kitchen door then followed her daughter.

"Mum, I love this room the best!!" Khusboo exclaimed as she switched on the light of the lounge, flooding the room with soft light.

The focal colour chosen by Sameera was pastel blue, with pale blue suede armchairs, cream carpet, and pastel blue curtains with tassels at the end with walls painted in cream which complemented the blue colour. There was a fireplace that was rarely used but gave the room a warm and cosy effect whilst in the middle of the room was a coffee table covered with a lace tablecloth and pastel blue artificial flowers at the centre.

"Mum did you furnish the room? It is very tastefully done; I think I have told you many times!" Khusboo sat on the sofa, fluffing the blue cushions on it before she leant back on them, then with a sigh, then blew on her mug before taking a sip of the much-needed tea.

She was still wearing her work clothes and wished she had changed into leggings or joggers, but as she had missed lunch, she had ignored her usual routine, at the same time aware that in the present time of Covid 19, infections were till prevalent, it was important to put aside her outdoor clothes, and have a bath after coming from outdoors. However, as they had all been vaccinated, she sometimes tended to disregard the guidance that was still in place but relaxed.

She shivered slightly as she felt a slight draught in the room so got up to check the windows and pulled the curtains aside.

"Mum! One of the windows is slightly open! If we had not come to this room, it would stayed open the whole night and we might have got burgled! You know the burglars prowl the streets looking around for something like this!" She closed it and walked back to the sofa. "Khushboo, you fuss so, your father usually checks the doors and windows at night before he comes up."

"Mum do you really think he does? He comes home late every night; has the dinner you have prepared for him than goes up to bed!" Khushboo retorted angrily.

"Khusboo, stop having a go at your dad, in fact I have noticed you do not miss any chance to fault him! Now we were talking about this room and yes, I did choose the colour and style, but that was many years ago, I am surprised that everything still looks brand new, maybe because we don't use it often? Now tell me why you are late? You are always punctual; is everything all right at work?"

"Yes, it is Mum" She quickly told her mum about her attending George Floyd 's rally.

Chapter 3

"You should have told me this morning before you left for work! What is happening in this world, what with the poor girl, Sarah, being murdered by a policeman, no less, and making all women feel vulnerable and concerned for their safety!" Sameera exclaimed. "Can you blame me for worrying, if you had told me I would not have been so anxious, anyway, I am proud that I have a daughter who supports such a cause, but in future if you do attend such rallies, be sure to let me know in advance. But at least people are recognising that what happened to George Floyd was cruel."

"It was, and the truth is that, that kind of brutality by the police is still present, but his case was only picked up because of the video taken by some bystander that went viral. I am sure you must have seen it too,

My god! That is so cruel, poor fellow he kept repeating I cannot breathe, I want my mother! People all over the world are protesting, showing how united the people are about the issue of racism in general." Khushboo sighed and put her mug on the side table. "Whew, I needed that cup of tea!"

"You know, Khusboo, I have never talked about it, but we went through discrimination too, when we first came to London, obviously not as extreme as what happened to Floyd. The attitude of people was quite different then and not at all what I had expected. Your grandparents, both from my side and your fathers, are from a village in India and I was from a modest background, so it was a delightful change to find that life in London would be so much easier!"

"I have only been to India once but thought that life there is only comfortable if one is rich, but yes, life here is much easier, in a different way of course, and one comes across obstacles here too again different ones." Khusboo remarked thoughtfully.

"Yes, I found that out, for soon after we arrived, we stayed with Adarsh, my father's cousin, for my family requested him to help us settle in a new country which he did. He offered Anil a job in his newsagent until he found a proper job and as there was a flat above, he proposed we move in. I was homesick so encouraged Anil to take the job with Adarsh. I missed my mother specially during my pregnancy and it was nice to have Anil nearby for I had not made many Indian friends either. I was not confident then as I did not speak English fluently and I am grateful that your father was patient with me, and after you were born, encouraged and supported me by getting me enrolled in English classes; twice a week he would drop and pick me up from the class however tired he was."

Khushboo found it difficult to believe that her father could be understanding and supportive, and now when she thought about it, she had attributed her mother's absence of friends to a lack of social skills, and as she was a minority would seek friends in the same community for with them, she would not be judged therefore would feel safe.

"Mum, I am surprised to hear that! Somehow, I cannot see Dad as being supportive, he must have changed."

"Khusboo you mustn't criticise your father so, and yes he has changed, but only because he works hard, but for me that was a happy time, for although we were not rich and it was not the kind of job your father was looking for, still it was enough to see us through and I saw more of your father. Oh, don't get me wrong, I am grateful to your uncle for it was nice of him to offer, but in that one month we met with so much harassment and discrimination; the like that I had not expected to witness in London"

"Why? what happened mum?" Khusboo asked with a frown. "Adarsh's newsagent shop was burgled at least one a month, and nearly every week stones were thrown by young boys shouting, 'go home pakis'!" Sameera replied. So, considering the money stolen and the money we had to spend on repairs, which, of course we gladly offered to help Adarsh, for it was the least we could do! Worried by the harassment your father upped his job hunting, and to be honest, I was relieved, for I was always frightened that someday a stone would hit your father! And every time this happened, Anil would run after the boys, who would just run away laughing and screaming. I can still see them dashing to get away and in their hurry some of them would often fall, but even though Anil ran after them with a stick, we knew that would not scare them and that they would be back again, throwing stones and rocks. And underneath it all this was the niggling fear that you would get hurt in the crossfire. And it was like I was forever holding my breath, waiting for something to happen!" Sameera shuddered

Khusboo looked at her in astonishment "How come you never mentioned all this before mum?"

"I knew you would worry, and anyway, it is all in the past now, but I cannot forget those days; the sound of stones hitting our window still echoes in my ears, the voices of the skinheads and sometimes even children as they dared each other to see who would be the bravest to throw the most stones."

Even though Khusboo knew discrimination existed, she had somehow thought her parents had not faced it, so remarked softly. "It must have been awful to feel that you were not safe in your home. A place where one is supposed to feel protected!"

Sameera shook her head and looked sadly down at her mug. "No, Khushboo, we were not, and as the throwing of rocks became frequent, your father vowed you would not have to face it, so when he told Adarsh, that he wanted to change jobs, he put in a good word for your father to his friend who had an IT shop. However, we could not move out immediately, and when Anil told his parents he wanted to move, they insisted they help which is how we could manage the deposit for this house which is in a better locality, and with the new job, Anil got a mortgage. That is why your father works so hard, he works two jobs to pay the mortgage."

Chapter 4

"Oh Mum, don't worry about it now, for now that I am working, I can help with the mortgage payment! Please tell Dad that he does not have to work two jobs, I would rather he spend time with us! But I thought you said your family were not well off?"

"No, mine are not, but Anils father are, they have ancestral paddy fields. but you know he would not take help from you, anyway he works two jobs not only because of the mortgage, he is saving for your wedding, he wants you to have the best. He believes in not only giving his daughter a good wedding, but also the dowry."

"Mum! No one believes in dowry anymore; in fact, it is illegal in India!" Khusboo exclaimed horrified.

"Yes, it is, but every parent wants their daughter to be well looked after, in fact that is how we came to be in London. As part of the dowry, my father gave us 2 tickets for London, to start a new life, and as his relatives were here, they would help us settle. In fact, they had told him knew there was a lot of opportunity for a better life here, at least more than if we had stayed in India"

"Mum I don't like the sound of the word 'dowry' but when you put it like that, yes, if one can afford it, I am sure many people do this but not under the term; 'dowry' Anyway you don't have to worry about me and please tell Dad not to work so hard on my account! Mum please…" however Khushboo knew her objections was futile, for both her parents were stubborn, but she loved them, even more so now when she knew what they had undergone in trying to protect her.

"I will speak to him about it, Khusboo but…"

"Does he still work for the friend of Adarsh uncle and how come we don't keep in touch with him considering he has done so much for us? I would love to know him for he is family, and it is not as if he is a distant cousin. But it was nice of him to give dad a job and a flat to live, I think he knew it was difficult for black and Asian minorities to get accommodation and you, like most Asian people, would have ended up by living in overcrowded housing!"

"We don't keep in touch because my cousins' friend who owned the shop where your father worked, was sold and he moved on without passing on Adarsh's mobile number or address. The only info I have is that he sold the IT shop to an English guy, William. But you know your father, he does not like to talk about work., all I know is that he still works there."

"He does not like to talk, period!" Khushboo exclaimed indignantly.

"Anyway, all this talk of racism is depressing, I would rather forget it and put it behind me." Sameera said.

"That is the problem, Mum, at home one can escape it for one does not have to face the attitudes and bigotry of petty people, but one cannot escape it outside where it is still prevalent, the only difference is that it is subtle but still flourishing nowadays." Khusboo remarked.

"What do you mean Khusboo?" Sameera sat up in alarm.

"You know you kept the knowledge from me hoping to protect me, well, I went through it too but did not want to tell you either for it would have hurt you. You faced the most obvious form of racism, throwing stones and shouting names, But I went through it in a subtle form; I suppose racism too has evolved and is now mostly implied" She smiled wryly "Racism is interwoven in major institutions like the police force, education, justice system and even in private offices sadly even in the arts, which only serves to stunt the creativity of the artist/artiste/writer.. The government takes out policies and makes discrimination illegal, but one can still sense the blinkered and biased attitude of some people!"

"Although I have faced it myself, sometimes I find it hard to believe, what with our chancellor, home minister being Asian. And now even the vice-president of a super state is a woman and of Sri Lankan heritage, and before him Obama..." Sameera remarked.

"I suppose things are improving and people are more tolerant like you said, mum, but it is in the day-to-day interaction with institutions that people face racism, that is in unemployment police etc. And yes, I have felt it at each stage, starting from school to college universities and now at work too".

"Oh my god! I would not have suspected that you were bullied and unhappy! I feel guilty because I know how it feels; you went through it alone whilst even though your father was there for me, I was frightened and often cried myself to sleep! You must have felt the same and I am sorry that you had to suffer alone. As your mother I should have sensed something was not right! I have often thought that we should go back home to India, you know, and this just confirms it, I will talk to your father about it."

"That is no solution Mum, and this is home for me, I have grown up with it and have accepted it, and truth to tell, it is not that bad for I have some genuinely nice English friends who have never made me feel like an outsider. That reminds me Mum, Aishya, my friend, who is in Dubai at the moment with her sister, might be coming to stay with us for a while."

"Oh, that will be nice, Khushboo, is she the one who was with you in law school?"

"Yes and no, she started of wanting to do law, then changed her mind and went into journalism and has now got a high-profile job but yes, we were, no, are very close, she went to Dubai to cover some story, but when I spoke to her last time, she sounded upset. I think she may have ruffled some political feathers, so I offered she come and stay. I don't know if she will take me up on the offer though."

"I remember her vaguely; she seemed a very nice girl."

"She is, both of us faced the prejudice of some people and because of it we connected and became good friends…" Khusboo said thoughtfully, then added. "You know Mum there is discrimination everywhere. You know how I told you earlier about Olga and how she escaped from her boyfriend Alexie? Well, the main reason he mistreated her was because he thought she was beneath him, for she is a Caucasian, and according to him, not ethnically a pure Russian!"

"Poor girl I am glad she has escaped and now has a chance to build a life here!" Sameera exclaimed "and the story this friend of yours is covering, could it be the same one that is being covered by TV? Oh, well, as long as she is safe. I don't know what is happening in the world even in India".

"Do you mean the farmers protest in Delhi? I did not know that my grandparents were farmers from Punjab. How are they involved in this particular demonstration?"

Chapter 5

"Khushboo, that is not nice not knowing about your roots! And yes, they are, both my parents and your fathers' parents, and they are involved because they insist on attending the rally being held in Delhi! It was your grandfather, my father, who feels strongly about the three agriculture bills which many people think is unfair, but, regardless of their feelings, the government insists on imposing them! Anil's fathers feel the same and when he heard his parents were going, Anil's brother Aarav, insisted on accompanying them!"

"But that is a good thing, Mum, and I admire them for protesting! I mean you agreed with me attending George Floyd rally!"

"It is not the same Khusboo, the mood of the protesters here is peaceful and the demonstration was only for a few hours. It is different to what is happening in India, they are planning to join the protesters for an indefinite time by living in tents and the weather at this of time of the year is cold and freezing."

"All the more reason you should feel proud of them Mum."

"Oh, don't get me wrong, I am, but my worry is that it will be very difficult for the women…I spoke to Anils mother, and pleaded with her not to go because, she, along with most of the farmers wives of our village have decided to join them. As usual, she did not think of herself, that she is not young and has arthritis, and the way my father-in-law treats her is shameful! But that is how women are treated back home, no doubt Aarav too will also treat his wife the same way!" Sameera sighed as she got up and patted her sari in place.

Khusboo was frustrated that her mother could not see that her father was treating her the same way and how she chose to blank out her father's treatment of her.

"Mum, I hope your parents are not going as well?" "Unfortunately, they are," Sameera replied sadly. "Everyone in the village, especially the elders of each family, feel very strongly about the bills. But I told her that it is not safe to be out in this cold and although this started off as a peaceful protest, now there is so much hooliganism attached to it I am glad your father is away from it all, Anyway, he is not like his father but, honestly sometimes these days I don't think he is not concerned about anything or anyone!"

"Yes, to me too it seems that Dad does not care about anything but his job where he spends most of his time! But he should care about his parents and us. And you are right about being worried about the protest, for I heard that the govt, is trying to control the protesters by cutting of their water supply and internet; plus, they have put nails around their site where the protesters are sitting. Horrible and cruel! Father is never at home, you never go out, he doesn't take you anywhere, yet you accept his attitude, in fact you even encourage him to behave the way he does! You wait on him hand and foot, have his meals ready for him when he does come home late yet you have never demanded to know where he has been…" she said breathlessly "I will never take that from my husband!" She added vehemently.

"We shall see, when the right man comes, you will forget all that; now tell me how is the attitude of your colleagues? Are they giving you a tough time?"

"Some of them, not all, but it is all very subtle…being a woman as well as Asian, the men in my firm are paid more than me and…!"

Sameera looked at her watched and gave a cry. "It is getting late, Khushboo!" she kissed her daughter on the head. "I think you have been very brave, but now that you have told me, remember you are not alone and you can talk to me anytime, but for now, you should go to bed, I will put out some dinner for your father for he should be coming anytime." But when she saw her daughter's annoyed expression quickly added "If he doesn't come soon, which happens often, I will leave it out for him and then I too am going to bed!" She said in exasperation "Khusboo?"

Khusboo arose from her armchair and kissed her mother on the cheek, "Sorry mum I heard what you said it is just that I get so angry when you indulge him so...Wow, I did not realise I was tired!"

She switched off the light and followed her mother where they parted, her mother went into the kitchen and Khusboo climbed the stairs to her bedroom.

After Sameera had put out an empty plate, cutlery rice and curry on the table, for her husband, she went up to her bedroom.

As she got ready for bed, she thought about the problems her daughter had faced. How could she not have noticed and what kind of mother did that make her; a mother who was not able to give moral support her daughter when she needed it?

Sameera thought how different her lifestyle now was to the life she had known., of her mother and aunts and how they would sit together at least once a week to share their experiences. They would talk in voices that varied from light to loud according to their mood. She thought nostalgically how they would jump up and down, whisper and laugh, but always, even when they recounted their painful experiences, they were confident they would not be judged but be given the much-needed moral support.

However, she was aware and hurt by Anil's attitude, but she wanted to give her husband the benefit of doubt, as she had been taught to do.

Khusboo, meanwhile, after having brushed her teeth and changing into pyjamas, climbed into bed and fluffed her pillows before she lay her head on them and closed her eyes. She was too tired and stressed to sleep but thought how what her mother had told her reflected the racist situation at present.

She hoped that the police officer who had so cruelly knelt on Floyd's throat would be convicted of murder, for what defence could there be when there was a video showing him pressing his knee on George flyrod's neck whilst Floyd cried out that he could not breathe at the same time that his shoulder moved, as if to give his lungs space to breathe,

As she tossed and turned, unable to sleep, she worried about her mother, for underneath her light heartedness, she had sensed unhappiness, sure it was due to her father for he was behaving secretively, the early mornings the late nights and excuses that he had to work over the weekends. However, her mother was so naïve that she ignored his conduct, so Khushboo thought it best to keep quiet about her suspicions thereby saving her mother from anxiety and worry.

As Khushboo drifted off to sleep, she hoped the farmers in India would realise that there were people whose aim was to malign the protest by spreading false rumours that religion and violence were being operated in their protest; which, if believed, would only weaken their cause in the eyes of the public.

Chapter 6

Khushboo's doubts about her father were well founded for he was having an affair with Aadrika, Anil found Aadrika not only to be lovely and affectionate, but also a very naïve and beautiful woman.

They worked at the same office, and they would meet twice daily; in the morning when Anil would arrive at Aadrika's flat after Aarush, her son, had left for school. They would then have a light breakfast, after which they would leave for work. In the evening Anil would walk her to her flat and if Aarush was staying over at his friend's. house, which was often, they would spend the evening together.

As they walked home one evening the sunlight bathed everything in a warm glow with a gentle breeze, a rare evening in London.

"It is so beautiful, Anil, I wish we would have more evenings like this" Aadrika said as she put her hand through Anil's arm.

They strolled past shops and restaurants then turned into a side road at the corner of the garage that sold second-hand cars. Some of them were displayed with yellow stickers on their windscreens with price of car on them hoping that would lure clients.

"You know Aadrika, this does not look safe here, especially if you are coming at night, have you thought of moving?"

"Yes and no Anil, to be honest, the rent is not high compared to other places." She sighed "but you know it is much too beautiful an evening to go spend indoors."

"You are right," Anil said just as they arrived at the flat. "It is a shame be indoors on such an evening."

"It is on days like this that I miss living in a house with a garden, where we could have barbecues and..." Aadrika sighed as she opened the door with her key.

"Granted gardens are nice, but they are a lot of work too, when there are strong winds, one has to clear up the small dead branches that had snapped from the trees, that is not forgetting the pruning of hedges that needs to do to keep the garden in a decent shape.",

"Well, I still think that there are more advantages than disadvantages maybe that is because I live in a flat, anyway I cannot imagine you doing all that."

"You are right, I get a gardener to do it." Anil grinned

As they entered her flat, Aadrika turned to Anil, "I am going to change, Anil, I'll be down in a bit."

"Of course, Aadrika, I will make us some tea, or would you like coffee?" Anil asked as he took off his coat and threw it on the banister.

"Coffee would be lovely Anil," Aadrika shouted over her shoulder as she disappeared into the bedroom.

Anil went into the kitchen and noticed that it had not been cleared for there was a breakfast bowl on the table, half a glass of orange juice and a small pile of books on it. He put the kettle on to boil then switched on the news to find out about what was happening in George Floyd case and the murder trial that was due to begin of the policeman who had put his knee on his throat.

He switched the radio off as Aadrika entered the kitchen having changed into black jeans and a pink t shirt. Her long black hair fell loosely down her shoulders.

"I heard you had the radio on and were listening to the latest news on the trial of George Floyd.?" Aadrika asked anxiously for she hated being in the kitchen.

She had often wondered why she hated it so, and the only reason she could think of was that she was fed up of cooking, for being the mother of a growing boy she spent half her time preparing meals for him, and the other half in throwing away his untouched food!

"I didn't know you were interested in what is happening Aadrika?"

"Oh yes, I have been through my fair share of discrimination, as have most of us, but we are the lucky ones, we went through it and at the very least it left us scarred, not like poor Floyd who lost his life because of it."

"Aadrika, you never did tell me much of your past, I mean are you from India?" Anil asked.

"No, I was born here but my parents died in an accident when I very young, and as they had no relations, I was put in a home."

Aadrika thought of what she had to endure in the care home, that hers had been a life of pain and twisted guilt over events that she had no control over. But Dhruv, her friend at the home, had often told her, to avoid certain pair of eyes and movements and meetings, as most of the men there ogled and leered at her, expressions that had made her feel uncomfortable and one, because of her innocence, she had not been able to identify.

"Oh, I am so sorry, Aadrika, that must have been awful." Anil put his hand on Aadrika's shoulder.

"It would have been worse had it not been for Dhruv, my husband, he arrived a few months after I did, so we actually grew up together. He protected me during those years and to a large extent, shaped my personality as it is So much so that as soon as we left the unregulated house at the age of 18, we had become so dependent on each other that we thought marriage was the answer, But in hindsight, I realise now that was a mistake for both of us were inexperienced to deal with the outside world, Dhruv, when he did get it, he was landed with the responsibility of a child and wife which he could not handle. We both were too young, and he was too immature." She sighed "Anyway that was all a long time ago and I do not blame him for leaving us."

Although she wanted to forget her time at the home, after talking in Anil about it, felt as if a load had been lifted, so continued.

"The care homes often became overcrowded, and when they were, it was usually the children from ethnic backgrounds who were sent to unsafe homes, called unregulated homes. And most of the children that did stay back were lost for the system! Instead of protecting them, the institution was damaging the vulnerable children, and we heard, through the care home grapevine, that many children committed suicide!"

"That sounds awful Aadrika! I am so sorry; no child should have to go through that kind of treatment." Anil repeated.

"I know, but I have since realised that life does not tailor to our needs or wants but that it has its own plan for you, in other words destiny, and actually I consider myself to be one of the lucky ones for I had Dhruv who looked out for me. I felt it to be important to have someone to look out for you and wanted to take care of Darpan, a young boy in the home, who, I thought was such a young and sensitive boy that my heart went out to him."

"Do you know what happened to him after you left the home?"

"Oh yes, he committed suicide!" Aadrika replied with tears in her eyes. "And I feel kind of responsible for it happened soon after we were sent to one of the unregulated homes.," Aadrika sighed. "I should not have left him because he had become too attached to me! One day, I had promised to meet him at the home, but somehow, I got late and when I got there, I found him hanging from a rope, his body swinging from side to side! If only I had not got delayed, I could have helped him! To this day I think his last thought must have been that I too had abandoned him!"

"Oh, that is terrible Aadrika!"

"Yes, it took me a long time to get over it, could not get over it, the only good thing was that Dhruv was with me wherever we were sent, even in the unregulated houses, but there were already nearly always three or four people already there!" Aadrika sighed. "I remember that in one accommodation there were 2 men, one was a drunk and the other who dealt in drugs, and both would look at me strangely, so much so that I was perpetually afraid that one of them, or both, were just waiting to take advantage of me, but thankfully Dhruv was there to protect me!"

"It really sounds a horrible, the government should actually ban the unregulated houses!" Anil exclaimed.

Chapter 7

Anil's opinion of Dhruv changed for it showed there was a decent side to him, and he felt relieved too, for he felt Dhruv was much too protective of Aadrika to abandon her for good.

Anil smiled slightly his eyes narrowing.

"It seems there was racism even in the homes," he remarked, "but people get away with it not realising the trauma their actions or words have caused! Example of that is George Floyds case, because the defence is trying to prove that it was not the pressure of the knee on George's neck, but other factors that contributed to his death, so Chauvin, too might just get away with it! And, yes, having faced racism, in whatever form, does leave one overly sensitive and scarred. I am facing it too, for when William my supervisor passes racist remarks, I feel that I too cannot breathe! It feels like his racist remarks have the same effect as cutting off one's oxygen, Covid 19, wearing masks and racism all rolled into one, but having said that, it is nothing compared to what you have been through..."

Aadrika smiled faintly. "That is why I do not talk about my past, I would rather forget those bad memories, and also why I feel I can forgive Dhruv anything. Anyway, do you mean William, the owner of our shop?"

"Yes, the very same! "Anil replied sarcastically. "Anyway, let's not talk about him, it is too depressing. By the way, I see that Aarush had his breakfast in a hurry! Are those his schoolbooks which he forgot?"

Anil asked admiring her for not only the way she, even in casual attire, had an air of style and elegance about her, but also how she had overcome the obstacles in her life. And what a big heart she had, the way she forgave Dhruv, although he had abandoned her and left her to bring up a child on her own.

"No, they are not, and he did not! I did not have time to clear up." Aadrika's nostrils flared, and her eyes narrowed and darkened.

Anil was startled and frightened when he looked at her; how could a minor annoyance she felt harden into something intense and vicious? However, her expression quickly changed yet again for when he looked at her, she looked so calm and beautiful that Anil thought he must have imagined it.

However, being a parent himself, he could understand how a child could be annoying and have that effect on a parent.

"Aarush did not need those books today and as usual I had to force him to have breakfast, he was in a rush to get to school and to meet his friends for this lockdown has been very difficult for him" She pushed back her hair that was falling loosely around her,

"I hope he remembers that it is better he wears a mask." Anil said as he watched Aadrika open the fridge door and take out eggs and some salad she had made the day before. "Everybody feels it is okay to relax and not wear them, but it is just as important now,"

"I do remind him, but you know how children are, anyway, would you like a sandwich, Anil." She asked. "Or would you prefer scrambled eggs?"

"Hey Aadrika, what is the matter and why are you fussing so? A mug of coffee is what I need, especially after a day with William! Anyway, Sameera will be waiting, and I will have dinner ready at home."

Aadrika twisted her long hair into a bun and looked at him angrily. "I am sorry, I cannot make the fancy dishes that your wife can, but I thought we had agreed that we were going to have something light. I have to make something for Aarush anyway. And I feel that any day now he might want to know about our friendship."

"Okay if you insist, a sandwich will be fine thanks Aadrika. I know how you hate being in the kitchen!"

"Anil, nice of you to have noticed!"

"Well, it is kind of hard to miss it when you would prefer eating out or get a takeaway!" Anil retorted with a grin and a twinkle in his eye. "As for Aarush asking about me, I don't think he will for we have not met! I come in the morning after he has left for school and leave in the evening before he comes home, and we don't meet on weekends anyway. "Anil replied in puzzlement.

Aadrika looked confused and flustered when she replied. "Yes, you are right, he does, I think I might have mentioned your name when I was upset, so knows you are a friend."

"Okay, so where is my sandwich, but no pressure, I can do without,"

"One sandwich coming up, Anil."

Reassured somewhat by his answer, Aadrika walked around the small kitchen, concentrating on making a sandwich.

First, she took the slices of bread that were lying on a plate, placed them on the bread board then spread some mayonnaise on them, on them careful to take the mayonnaise right to the crust of the bread. She then chopped up uncooked frankfurters which she had taken from the fridge and cut them into round pieces which she then placed on top of the slices of bread. She had taken out some cheese from the fridge earlier which she cut into square pieces and placed them on the rounded frankfurter.

After Aadrika had finished, she wiped the surface top clean and cleared the bed crumbs into the palm of her hand which she then threw into the sink. She opened fridge door to put back the rest of the things and as she was closing its door, the black marker pen that was hanging on a string fridge next to a clean board swung from side to side reminding her to make the shopping list.

Whilst waiting for the sandwich, Anil sat idly at the table, then began fidgeting; his fingers could not keep still so he kept moving coasters that were lying on the table. Next, he took out his cigarette packet, but finding it empty, twisted its wrapper into knots and when that did not calm him, he knotted his fingers together.

Aadrika meanwhile had cut the sandwich in half, and as there was some left-over salad, placed some of it beside the sandwich and placed the plate on the table.

"My, you are restless Anil! Still thinking of William, don't worry about him. Now, would you like some ketchup to go with the sandwich?"

"Aadrika, that sandwich does look delicious! I should have made the coffee while you were making the sandwich. I will do so now, you start, and I will make the coffee."

Whilst Aadrika put some salad on her plate Anil came over with 2 steaming mugs. "What about you, no sandwich?"

"No. I will just have the salad., thanks, I am on a diet." Aadrika replied as she put some salad dressing on the salad. "Sorry, this is only a sandwich, nothing like the fancy stuff Sameera cooks." Aadrika remarked but Anil could sense the slight tone of jealousy in her voice. "I don't know why you have to go to her." she muttered.

"Yes, Sameera cooks for me but that is all. I told you in the beginning what the situation was. I have been married too long and the marriage has now become so boring and routine it is virtually dead but being with you makes me feel alive! But Aadrika coming back to Aarush, if the subject ever comes up, you should tell him that we are casual friends who work at the same place so travel to and from work together.

Chapter 8

"Yes, I will but if that is how you feel, about your marriage, Anil, why don't you leave her?" Aadrika looked at him angrily not knowing whether to take that as a compliment or not.

Anil shrugged his shoulders and looked down sheepishly than raised his head. "Aadrika, don't make me feel guilty, you too are still married and not divorced!" Anil came up behind her and put his hand on her neck and kissed her lightly on her cheek. "I don't know what kind of man your husband was to leave you to bring up your son on your own! But I cannot leave my wife because, one, the tradition and attitudes of our culture makes it impossible for me to do so and secondly because Sameera cannot take care of herself, Aadrika, she is not like you. and anyway, why are you bringing this up today?"

"I don't know why, maybe because I am feeling depressed Anil! Maybe it is the change of weather for you know my mood and behaviour change accordingly!" She looked thoughtfully as she opened the window and inhaled the fresh cold air. "But actually, I don't think it is the weather for it is cold but pleasantly so." She closed the window and looked at Anil.

"Aadrika, you know I am fond of you for you are a very kind caring woman, without being needy and clingy. I have appreciated the fact that you cared about me without making me feel you were interfering or being nosy, that is till today, for I thought you understood the situation. In all the time I have known you, you never once criticised, nagged or even made a suggestion.to that affect."

They ate in silence, and after Anil had finished, he licked his fingers tipped back his mug and drained the last of coffee. He put the empty mug on the table moved over to sit beside Aadrika., putting his warm hand on the back of her hand and pulled her close to him.

When Aadrika glanced at him, there was such a serious look in his eyes, that she looked away, got up and reached for the coffee pot, taken aback by the intensity in his eyes and poured the coffee in two mugs and handed one to Anil.

"Another cup of coffee? I wish you could stay longer, and we could have proper dinner."

"That would have been nice, but you know I never stay for dinner, your sandwich will tide me over till I reach home, but another cup of coffee for the road will be fine." Anil said with a frown as he took the mug from her.

Aadrika tried to work though her feelings for him, for she felt miserable each time he left her, although she knew she should brace herself for the time when he would end the affair. And when she saw how thoughtful Anil looked, she was sure that day would not be far off.

Therefore, she reminded herself, she must take over her finances, for earlier on in the relationship, when she had grumbled that she did not have enough time to deal with her bills and rent because she was overworked in the office, Anil had been kind enough to offer and she had only been too glad to hand them over. And ever since, things had been running so smoothly that she had not taken the responsibility back and as Anil seemed to be taking care of them so effortlessly that she thought she would leave things as they were.

"Anil, don't you realise how I feel every time you leave? You know, I too, like most women, desire to be a wife?"

"Hello, Aadrika, look who's talking, you told me you were still married!"

"Married, without a husband…" She said wistfully. "Mother without a child, now that Aarush is growing up, he is never home, and I hardly ever get to see him."

"He is growing up and needs to be with his friends, especially now that Lockdown is over which you are wise enough to figure out. But now that you mention it, I too barely see him, which is good under the circumstances, I suppose?" He winked.

Aadrika smiled for she knew he was right for the situation of being separated and a mother plus having a relationship with Anil was a difficult one to manage and Anil had been understanding and was not demanding. He knew she was still married to Dhruv, that he was her first love, and she even suspected that part of her heart still belonged to him, however badly their relationship had ended and was hurt when he did not contact her again. Nevertheless, she was surprised that Anil was unaware of her feelings towards him, but then she herself did not know what she really felt about Anil. Maybe she was only with him because she felt a sense of gratitude because he had saved her and because it was nice to have a decent man around the house? "

So, you were telling me that William is a racist? Aadrika tried to change the subject,

"Yes, and I also said I do not want to talk about him!" Anil said looking irritated, "But now that you have mentioned it, William always passes racist comments or does something to annoy me! Let's drop it shall we?"

He went to the sofa and sat down after placing his mug on the side table. He heard brakes as a car crunched to a halt outside and wondered how Aadrika could sleep despite the noise of the traffic., But when he had pointed it out to her once, her answer was that it had been difficult when she had just moved in but had since adapted to it.

Aadrika's rented flat was small but cosy, with just enough room for herself and her son. The lounge was large with concrete walls and unshaded lightbulbs hanging from the ceiling. The carpet was beige with brown curtains and to cover the faded bits, she had laid out brown rugs in the hope of covering them. There was one two-seater faded deep brown sofa, an armchair and a TV.

Aadrika looked up at the ceiling of the room and when she saw the unshaded light bulbs, made a note to buy some, hoping that would make the room more liveable but then thought to herself 'who for? Suddenly there were tears in her eyes and she turned her head, trying to shield her face from Anil so he could not see the tears that had suddenly welled up in her eyes.

But Anil had noticed them so put his hands under her chin and turned her face towards him then kissed her on her lips, the salty tears stinging his lips.

"Oh, come on Aadrika, don't be angry with me. We both went into this knowing my situation and we have been together for a long time."

"I agree and I won't blame you when you did put an end to the arrangement, Anil you have been very nice to us. I thought I was prepared for it but when I noticed recently that you are becoming more and more aloof, I didn't like it! I feel that you have compartments in your life, your wife, daughter, work, parents but you don't have one for me, and even if I had a compartment, I feel the door would not close on any of them but on me, in fact, I am expecting that to happen!!" Aadrika wiped her eyes.

"Aadrika, you know that was the case, but please don't worry, and yes I do have something on my mind, but it has nothing to do with you."

With those abrupt words, he got up, kissed her lightly, brushed his hand through his hair then began rummaging around in his pocket making sure he had his wallet.

He then put on his coat and gloves and left, closing the door behind him. He looked at his watch with a frown for the sky was darkening, turning to inky blue which in turn would turn black.

He walked thoughtfully towards his car, for there was something weighing on his mind, something he was planning but did not want to disclose to Aadrika yet, because he thought, like today, she might throw a tantrum, become unpredictable and emotionally volatile and if she did, she could become an obstacle to his plans which were still hazy and unclear as he had not decided what path he was going to take, He realised that although he was central to Aadrika's life, she was just outside his. He was fond of her but now he felt she had become a messy thread on an otherwise neat hem.

But before he cut her off, he had to talk to his friend who had warned him that she was like a black hole that could drain the energy out of anything that came too close. Till now he had thought his friend to be wrong till he remembered the momentary look that had passed across Aadrika's eyes. Plus, he was spending a lot of his energy and time in trying to avoid detection of his affair from Sameera, although he often thought that Sameera must know about the reason for his late nights and early mornings.

But she never complained about behaviour, and by keeping quiet he thought that Sameera gave him her silent agreement as if she was saying' don't tell me about it and I won't complain! But Sameera was a naïve woman who trusted him and the mere thought of his having an affair would never occur to her. He concluded that maybe he was only placating his guilt by believing she approved, and it was this guilt that was making him paranoiac!

Anil had brushed the raindrops off his sleeves and climbed into his car sweeping back the hair that had fallen on his forehead.

As he drove home, he found the roads were deserted and there were only a few cars on the road, but suddenly he had to brake suddenly for a driver in front of him had stalled, screaming with fury into his mobile, ignoring the fact that it was illegal.

Chapter 9

After Anil left, Aadrika made herself another coffee and with unsteady hands, came to the table where she sat on a chair and stared at Anil's empty plate with eyes that shimmered and swam. She was amazed at his nonchalant attitude, the way he had suddenly left without a word to her!

Aarush was still at his friend's house and would not be back for some time, so she took her coffee and went back and sat on the sofa, reminiscing about the time they had first met.

She was a secretary in the IT place he worked and was a shy woman and had few friends in the office. She kept herself busy with her work, so Anil had barely noticed her, and they had only exchanged an occasional smile and greeting.

However, one evening, she left office and was walking towards the underground when she looked back and noticed there were some men behind her. Under normal circumstances, that would not have worried her, but they were drunk and were holding bottles of beer in their hands. They caught up with her and encircled her, looking and behaving so menacingly that Aadrika looked around for help, then shouted for help, hoping that someone passer-by would hear her, but the street was deserted.

Anil was close by when he saw Aadrika surrounded by ruffians whooping laughing and whistling. They were all dressed in what looked like a heavy metal band, wearing black t shirts and arms so full of tattoos up to the elbows they were almost blue. When one of them had held Aadrika's arm and thrust his face near, Aadrika noticed, in terror, that he had a silver stud not only in his ear but also through his cheeks and eyebrows. and all the men had hair that was shaved at the sides but grown long on top and tied back with elastic bands.

Their attitude looked so menacing that Anil had intervened quickly, thereby preventing a situation which he was sure could have turned ugly and the men, when they saw she was not alone, turned on their heels and fled.

The incident had left Aadrika so shaken that she was clinging on to Anil's arm whispering 'Thank you, oh Thank you.'

"It's all right you are safe now; look they have gone." Anil tried to reassure her. But she looked so pale that that Anil had insisted they go to a nearby café.

"Sit down Aadrika, whilst I will get some coffee."

After Anil had gone to get the coffees and the shock had worn off, Aadrika thought she would freshen up so took her purse and overturned its contents; and out tumbled her lipstick, compact powder, some tissues a packed of mints and her mobile on the table.

After she had wiped her face with a tissue, she opened her compact dabbed some powder on her face then applied a fresh coat of lipstick before she quickly put everything back in her purse.

She looked at Anil in admiration as he carried the cups over to her table. He was wearing a red sweater and his hair was dark and curly although Aadrika thought he was about 40 years of age he looked younger for he had a black fringe falling on his forehead that he constantly swept back with his right hand.

When Aadrika saw Anil look at her in surprise, she smiled faintly. "I don't feel strong enough so thought I would freshen up here. And whew! I feel better now, but sorry about this Anil, I hope you weren't embarrassed, I tried to be as discreet as possible"

"Not at all Aadrika." Anil replied, wondering why he had not noticed her before for not only was she kind and gentle but was also a very beautiful woman.

"Thank you for saving me from those hooligans, Anil, they have been stalking me for a long time but today was the first time they came close and oh my God, looked so dangerous! I don't know what would have happened if you were not there!"

"My God, Aadrika, I thought this was a one off, but if you have had trouble with them before, you should have reported it to the police, I am sure they will help."

"I did report it, Anil!" Aadrika replied impatiently," but they have taken no action, I don't know if it is because I am a lone Indian girl or if they do not consider it to be serious or violent enough to pursue! How hypocritical that is for one hand the govt is saying that women's safety is paramount and on the other…"

"Aadrika, you must take this seriously and if they cannot help, you need to take precautions yourself to protect yourself against something like this happening again."

"Yes, I do most of the time. but there are some things that one must get done, for example, today, there was no other route for me to have taken to avoid that deserted street. Anyway, thank you again, not only for rescuing me but for the coffee, I feel better now." She smiled as she rose.

Anil insisted he take her home and as he walked her home; he noticed the beautiful scarf around her neck and wrinkled his nose in appreciation as he got a whiff of the scent that was drifting around her. As Anil walked her to her door, she turned and looked at him and caught her breath as their eyes met.

She remembered she had had a funny sensation in her stomach, and felt there was something huge between them that she could not define, could it be passion or chemistry or both? Whatever it was, Aadrika would not be able to recognise it for Dhruv had protected her from exploring any kind of emotion.

Anil had told Aadrika later that he too had felt something, and it was the first time in all the time he had been married he wanted and needed to have an affair with a woman, an affair that would be smouldering at first then sweaty and sticky and sleazy. What he did not tell her was that he was sure that it would gradually turn into something boring and dull, but by then Anil would have got it out of his system so he could return to his mundane life with Sameera.

Aadrika had been grateful when Anil walked her to her apartment and having thanked Anil again, she entered her flat whilst Anil walked home thoughtfully, unhappy at leaving her for he had enjoyed her company but happy in the knowledge that he would be seeing her the following day.

So, when they met the next morning, they were merely polite for neither was going to admit or let the other know of the depth of their attraction. However, as both enjoyed each other' company, they found they did not really want to ignore each so one afternoon, Anil joined her during their lunch break in their canteen.

Aadrika had not been so relaxed and happy since Dhruv left, so when Anil proposed they meet for lunch once a week. Aadrika agreed happily, for her only friend Anika had gone to stay with her mother in Kent soon after Anika had stayed with her after Dhruv left.

Aadrika changed her position on the sofa, rested two fingertips to her forehead and closed eyes thinking that she had been so busy recollecting how the affair had started that her neck ached as she most probably lay at what must have been a wrong angle.

 She got up and went into the kitchen, held a towel under the cold tap the held it to her face and placed it on forehead for a minute before she made herself another cup of coffee and returned to the sitting room and looked out at the window.

She turned away from window returned and finished her coffee, closed her eyes and lay back trying to find a comfortable place not only physically but mentally for her. mind kept racing back to Anil and wandering over the many conversations they had had when Aadrika had confided in him.

Chapter 10

It was during lunch one afternoon that Aadrika suddenly started crying.

"Aadrika, what has happened are you all right?" Anil asked in alarm. "Is it those hooligans again, are they harassing you?"

"No, it is not them Anil, but today is my wedding anniversary and…" she gulped as she wiped her eyes.

"I am so sorry, Aadrika, but are you not better off without him?"

"Maybe, but I still feel so lonely sometimes, and we were happy at first, that is before everything went wrong!" #

Anil put his hand on hers when she broke down and she told him, her voice breaking and in between deep shuddery breadths, that there were times when she missed having no family, that she found living with a young son to look after difficult on top of which she was struggling to meet ends meet. "

"Doesn't your husband help you financially?" Anil asked, wondering how anyone could abandon such a beautiful and gentle girl.

"He is legally responsible to pay maintenance for your son and there are agencies which would make sure he does! Have you contacted any of them?"

They were sitting at a restaurant at a table that faced the window overlooking the pavement and as Aadrika looked out she saw shoppers laden with grocery bag, and women with prams and push bikes walking past

"No, I have not," Aadrika replied sadly, "but he is not a bad person really, he is immature and irresponsible, one who is afraid of commitment. We were happy till our son Aarush was born and when he was a few months old, he said he was being suffocated in the marriage, basically that we were suffocating him!" Aadrika gulped. "I had no idea he felt so strongly about it, anyway, that same evening he packed his bags and left. Just like that without a backward glance, not at me nor his son."

"How did you manage? I mean leaving you alone with no family for support?" Anil asked as his admiration for her grew.

"It was horrible, more so because I thought we were happy." Aadrika choked, tears in her eyes. "I had no family no friends, no, fortunately I had a good friend Anika, who I phoned the evening that Dhruv had left. She was so worried that she immediately packed her bags and came to stay. She bought her son with her who is the same age as Aarush. I don't know what I would have done without her. But I thought that maybe Dhruv had left in a huff and would come back! But when after a week, I heard nothing, I knew he had gone for good and could not expect any kind of help from him emotional or financial. And with that came the realisation that I had to look after Aarush so decided that as soon as Aarush started school, I would start working."

"I am sorry it must have been very difficult on your own., I think you are very brave to have faced this on your own."

"Thank you, and yes it was, but Aarush had started nursery by then so that kept me busy, dropping him and picking him up and sometimes meeting some of the mums. We did get together socially sometime whilst the children played outside, but I found making friends difficult, for my childhood had been spent in an orphanage. I was uncomfortable in their company because I felt that beneath their laughter and smiles there was spite and viciousness for, they kept wanting to meet Aarush as if wating to point out that I was not bringing him up well.!"

"That was not nice of them!" Anil was horrified that there was racism even among the women. "I would have thought they would have sympathised at the terrible position you had been left in!"

"I thought so to and wanted so much for them to understand, but they would look at me and whisper amongst themselves, for I was an Asian, single and a woman struggling to bring up my child. However, something good did come off getting together with the ladies, for that is where I met Anika and from then on, we became good friends," She stirred her coffee thoughtfully. "I thought I would have got over it by now but being scorned by the person I loved and then abandoned still hurts, and now that Aarush is growing up, he will want to know about his father and what will I tell him, that his father abandoned him?"

Chapter 11

Anil felt sorry for her and. wanted to protect her from the men that Aadrika said were stalking her. As Aadrika needed a friend, gradually they began to find time to spend together for lunches or coffee, however keeping in mind that they stay within the boundaries of friendship.

But one day, on their afternoon off, having finished lunch they walked out of the restaurant and got caught in the rain. Being unprepared for the sudden change in weather and with no umbrella to protect them, they were soaked by the time they reached Aadrika's flat. Aadrika invited him in as her son Aarush was planning to spend the evening at his friend's house directly after school.

Anil had readily accepted for he enjoyed Aadrika's company and found, when he entered the flat, that like her, it too was warm and cosy. "Anil, I will get a towel so you can dry yourself and I will make some tea after I have changed."

Aadrika quickly ran into the bathroom and came out holding a towel which she handed Anil, who began rubbing his hair.

Having towelled his hair he went into the kitchen where he found Aadrika had changed into casual black jeans with a pink tank top, which he was to later learn were her favourite casual outfit.

She looked beautiful as she stood in the kitchen waiting for the kettle to boil, opening the kitchen units, taking out the mugs and putting them on a tray.

She did not hear Anil come up behind her and quietly put his hand his hands round her waist. And, when she did not resist, he kissed her gently on the lips and the boundary of friendship was crossed!

Although both had wanted this in their heart, theirs had been a platonic friendship so far, the only touch exchanged was an occasional casual hand on the shoulder and an innocent hug, however, there had always been an underlying attraction that both had ignored, but now both felt their emotions clouding and as they did, their bodies leant towards each together hungrily.

"Come with me, leave the tea, that is not what I need." Anil held her by the hand, his eyes glittering with desire for the pink tank top moulded her figure and her black hair rippled down her waist.

Aadrika followed him silently, her mind telling her was married, as was she, and she would only get hurt. But she had been alone for so long that she found she could not turn off her feelings of passion and desire which made her vulnerable.

Anil led her to the sofa where there began a loving war between masculine and feminine bodies twisting trying to hold on to something that neither could hold on to, and after a brief break when they had regained their breadth, the internal and physical battle would begin again.

At first, Aadrika's body was stiff and tight than gradually she relaxed and when Anil kissed her tenderly on the lips, she groaned with pleasure and a sigh rippled through her. Anil made her feel alive, secure and warm and suddenly it seemed as if the air was charged, electrifying and pulsating with what was in their minds, something they could not recognise but their hearts did, expressing what their tongues could not but hands could, and finally both Anil and Aadrika were overpowered by their feelings and practicality and logic vanished into thin air.

An electrical impulse swept through their bodies as they clung to each other, and it was as if the storm of their pleasure and pain gushed out from them and spilled across the room. They clutched and held each other, not willing to let go, and finally when their passion cooled, they clutched and caressed each other, then lay back contentedly still holding on to each other peacefully knowing, understanding and embracing the complications of their situation.

Aadrika put her hand on Anil's cheek and gently stroked it, and for the first time she thought there was pleasure to be had in life after all for, after Dhruv left, she had not thought there would be any kind of happiness for her, but this was soon followed by a sense of guilt as she thought of Anil's wife.

Anil abruptly got up, and as he got ready to leave, she felt as if his manner had changed and the romantic ecstasy had left not only him , but the room, leaving it empty, Aadrika's heart ached, for till now, she had been successful in closing the doors of her heart, for she was aware that opening them would surely lead to hurt, but somehow Anil with his intelligent engaging boyishness had let himself in.

"Aadrika, I am sorry, but this must never happen again." Anil said as he tucked his shirt in his trouser and combed his hair.

"Yes, you are right, I don't know what came over me." Aadrika replied, putting on her clothes that had been discarded in a hurry. "I have been in control for so long, that in the heat of the moment, it eluded me, though that is no justification!"

"It was not only your fault, Aadrika, but you looked so beautiful that I..." Anil smiled and winked. "Anyway, Aarush will be coming any minute?"

"Oh yes, I forget! I have to make dinner for him."

However, Aadrika felt hurt and disappointed for she had thought Anil to be too kind a man to blank her out or treat her as a piece of furniture, but it seemed she was wrong, for he just had, and even if they did continue to see each other, the limited amount of pleasure would only serve as a thin strip of elastic stretched to cover Aadrika's pain, for each time he went back to his wife would only puncture the wound of being abandoned again. 'I too do not want to get involved with a man who thinks I am a convenience nor care how I feel. 'She thought to herself trying to regain some control of her emotions which had let her down.

Therefore, she had nodded her head as she looked at him getting dressed. "You are right Anil, better to nip it in the bud to save us from hurt."

"I am glad you understand, Aadrika, you deserve better." He kissed her on the head and left.

However, when they met the next day at the office, both felt the reoccurrence of the electricity between them and Anil asked her out for lunch on the spur of the moment, it was not as if he was asking for affection and love!

"I don't know what you feel," Anil asked her as they had quickly gone out for a quick lunch." But I don't want to fight or ignore this feeling I have when I see you so, although we had decided not to, I would like to see you again."

Aadrika had looked at him dreamily and thought there was nothing better than to feel wanted,

"I agree, Anil." She had whispered and gradually their one-day liaison became an affair which Anil thought would run its course with intensity then dwindle and fade away, for both had family priorities.

Aadrika had become so absorbed in her thoughts she had dozed off and suddenly gradually got up with a start, finding herself in a foetal position on the sofa, but feeling refreshed and strong after the short nap to face anything that life targeted her with, for she knew in her heart that it was only a matter of time before Anil ended the affair.

She hurriedly went into the kitchen to prepare dinner for Aarush, though she knew that she would have to throw most of it away for Aarush, unlike most children, did not like any kind of food.

Chapter 12

Anil droves home perplexed and at the same time ashamed of the lie he was living, the lies he had to tell so no one would get hurt. He should have put a stop to the affair earlier on, but it had started off as being platonic then become intimidate.

They both had felt guilty to start with, Anil because he was cheating on his wife and Aadrika, because she was sleeping with a married man. Anil wondered when his double life had started, there had to be a time when he had first lied, when he had deceived Sameera who was very naïve, loved him unconditionally, plus he had a grown-up daughter Khushboo whom he loved dearly.

There were road works ahead so the road was jammed, and he sat impatiently, first putting on the radio then tapping his fingers on the steering wheel as his thoughts wandered back to Aadrika who had only shown her feelings once when she told him that she did not like this arrangement and nagged him into leaving Sameera.

He pushed back the hair that was falling over his forehead as he recalled the conversation.

"Aadrika, you know very well that I won't, we have been through this before! I have spent more time with you over the years than with Sameera and Khusboo!"

Anil rose from the sofa angrily and ran his fingers through his hair. "I don't know what else I can do. You knew how it was going to be from the start and had agreed that you would make no demands! You know where Sameera thinks I am whenever I have not been able to make it home? She thinks I am working two jobs and I have missed so much quality time with my family because I was here with you! That is how naïve she is, not once did it occur to her that I might be cheating on her!! And if she ever found out it would break her for, she depends on me, and I appreciate the fact that she left her family to be with me and I repay her by cheating on her…!"

"Anil, you should have thought of that before we started this affair and I know I agreed to go along, but I too long to have an ordinary life, even the little things like the problems of marriage as mother and wife. How nice it would be to come home to a family after having been out to a party and whatever worries there would be, would be rightful and legal!"
"You knew from the beginning that would not happen!" Anil reminded her again, ran his fingers through his hair in perplexity. "You don't know how guilty I feel for deceiving Sameera."

"But it is too late to grow a guilty conscience don't you think? And I don't like the fact that you seem to put all the blame on me, when all the time I was nothing to you but a…!" Aadrika had tears in her eyes which she wiped with the back of her hand. Anil went to her, put his arms around her and wiped the tears from her face with his hand.

"Aadrika, please don't cry, you know that I hate to see you cry, come sit." He led her back gently to the kitchen and sat her on a chair tenderly. "Aadrika, you know that in my own way I do love you and we have been through so much over the years."

"It is not easy for me. Aarush is growing up and is going to question our relationship and I want the world to know about it for I am not ashamed of it."

"And neither am I, Aadrika," Anil lied, for his feelings for her did not run deep... "As for Aarush, I have not even met him for he is always at his friend's place. I think you are too lenient with him anyway, the last thing I want to do is to teach you parenting classes, but I am caught in the middle here maybe we should not have let things get this far. Leave it me, I will think of something, though all I can foresee, if we bring this to light, is heartache for everybody!"

However, he found Aadrika to be such a gentle and beautiful girl he found it difficult to end the affair, and soon they had settled into a comfortable routine without ruffling any feathers and years had flown with Anil alternating his time between Sameera and Aadrika. But to do so, he found himself lying to Sameera, who did not question him when he explained that he had to work two jobs to pay the mortgage.

But eventually, as his life fell into a pattern, something he had predicted would happen, and he began to find his life suffocating. He began to resent the drainage of his energy into an affair that was going to end in boredom or scenes of passion as the one Anil had witnessed; and he just did not have any strength to calm her or feel guilty about it. But he knew he was a coward in letting things get so far and wondered how much further he could continue, for he felt sandwiched, and it was now becoming so suffocating that he felt he could not breathe and was trying to find a solution.

The traffic started moving and Anil heaved a sigh of relief but found that it was still progressing too slowly. He looked out the window and the few faces that he could see were beginning to grow dim and shadowy as the sky began to prepare for the darkness of night.

Even the trees were forming dark patterns of their leaves whilst birds were beginning to disappear into the silence of the cedar leaves who were forming dark patterns and Anil marvelled at how quiet it had become for, he could neither hear the rustle of a leaf nor the chirp of a bird. As he put down the silence to his being in a car, his thoughts turned to another problem.

He was worried that his family in India were in trouble as they had all gone to join the protest in Delhi. He had spoken to his brother, Aarev, and tried to tell him to persuade his parents not to attend the rally for they were old and fragile and to sit out in the cold would be harmful to their health. But Aarev told him that he had already done so and when they still insisted had suggested that he would go with them.

"Anil, father is adamant, he feels it too be his duty, not only because he believes that the bills were passed illegally amidst a pandemic, without consulting the farmers and also, as he is the elder of the village, he feels it is his duty to set an example for the others in the village."

Anil knew what he said was right for he knew his father to be a stubborn man, one who could not be deterred from his goal

Chapter 13

. Anil's thoughts turned to his daughter, Khushboo, who he thought had taken after him, for she too was strong and stubborn, a young beautiful intelligent woman who he was proud of. But sometimes, when he spoke to her, he could see her look at him strangely, at other times sadly as if silently reproaching him? Sameera was naïve and trusted him when he rang up to say he was going to be late, but Khushboo, he was sure, was suspicious of his behaviour, although, out of respect and love of her mother, she did not talk openly about them.

Finally, the traffic moved, and he went past the repair work that was being done, after which the roads were clear. As he neared his house, the plan that had seemed so hazy and unclear in his mind at the start of the journey home, began to unfold, however, he needed to process and filter it before he was ready to make it public.

He felt sorry for Aadrika when she had told him how she had suffered during her time spent in care. However, Anil admired her, for regardless of what she had been through at the care home and then being abandoned by Dhruv, she had endured and then overcome all obstacles that came her way. Sameera, on the other hand, was dependant on him, and if he chose to leave Sameera, she would be devasted although he was confident that Khushboo would take care of her. But he could not envisage Sameera, a proud woman, accept being cared of by her daughter who would, anyway, eventually marry.

After Anil had parked his car and opened the car door, he got out, running his fingers through his hair, vowing to himself that he would sort out the situation soon, in fact he was sure that by morning he would have.

He opened the door of the house quietly with his key then tiptoed towards the kitchen, knowing that Sameera, before going to bed, would have left dinner for him. And as usual, she had laid out a plate, cutlery for him with some lentils curry and rice on the table. He dished out the rice and curry on the plate and put it in the microwave to be heated and sat on the table then restlessly got up feeling thirsty for it had been an unusually long drive in the car.

He opened the fridge, got out a cold bottle of beer and placed it on the table, then opened the microwave door when he saw the food had heated, brought it over to the table and sat down. The food was delicious for that was one thing he liked about Sameera, she took care of his needs unconditionally, knew his likes and dislikes whereas, he, on the other hand, had cheated on her and spent so little time with her.

She had stood by him when he had worked in the newsagent, with her father's cousin Aadarsh, looking after the shop so that he could rest as the shop was open 24 hours, They lived in the flat above the shop, so she brought Khusboo down with her to the shop so she could keep an eye on her whilst Anil rested, willing to face bravely the danger posed by gangs who he was sure were skin heads always loitering around the shop shouting "go back home pakis!

Anil had had an affair for years, yet had not cared what effect it was having on either woman or wondered why he was disturbed by it now?

He thought of his parents again, sleeping out in the cold for a cause, and how ashamed they would be of him. And one of his friends had just told him about the disaster in Uttarakhand and the many climate disasters around the world, he realised how fragile life really was. Maybe he would return to India, and he had the perfect excuse, for both women knew how he felt about the farmers agitation, but now it was not only the women who were the problem, it was William at work who was humiliating him by passing derogatory and racist remarks.!

After he had finished his dinner, he threw the empty beer bottle in the bin and washed his plate in the kitchen sink. After he had dried and put it away, he switched off the light and slowly climbed the stairs, but before going to his bedroom he went to his study. After spending a couple of hours going through his paperwork, he went to his bedroom having decided that he would not go into work the following day.

As soon as he entered, Sameera called out sleepily. "Anil is that you, have you had your dinner? You are very late, and you have to go to work in the morning."

"Shhh Sameera, go to sleep, yes I have, thank you and don't worry I am not going to work tomorrow."

After he had brushed and changed into his pyjamas, he turned back the quilt and got into bed. He closed his eyes and drifted off to sleep, and as his plan had begun to take shape, his worries vanished.

For since the last year, Anil had felt trapped, he felt like a bird in a cage, the only difference being that his cage not only had bars of hate and power but also of the needs of the people around him, all closing tightly around him so that he could not breathe.

He began to panic till he went over the plan he had cleverly crafted in his mind that he hoped would free him so he could safely breathe again!

Chapter 14

Anil walked into the kitchen the following morning rubbing his hair with a towel to find Sameera making breakfast and the aroma of stuffed paranthas (stuffed chaappitis) wafted over to him, and he suddenly felt feeling hungry.

"How come you are home today, Anil? Everything all right?" Sameera asked anxiously.

"Yes, it is, Sameera, I will explain after I have your delicious breakfast!"

He sat down quickly at the table whilst Sameera placed a hot. Parantha on a plate. Sameera had already placed a bowl of curd and a jar of pickle on the table, which usually were taken with Paranthas. This was a treat for him for he, since he met Aadrika, always left early in the morning, had breakfast with Aadrika.

"Has Khushboo already left for work?" he asked as he added some pickle on his plate... "Can I have some curd please Sameera?"

"Yes, she has," Sameera replied handing him the bowl of curd. As he ate, Anil thought how warm and cosy it was sitting with Sameera, a rare occasion, who had joined him at the table with a pot of tea. With Aadrika, breakfast was a quick affair with cereal, a cup of coffee and toast.

"Anil, how come you are home today?" Sameera asked again as she poured herself some tea. "You never take a day off, you are not coming down with something, are you?" Sameera asked anxiously,

"No, I am fine, Sameera, I had to talk to you about something that has been bothering me for some time. You know Dad and mum have gone to Delhi for the Farmers protest? Although Aarev is going to accompany them, I don't know what they are thinking of at their age to sit out in the cold!"

"I know! I too spoke to your mother Anil, hoping that I would convince her otherwise, but she was adamant, felt it was her duty to support her husband!" Sameera was fond of her mother-in-law and smiled affectionately. "Everybody's emotions in Punjab are stirred against what they feel are unfair laws, my parents, too, have gone and I am just as worried for they are stubborn and will stay there as long as it takes and from what I hear, neither side wants to give in."

"You are right, Sameera, and I am worried too, for now I heard that they have switched the internet off as well as cut of their water supply! They have put in nails around the area where the protesters, thereby making it impossible any to leave that area! What started off as a peaceful protest has become intense and violent."

"Yes, Khushboo told me about that! But is there nothing much we can do from here?" Sameera remarked thoughtfully. "There was a protest march in London too, but I think you were working so could not attend." "No, actually I did attend it, I left work early, but like you said there is nothing much we can do from here so I was thinking that maybe I should go be with my parents? They have always listened to me more than Aarev, maybe because I am elder of the two? But that is not the issue, I feel I should be with them at this time"

Sameera smiled slightly, "No I think it has more to do with the fact that you are sensible, not that I am saying Aarev is not but…" Anil was touched that his wife thought so highly of him followed by a pang of guilt. "But it is strange you are talking of going to India for I was thinking the very same thing! In fact, I was talking to Khushboo about it."

"You mean going to India?" Anil was surprised. "Why were you thinking about it Sameera, surely you are happy here? Or are you feeling homesick? You are not thinking of leaving me, are you?" Although Anil said it lightly, he could not help feeling that it would solve all his problems? Or would it?

"Of course, I am, Anil, but like you, I was worried about the situation back home, and since we got married, I have only been back once. Also, this is something Khushboo did not talk to me about, apparently, we were so occupied with what we had been through at the newsagent and all the racism that was hurled at us. Anyway, I think by moving here both of us thought that those days were over, and we had protected Khushboo, but she went to through the same ordeal, not the same as ours of course,"

Anil poured tea from the pot and helped himself to another Parantha (stuffed Roti) and added curd and pickle on his plate then asked with a frown "What do you mean Sameera?"

"She was bullied all the way through her childhood to university children teachers making comments about her race and background and now she is also facing it at work, so I suggested that maybe we should go back and not just for a holiday, I mean permanently."

"Sameera, you know if she is facing it at work Khushboo, as an employee who has experienced or is experiencing racism - even if it is not directly aimed at her - should be able to raise her concerns with her employer and I never thought…" Anil ran his fingers through his hair." Everyone in an organisation has a role to play in treating everyone with dignity and respect, having said that, I know the problems of raising the issue in the workplace, I myself am having the same problem at my workplace, Sameera!"

"How terrible! Is that the reason you wanted to go to India?" Sameera asked.

"Yes and no, the main was to see my parents, I only mentioned it because you said that Khusboo was going through it, anyway, being a lawyer, she would know all the legal issues surrounding it."

"I am sure she does, we have a very intelligent and capable daughter, Anil, what really saddens me is the fact that I could not see the pain she was going through, for when we went through it, we had each other through those terrible days, but Khusboo endured it alone." She wiped the tears from her eyes.

"Sameera, don't worry, she is a very strong girl and will know how to deal with it, now this is delicious! And to think I have been missing all this just to get to work!"

"And maybe that is another reason we should go; it will not only put your mind at rest when you meet your parents but will also be a holiday for us!"

"No, Sameera, I was thinking of going alone, someone needs to stay with Khushboo.

Chapter 15

"Oh" Sameera replied surprised. "But she is not a child, Anil, she can look after herself, anyway, her friend, Aishya, will be visiting from Dubai and will be staying here for some time"

"That is the first I have heard about her!" Anil asked protectively. "Where does she live and how does Khushboo know her?"

"I am surprised you are asking me that, Anil, but then you barely know your daughter! She missed not knowing you for all through her childhood, you were too busy to spend time with her. In fact, in our conversation, she mentioned taking over the mortgage payments, so you do not have to work two job and…"

"That is very nice of her, but you know I would never do that! She is my daughter, and one does not take money from one's children. It is about time she got married and it is my responsibility to see that she gets married in style, in fact that is what would be expected of me, us."

However, Anil had not thought about it at all. Could he use this to his advantage too? "And back home, I will not only look after my parents but look for a nice decent boy for Khushboo."

"And good luck with that! That is what I mean when I say you do not know your daughter for, she does not want to get married, at least not in the traditional manner. I spoke to her many times about it and her only answer is 'Mum, don't keep on and on about it, you are suffocating me, and I cannot breathe' She insists that we should not worry, and she will get married in her own way. As for the mortgage payments, I told her that you would not agree, and I was right!"

"Sameera how can you accept her attitude on marriage??" Anil exclaimed angrily. "It is not only what we expect, but also my parents and I am sure yours too and of course their grandparents,"

"Yes, but Anil, things are not what they were, we obeyed out parents, children nowadays are independent and know what they want. I think we should not force them, anyway we cannot."

"Ok I suppose you are right, but I still think I should go to India, alone! Sorry Sameera, I think that came out all wrong, but I think it best you stay behind with Khusboo, and I will make sure   that your parents are looked after. Anyway, I will finalise later, I don't even know whether I can get leave."

Sameera was silent, looking thoughtfully and sadly out of the window, knowing he would not bother to find out about her parents for he did not like them, something he had not hidden from her. He had only met them twice, once when he came to see her and the other at their wedding and whenever she called them, which she did once a week, he never tried to speak to them, even if he was in the same room. And she was tired of making excuses about his behaviour to them and to Khusboo, maybe she needed a break from him too for the stress of keeping up appearances was getting to be too much!

"And when are you planning to leave?" She asked pouring herself a fresh cup of tea.

"Sameera! I just ran it past you, now that you are on board with it, I can see to the details, the first one being about my jobs…in these times they are not many people taking holidays. I might have to take unpaid leave! Now, I am going out for a bit."

He went upstairs to change and when he came down found that Sameera was still sitting at the table and as soon as he had worn his coat and gloves, slammed the door behind him and left.

As Sameera got up from the table to clear the dishes, she could not but help feel sad, for the idea of going to India had excited her, but after her conversation with Anil, was unhappy that Anil wanted to go alone.

Sameera was not as naïve and innocent as Anil and Khushboo thought and felt that he wanted a break from their marriage, from her, and that the protest and wanting to take care of his parents was just an excuse.

Chapter 16

Anil was excited at the prospect of going to India, now all he had to do was tell Aadrika, so had sent a text to her in the morning not to expect him for breakfast as he would not be going into work but would like to meet her for lunch at their favourite restaurant.

As she had texted back confirming the arrangement, he drove past the local garage and chip shop on his way to the restaurant passing a park where he noticed that the leaves from some trees had fallen due to the wind and a couple were pushing a crying toddler in a pink pushchair.

Anil parked his car and walked on the pavement that was crowded with people; and as he crossed the road towards the restaurant quickly, some motorists beeped their horn in irritation, and he heard a man's angry voice muffled from behind the window of a car. Anil smiled, waved to him and quickly finished crossing the road.

He entered the restaurant through the swinging doors and stood awhile trying to locate Aadrika, for the restaurant was full and the tables were set at a distance, the restaurant carefully adhering to the social distancing guidelines for although restrictions had been lifted people were still wary of how quickly and easily the infection could spread.

He took out his mobile to phone her but then spotted her at a table wearing a light blue sari, her head bent over the menu, her hair escaping in strands from pins that had kept it knotted it in place but now lay untidily about her cheeks and neck…

Aadrika too had seen Anil, his eyes hidden by a baseball cap, wearing jeans, shirt with sleeves that were rolled up to his elbows under his favourite leather jacket. He walked across towards her with a smile that spread across his face and crinkled the corner of his eyes that hid his anxiety.

As he walked towards her table, Anil thought that Aadrika would not take the news of his going lightly, as had Sameera, maybe because she knew that Khushboo would look after her mother, whereas Aadrika had a young son to look after and no one she could depend on.

He wondered, if, since Khusboo was independent and broadminded, she would understand his situation? However, he dismissed the thought for no one, least of all Khushboo would tolerate her mother being treated the way he did. However, he could not but feel that Khusboo would understand Aadrika and even admire the way she had survived so many obstacles., for she believed in women empowerment.

"Hey there, Aadrika, anything interesting on the menu today?" He kissed her lightly on the head, patted her hair than wound a strand around his finger before sitting in the chair opposite.

Aadrika's almond eyes had lit up when she saw him and smiled, her big, dreamy eyes looking up at him "Hey, you are forgetting social distancing!" she grinned impishly "You know I only like their specials, which is always delicious! I know what I want but was only waiting for you to order."

"You go ahead, Aadrika, I will only have some coffee." He took off his jacket and placed it at the back of the chair and gestured to the waiter who came over with a tablet in his hand, which had now replaced notebook and pencils in most restaurants. After placing their order, Anil leant back in his chair.

"How come you are not eating, Anil? You too like their specials." She looked worried for he looked tense.

"I do Aadrika, but Sameera made stuffed Paranthas this morning and you know how l love them; so, I am full up!" Anil grinned.

Aadrika had flinched when she heard Anil say 'Sameera' and thought she detected an undertone of affection in his voice. The truth was that Sameera loved and cared for him and cooked delicious dishes for him whereas Aadrika only knew the fundamentals of cooking.

She sounded like a nice woman which made Aadrika feel guilty that she was breaking up a family, quickly followed by the thought it was Anil who had instigated the affair and maintained it.

Anil was a kind decent man, and he reminded her a lot of Dhruv, for in the orphanage, she had only come across men in authority who would leer and ogle her as soon as she reached puberty, but Dhruv had protected her from them, for no matter what had gone wrong with Dhruv after marriage, she would forever be grateful to him for keeping her safe and protected from those lecherous men.

And, when white children ganged up on her and told her that her parents did not want her and that is why she was in a care home, Dhruv would put his arms around her and tell her that was not true and that he wanted her. And when they taunted her by passing comments that she was from a low caste family, and when she cried, Dhruv would tell her that she was his princess.

Consequently, even the few Indian children in the care home stopped speaking to her and often turned their head when she passed. She felt obligated to Dhruv for she would often see him talk to those very children on her behalf.

Aadrika felt angry at herself for thinking about Dhruv, so put him at the back of her mind and pushed back her long hair over her shoulder, noting that Anil looked restless.

"Anil, there is something worrying you, tell me what is it? Are you feeling all right?" she asked in alarm for since the start if the pandemic, she was afraid that one of them would get covid although they strictly followed the national guideline and had had their vaccinations.

"I am fine Aadrika, you worry too much! But yes, there has been something on my mind, but have your lunch first we'll talk afterwards."

The waiter had placed the food and two cups of coffee on the table, and after he left, Anil pushed the food and curry towards Aadrika whilst he took the cup of coffee, added some sugar in his cup and stirred it thoughtfully, how was he going to tell her that he was planning to leave her to fend for herself in a world full of vultures?

Suddenly, he had an idea, before quickly dismissing it. What if he stayed with Aadrika and told Sameera and Khusboo that he was going to India? And later, he could always say that he had decided to stay on and with WhatsApp it was easy to deceive a person as to the location.

Aadrika had eaten quickly for she had left home in the morning without breakfast as she hated eating alone. Anil came every morning and she missed him when he did not, but luckily that did not happen often. She sipped her coffee and looked at Anil from under her long lashes.

"Now, Anil, what is the matter? You said you had something to talk about, nothing serious I hope?"

"No, it is not, I don't know how to put it, so I will come out and tell you…I am planning to go back to India and..."

Chapter 17

"What!" Aadrika exclaimed choking on her coffee. "That is a bit sudden, are all of you going? How long will you be gone and when will you be back?"

"One question at a time please Aadrika, I have been thinking about it for some time, at least since the farmers protest started and my family decided to get involved!" Anil lied "And you know I have been having problems with William my supervisor, I think, no I know he is a racist, he is always finding fault with my work, and I am just plain fed up! If he did that with the others, I would not mind but to be singled out, it is humiliating! When I come back, I will find another job, a less stressful one."

"Yes, you told me about him earlier, but I did not know that things were so bad, the atmosphere must be awful, but somehow, I cannot see him as being racist, womaniser yes, but if you get another job, we won't be able to meet easily."

Anil ignored her last comment and decided to concentrate on William "Maybe because you are a beautiful woman, maybe because you are not directly under him, who knows how his mind works but either way, I am surprised he has not hit on you, I would not put that past him!" Anil snapped. "He feels he is superior and much too occupied with maintaining the power he holds, and he is not subtle about his opinions either, for he is always passing racist remarks,"

"That does sound horrible, I can see it must be very demoralising to hear those cruel remarks day in day out and I can see why you would want to change jobs..." Aadrika shuddered, reminded of the comments that had been thrown her way at the care home and later by the women when they met weekly to discuss their children.

"It gets worse, my colleagues, even though they do not pass any remarks, keep quiet and look the other way when he does, which actually proves that they agree with him! And I am sure they do because during lunchbreak they all sit together laughing and whispering. It does not stop in the office either, in the evenings they go the bar for a drink or sometimes William has a barbecue on a weekend at his home, one to which I am not invited, but he makes sure I know about it for he invites the others in my presence, and on Monday they joke and laugh about the good time had!"

"Oh, you poor thing, is that why you were so keen that we should come out for lunch? I always wondered why, if not at this restaurant you always insisted, we go for a walk in the park."

Anil nodded his head miserably. "I am used to this attitude, for before I joined this office, I was working at my wife's cousin's newsagent, and nearly every day there were bricks thrown at the shop, told to go back home by gangsters who I am sure were skinheads!! That was a terrible time we went through, Khushboo was only a baby, yet Sameera stood by me. looked after the shop and the baby so I could rest! I will always be grateful to her for that for to have left her family in India to come here only to be face such violence…! "He shuddered."

Although Aadrika felt sorry for what he had been through, she selfishly thought of herself. She would miss him for only had he been a good friend and companion, he had taken care of her finances so she need not worry...

Although she smiled her approval, she was calculating how to capture and hold on to Anil who suddenly seemed so elusive. She began to think of ways that she could tie him to her with unbreakable bonds. And from her experience with Dhruv, she felt she had succeeded in binding him to her by exposing her vulnerability and weaknesses? From an early age, Aadrika had discovered that there was no greater power over another than the power of submissive dependency on them.

"Yes, I faced that too, in fact that was the reason Dhruv and me became close for both faced the same kind of discrimination... At least Dhruv protected me at that time, pity he did not feel the same once we got married." Aadrika looked sadly out of the window "But somehow after marriage, we could not live in peace and now I realise that maybe that was because as long as there had been a pattern or regularity to the problems that arose, which we had in the orphanage, we made a good team but, I have had a lot of time to think about why things went wrong with us and the only reason I could think of was that we were only good together because there were obstacles and problems and that is what we needed to make the relationship a success? Maybe our relationship required that to develop and nurture? I don't know if that makes any sense? One would think that by not having confliction and friction in a relationship that it would it develop! But I think Dhruv had become so used to protecting me that when he did not need to, he could not deal with it. I thought that things would improve after Aarush was born, but he completely ignored him!"

Aadrika's mouth trembled, and tears began to ooze into her eyes but did not fall. "You know that institution bruised my soul and stole my dreams, but not for Dhruv, he was strong and still clung to his dreams, whatever they were, which is why he left, to chase them!" she added bitterly.

Anil wiped his face, for although Aadrika had told in about the care home, he was horrified at what Aadrika had had to endure and its damaging effect on her. She had not had a normal happy childhood, which he and Sameera had been so careful to provide for his daughter

"How do you know that Aadrika? Did he tell you?" Anil asked, idly glancing at the couple who sat at the table next to theirs looking happy and oblivious to everything around them.

"No, he did not, but he said something to that affect!" Aadrika said sarcastically, "he looked so intense and angry when he told me before he left was that one never knows what will happen tomorrow so might as well achieve all one can today! And I am beginning to think he was right for what makes people live to the full is knowing it is limited and what makes it pointless is lack of purpose, like me. I think it has made me a prisoner and my own keeper too!"

"Aadrika, don't be too hard on yourself, I think you are doing the greatest job of all, bringing up a boy alone and under these circumstances" However although the words Anil uttered were sympathetic, the expression on his face was distant. Aadrika looked at him in confusion for she had literally sprawled her pain for Anil to see, yet, he had remained steadfast and had only flinched once momentarily.

Aadrika marvelled at his control, if it was that, but continued nonetheless, "When Dhruv left me, I came across discrimination where I worked, that is before I joined this job I used to work as a temp in various shops, and of course, the men you saved me from. Well, they had been stalking me for a long time and if you had not saved me, I am sure they would have raped me!" There were tears in Aadrika's eyes.

"Aadrika, I admire you for being so brave and facing all this alone!" Anil put his hand on Aadrika's delicate hand which was lying on the table.! "I am so sorry, at least I had Sameera and my cousin, but you had to face this alone."

"I know it was, no is a terrible time, but never mind about me, Anil, are you serious in going back to India? I am selfish for I am thinking of myself for I don't want you to go! Even though I only get a little bit of your time, since I have met you, I have never felt lonely! You have been so kind and..." Aadrika gulped and blinked back the tears at the thought of life without Anil, for without him there would be. no one to share breakfast and occasional snatched coffees and lunches!

"Aadrika, I too will miss you!" he smiled affectionately pushing back the hair from his forehead. Anil looked around at the restaurant at all the tables, at the couples who were laughing and talking. "Anyway, you will not be allowed to travel, I think India is going on the red list.

"No, I found travel is now easy as long as one is tested and if need be, quarantined at both ends, it should be okay."

"So, you are definitely going?" Aadrika asked hopefully than added as an afterthought "I don't think it is only Williams attitude that is making you go to India...could it be the Farmers Protest? I know you feel very strongly about it and also because your family is there??"

When Anil nodded, she continued "Anil, you know there are demonstrations and protestations everywhere. That is happening all over the world, the riots in America, because of George Floyd being killed by a police officer the mob hysteria and violence, people get over it, you don't have to uproot your life because of it!

Chapter 18

Anil smiled at her naivety and how oblivious she was to the fact that he was escaping, not her, but the dilemma he found he was finding himself in...he felt he was suffocating, oh God, how could he tell Aadrika that he felt the same as Dhruv, that he could not breathe? This was quickly followed by the thought that now was not the time should do the decent thing, that would disrupt his plans...

A man wearing a thick navy polo neck sweater and denim baggy jeans passed their table, glancing at them curiously for they were talking fervently, oblivious to everybody around them.

"Aadrika, yes that too, and you are right, the situation in India will, hopefully blow over, but till then, I need .to get away from William and to spend some time with my parents, Khusboo will be working from home most of the time so will be with Sameera, and you can too as you can do flexible hours to work from home to look after Aarush as the schools will be shut too. And I will be back in no time at all, I have spoken to Sameera and..."

However, seeing the look on Aadrika's face, he bit his lip and cursed himself for being so insensitive… It was not fair on her, he thought, to talk about Sameera, so tried to change the subject.

"I also have to speak to William as yet, and knowing him, he will try and make it as difficult as possible for me!" he sighed "You know I thought I had left that kind of attitude behind in the days when I was working with Sameera's cousin, but I guess it is still prevalent everywhere."

"Yes, it is, and a lot depends on how one is brought up too, values of the parents and what they teach their children about diversity."

There was a note of longing in Aadrika's voice for she had not experienced the love and warmth of a family life. That is why, having lost Dhruv too, she clung on to Anil, even if it was for a brief time, since even the slightest atmosphere of family life alongside him satisfied her and she felt complete.

Anil, meanwhile, although he had dismissed the idea of staying back in London, thought about it again, it would solve all his problems, for he found his life, alternating between the two women, to be suffocating. Although he had enjoyed Aadrika's company early on in the affair and felt that there was chemistry between them, and she stimulated him, he was even fond of her, in his own way, he had become bored for Aadrika had become too clingy, and with the help of his friend he could, so decided to talk to his friend as soon as possible before he came to any decision.

He thought about Sameera and how different in temperament she was compared to Aadrika. When he was young, he had never considered himself to be the marrying kind and was content to stay in India with his parent and when they had brought up the subject of marriage, he of course, had refused profusely. However, his parents had persuaded him into at least meeting Sameera before deciding and when he had, found her to be a pleasant woman, but the deciding factor had been when her parents were offering, as part of dowry, two tickets to London, where, should he agree, they had some relatives to help them settle.

It had always been an unattainable dream of Anil's to come to London so had, to his parent's delight immediately consented. Anil had always thought that he was in control of life, and it did not occur to him that he was doing exactly what society determined and by consenting, rather than taking control was surrendering to its rules

He shook his head as he thought that he would deal with the problems as and when they arose.

"Aadrika, shall we leave?" And when she nodded continued

"Right, wait for me here whilst I pay the bill." He went to reception and after sanitising his hands, returned to their table where Aadrika was waiting, tapping her foot impatiently.

"Anil, I have just remembered, I need to be home by 3 pm Aarush will be home."

"Do you want me to drop you home?" Anil asked as he put his under her elbow and steered her out of the restaurant.

"No thanks Anil, it is not too far, but if it not too much trouble can you drop me at his school? That is only if you have time, I know you will have to make travel arrangements and shopping." Aadrika asked as she turned to him. "You will let me know when you are going? I will come to the airport and oh, I will miss you." She stood on tiptoe and kissed him lightly on his cheek.

"Yes, of course I will take you to the school where you can pick up Aarush. Do you want me to wait for you whilst you collect him, then I can drop both of you to your flat?"

"No thanks Anil." Aadrika replied quickly. "He might have some extra class, so we will walk back home."

"As you wish, Aadrika."

As they walked towards his car, Anil could not help wondering at the strange look that had crossed her face when he had suggested he would drop both of them home. However, he quickly dismissed his concern as he had other things to worry about.

Anil stopped the car just outside the school and was glad they were just in time for the children were coming out of their classes amidst the buzz of childish voices.

"I can drop you back Aadrika, I will wait for you whilst you go collect him." Anil asked again.

"Aah, that is so sweet of you Anil, but we will manage, thank you, don't worry." Aadrika smiled sweetly.

She got out of the car, pulled her coat tightly around her for the wind was cold and biting, and with its force, was hurling the litter along pavement. Aadrika turned and waved him a kiss, shoved her hands into her coat pockets and disappeared into the school grounds.

Rather than going back home, Anil thought he would go and see one of his friends, Reyansh.

As he drove towards his office, he passed houses and parks, the houses he noticed were clustered together, some with messier gardens than others. In the park there were dogs barking and children zigzagging around the trees and bushes.

He had to brake suddenly as the truck in front of him stalled and he noticed that it had building implements, bricks and spades that were piled at the back of the truck, and most probably was on its way to a construction job.

Chapter 19

Reyansh was a good-looking man with brown wavy hair that was dark and shiny, with a strong straight nose, prominent jaw, and a dark neatly trimmed beard and although there was usually humour in eyes, he looked impatiently at Anil.

He frowned slightly squinting against the cold light that was streaming from the window, impatiently tapping his pencil on his desk. He swivelled his chair to look at Anil, who was sitting on the other side of his desk.

Anil quickly told him about his plan to go to India.

"What do you want me to say Anil" Reyansh frowned after Anil explained his plan.

"I got the impression that somebody should go to India to set the record straight, when we met at the protest rally here in London."

"Yes, about that, you do realise that I have a full-time job here and am only partly involved with a cause in India. Through my organisation grapevine I had heard that there are some elements who only want to exploit the situation for their own benefit. I deal with clients who have families back home who are worried, And I was worried because it is being rumoured that my organisation is funding it, and that the rumour is being fuelled by people for their own ends at the expense of the poor farmers! I believe your parents are also involved in the protest?"

"Yes, they are and that is why I am worried, for like you pointed out, some people are exploiting the protest for their own ends, innocent people are getting hurt and because of that I am afraid for my family,"

"It is understandable that you should feel strongly about it, but we are only concerned with the politics here in the UK, for we know that ethnic and racial inequalities continue to exist, no thrive, in employment, housing and the justice system! In addition, we now must address the issue of ethnic disparity in deaths from COVID-19. So why we would interfere in another country's politics or why anyone would even think so is beyond me." Reyansh said in frustration as he put the pencil back in its holder.

"But like you pointed out, the protest in India is personal to most of us, my parents too are farmers, and feel they should raise a voice. Anyway, I personally don't know enough of the bill and whether a protest is justified."

"Oh yes, it is justified and there is money being sent to them from abroad, but it is sent to the farmers direct and only because most of us here are from villages back home and our parents are farmers, so it is but natural to send them money to care for them Anyway, that is not I wanted to talk about, I was wondering if once I am back from India, that I could work for you ?"

Anil explained the problem he was facing with William. "I feel I can do good here for I have experienced it first-hand for before working for William, I was working with Sameera's cousin at his newsagent where every week there was a burglary and children or skinheads, sometimes both at the same time, threw stones at the shop and wrote graffiti on the shop window."

"I am sorry you had to go through all that Anil, Anyway, although most of the people in our organisation are volunteers, who raise awareness of the problems that face ethnic people, I think we can find a job for you here and your experience would be invaluable for we do realise that it the bigot of today, by voicing racial jokes, not only show their mindset, but that these everyday humiliations that people like us endure only helps to create that it is normal to do so. And what saddens me is that people like him prove to be successful in resisting the awareness that our people are trying to raise and that is very frustrating! So, we will welcome someone like you, in fact we need more people like you, we need to stop this for if we don't it will continue and increase! We cannot afford to ignore it, take the case of George Floyd for instance."

"At least they found the policeman guilty, a verdict no one predicted! But that is not the end of the matter, for I believe he is appealing, and one never knows, he might still get away with it!"

Reyansh got up from his chair and held out his hand with a smile. "Let's hope not!"

"I admire the work you are doing Reyansh, and I look forward to working with you," Anil replied as he got up and shook Reyansh's hand. As Reyansh walked him to the door, he said "We are getting there, Anil, slowly but surely!"

Anil droves home, happy in the knowledge that his plan was coming together and that at least he would have a job, when he decided to return. He would enjoy this job he mused, for after his experiences and what Sameera had told him that morning about Khushboo going through the same thing, he was impatient to help challenge inequality so that the minorities could demand human rights and social justice, something that was their basic right.

He decided that after dinner he would tell Khushboo and Sameera part of his plan, which would be easy as he had already prepared Sameera, however, asking William was going to be difficult for he was sure to make matters difficult.

He was in a dilemma, if he asked for leave, William would most likely refuse or force him to take unpaid leave and he needed the money, although he was sure once in India, his parents would help, but of that even he was not sure as they had been on protest which would surely have affected their income such as it was.

So, as it was only 5:30, he decided to visit William and get it over with, so that he could plan accordingly, and much to his surprise, William approved his leave on compassionate grounds.

After he had been to see William, it was still early so decided to go to the travel agent after which Anil turned his car into a side road and the throng of people disappeared as the noise of the main road became a whisper of a residential area.

Chapter 20

William was a large man with big bushy black and white beard and intense blue eyes. He was wearing jeans with a shirt that was open at the neck from which dangled a gold chain. His hair was pulled back into a ponytail, his forearms were covered with tattoos, and he usually wore three or four bracelets on each of his wrists.

He parked his car, opened the door of his house and entered, but the house was unusually quiet, so assumed Mary, his wife, must be out. The thought angered him, and his hands turned into fists, the nails digging into his palms for she knew that he came home at 6.pm and he expected her to be waiting for him.

He went straight into the kitchen, opened the fridge, and took out a cold bottle of beer, and before taking it to the lounge, looked out of the window and saw his two sons, James and Oliver playing in the garden. He took a swig from the bottle, wiped his mouth and after putting on the TV sat on the sofa with his legs on the coffee table.

He lit a cigarette lifted it to his mouth then prodded it lightly before pursing his lips and bringing the cigarette to them with his arm, and as he did so, watched in admiration the bicep on his arm that had enlarged and curled. His training was paying off!

He switched the channel to the one that was reporting George Floyd's trial with interest for William was a man who endorsed inequality and it was with surprise he heard the channel report that a guilty verdict had just been pronounced on Chauvin.

William was dumbfounded for he had been sure that Chauvin would not be found guilty; at the very least would only be given a minimum sentence as a matter of formality. For George Floyd was a black man who had been on drugs, which the defence was claiming to be the cause of death, whilst the prosecution were claiming that Chauvin was only doing his duty by restraining George by placing his knee on George's neck! And yet he had been found guilty, William thought angrily as he got up to switch of the television.

William's face was distorted with rage for he believed that people of different races possessed certain characteristics that, according to him, separated them as being inferior to the white race; thus, he thought that they were only born to be subservient to them, and that Chauvin had only shown his superiority by putting his knee on George's neck... William was glad a couple of minorities were his employees for it give him a chance to wield his power over them. He was aware that to do so was illegal, but he also knew that most ethnic people were too docile and meek, thus making it easy for him to do so without fear of repercussion. Of the two in his employment, he thought Aadrika to be beautiful and exotic, unlike his wife, Mary, but she was also inaccessible as she worked in another department.

William, although married, was a man who liked to have casual affairs with women. and was so arrogant that he thought if he wanted to have Aadrika, he could do so, for her docility would make her an easy target. He thought Aadrika to be like an injured sheep that has stuck out on the edge of the flock that is just waiting to be picked up! He even had had some of his friends follow her to find out where she lived, and to his surprise and delight, she lived in a flat that was in a remote area and was not far from his house. So, it was only a matter of time before he….

Whilst Aadrika was exotic, Mary, his wife was ethereal looking, with pale skin and long blonde hair, a woman who was neither beautiful nor ugly but had the possibility of being both...She was so meek that he could control her easily, although, to William both, being women, were obviously inferior, Aadrika more so because she was 'one of them'

William did not recognize the strengths and value of the diverse cultures and what they could bring into his culture. There was no doubt in his mind that it was only biology and anatomy that shaped people's destiny, and not that they might have potential, and that they might have a talent, ability or skill that would form the basis in creating a better future for themselves and their children.

William believed strongly in genetics, for that would explain their physical attributes, inherited traits both mental and physical. His biggest fear was the that the minorities were destroying his social privileges, thereby the balance of society, and he knew many people felt the same, and he admired Chauvin for arrogantly airing his superiority.

William was intent on humiliating Anil, and by doing so, reaffirming, and taking back what he thought was rightly his position, overlooking the fact that Anil was no threat to him. But this attitude had been taught to him by his parents and he was making sure that not only was he living by them but that the same beliefs would be passed on to his children. He thought about his conversation he had with Anil who had put it an application for leave.

"You know we are overworked here; this is no time to be going on holiday" he had barked angrily...

"It is not really a holiday sir." Anil had answered meekly. "My parents are in some kind of trouble, and I need to be there to look after them..."

William had unwillingly approved of the application knowing that Anil was within his rights to apply for compassionate leave and that he could create a problem for their office if he refused.

As he sat waiting for Mary, William thought it was perfectly natural to behave and think like he did, for although he was not by nature a racist, he was born to parents who were and in a society that embraced and nurtured racist attitudes and ideologies which then trickled into schools, media and culture before finally inching its way into institutions of power.

His parents had raised him to look down at people who were different to him, and he had resented them when they began calling Sahil, his best friend, 'your brown friend' followed by 'you can do better than him, son'! William had been hurt because he had liked Sahil and wanted his parents to like him too, he was his best friend who was kind and helpful. He liked is parents too, for they welcomed him into their home and fed him milk and cakes, and if his mother was cooking an Indian dish, would let him taste it and if he liked it, fed him...

As a young impressionable child, it was confusing and disturbing for William to hear his parents pass racial remarks, however, he felt there was an unspoken line he could not cross, a line that existed when interacting with others and his parents. William could not ignore his parents' racial comments as one could from a stranger. because, unlike arguing with strangers, it was impossible for him to completely disregard his parents' bias against people of dark skin. An attitude which first had first only overshadowed but then replaced Williams flourishing attitude of anti-racism.

His mindset had interchanged only because he cared what his parents thought and because there existed in him, as it does in all children, a small child that longs for validation from its parents. An authentication that he still needed, although his parents were not alive, he felt that by adhering to their values, he was keeping them alive...His parents had wanted him to either deny, negate or at the very least trivialise a minorities existence, and gradually they had begun to succeed and as soon as William had been fully shaped by his parents' intolerance, he began to taunt and bully Sahil, his onetime good friend, who could not understand the sudden change in him.

The cruellest thing that occurred because of William's bullying was that the other children followed his lead in harassing Sahil, because of which his parents had him transferred him to another school.

They still lived nearby, and William would often see Sahil walking home, his head bowed, not daring to look up, and if he ever saw William, would turn his face. Sometimes William did miss him, how he would greet him happily with a huge grin across his face with one tooth missing. But once he went home, Sahil was forgotten, but not his parents' ideology, and now that he was all grown up, he had fully embraced the values of his parents.

However, although his parents had ensured that their beliefs were firmly rooted in him, they failed to infuse in him what constituted a loving relationship and how to maintain it, maybe because the only way of communication his father had with his mother was with his fists?

William remembered vividly his father raising his fist on his mother whenever he did not like her cooking or for his perception of what he thought constituted disrespect.

Chapter 21

Therefore, his relationship with Mary was like that of his father, he believed that to abuse his wife was his entitlement and that, should she ever think of reporting him to the police, his actions would only be acceptable and justified, for was it not Mary's behaviour that provoked him to hit her? He did not realise that his bullying was having the same effect on her as it had on Sahil for Mary had become a scared and submissive woman.

As William waited for her, Mary, having done her grocery shopping, was driving home anxiously for she was held up in a traffic jam. She sat impatiently tapping her fingers on the wheel and biting her lip for she had planned to be home before William arrived home.

She always made sure she did not displease him in any way, but nothing ever satisfied him, and he was constantly criticising her. In fact, things had got so bad she felt she could not breathe and that if she did, that too would only make him angry! She had considered going to the police but knew that no one would believe her for he made sure that he only hit her where it would not show; added to it was the fact that he could be so charming and polite that people would find it difficult to believe that he had a dark side to his nature.

She was exasperated and enraged by his constant threats and humiliation of not only her but her friends too who had felt so offended that they had stopped contacting her in fear of him. She could not even meet them for coffee or lunch for William constantly phoned her to find out that she was home.

She had often thought of leaving him, but because she felt her sons needed her, was willing to endure William's beatings and humiliation vowing that as soon as her sons were older, she would leave, and in readiness of the day had begun putting aside some money for that day. But lately, William had upset her plan of escape for he had stopped giving her housekeeping money, and she suspected that it was because he had somehow found out about her savings, and if he had, today would only confirm it for she had had no choice but to use it.

He was not only going to get angry that she had left the house, but that she would have spent money without his permission, blind to the fact that it was only spent on necessities. Mary thought how manipulative and sly he really was for with him, everything was a test, which is why she felt she always felt she was walking on eggshells. She identified herself with George Floyd and how he must have felt in the last minutes of his life, that it was William's behaviour that was so suffocating she could not breathe; it was not for nine minutes that she could not breathe, her life with William was continuously stifling her!

His affection for her, if there was any, was measured against what was given to him, and William evaluated that against what he had not received, and the balance always disappointed him. Mary was beginning to think that even his children would disappoint him one day and dreaded the consequences of that happening. Maybe she should take them and leave before that happened?

After what seemed to be an awfully long time, the traffic started to move, and she turned off the main road by pub and drove up the narrow road that had overgrown hedges on either side that led to her house.

She hurriedly got out of the car and saw her sons playing in the garden, praying that William had not reached home, however, with dismay, saw his car in the garage so parked on the driveway.

Her long blonde hair was tied at the back with a red and grey scarf, and she was wearing a coat above her tight blue jeans and boots

"James. Oliver come help me with the shopping" she called out to her sons quickly as she opened the car door and started taking the shopping out of the car.

"Coming, Mum!" they answered as they threw the ball on the floor and hurried to the aid of their mother. They were old enough to understand how their father treated their mothers and saw with dismay the frightened look on her face.

William had heard her voice and was standing at the doorway hands on hips, his face thunderous. He let James and Oliver through, but when Mary tried to pass, held her arm and hissed under his breadth "I will see to you later!"

Mary flinched as she felt Williams hands grip her arm tightly, his fingers and nails digging into her soft skin

"William, leave me alone, you are hurting me and not in front of the boys please!" she whispered, hot tears gathering in her eyes as William loosened his grip on her arm.

After the boys had placed the shopping on the kitchen table and run out, Mary looked at William anxiously

"William, there was a lot of traffic on the roads because of a burst pipe and..." she said faintly, but when Mary saw the look of anger on William's face, aborted the sentence for fear she might say something that would only aggravate his anger.

However, he did not answer but just stood glaring at her whilst Mary nervously stumbled across the kitchen afraid of what was to come. William slowly walked towards her than stood in front of her, so huge that his frame loomed over Mary, blocking her vision. his face expressionless, looking at her with burning intense eyes.

"William, I need to put the shopping away in the freezer than cook dinner for the children." Mary said quietly as she tried to get past William

"You should have thought of that before going out when you knew I would be home!" William thundered, looking at the shopping." And if you had to go you should have run your errands in the morning, did you have to buy the whole shop, you spend too much money!" he said angrily as he caught hold of her arm and pressed it hard. "How did you get the money for I did not give you any! You must be having an affair and it must be your boyfriend who gave you the money? Where do you meet him, do you bring him here or do you go to the park?"

The back of Marys legs pressed against a chair, and she tried to get away, but William grabbed her shoulders and shook them.

"Ouch William you are hurting me! I could not go in the morning because James had a fever and I had to call the doctor than go the chemist." Mary tried to explain but knowing it was useless. "How dare you accuse me of having an affair, I had some savings from the housekeeping you gave last month which I used to buy groceries for there is no food in the house Anyway, please keep your voice down for the boys see how you treat me, they need to see how a woman should be treated, with respect."

Suddenly Mary there was a blur at the corner of her eye and her head cracked to one side. and she felt the pain searing from jaw. She stumbled and clutched the chair, whimpering and closed her eyes when another blow hit her. She waited with baited breadth for another. but when none came, she opened her eye slowly and saw William move away from her.

William looked at her in disgust from the doorway. "This is how my father kept my mother in line and it did not break her, I don't know why you complain! Now where is my dinner, I am hungry! I go to work to provide food and shelter and you can't even bother to be here when I come home!" he raised his hand again.

"It is ready, William, I put it in the oven before I went out to keep it warm. I will bring it out immediately." Mary said meekly.

"There you go, lying again! You just told me that you have to prepare dinner!" William's face clouded with anger. "And get me another bottle of beer from the fridge, and it better be a cold one!" He shouted as he sat on the table.

"I prepared your dinner before I went out, I was talking about dinner for the children." Mary flinched as she put her hand on her forehead and felt a cut for, she had hit her head against the table.

She went to the fridge to get a bottle of beer and after she had handed it to William, wore her oven gloves to take out a plate of food and laid it on a tray. She lay everything in front of William than ran upstairs to cover up the bruises and cut with make up for she did not want her children to see them.

She was not scared for herself as she was for her children, for although she tried to keep William's beatings hidden from James and Oliver, they were aware of it, for she often had bruises and cuts. And once they had walked in the middle of it, were terrified and tried to protect her but William had turned his wrath on them. Somehow, they had escaped that time, but Mary had made them promise that whatever happened, they were not to interfere.

As she finished applying the makeup, she thought to herself she could not take any more of this She had read about an organisation that offered help to victims of Domestic Violence and had memorised the number for she was terrified that if she wrote it down and William found it there would be hell to pay.

Chapter 22

Anil droves home in the evening satisfied with the outcome of the day, starting with his meeting with Aadrika, Reyansh, getting his leave approved by William and finally his visit to the Travel Agent where he had booked his ticket to India that would depart in two days' time...He was impatient to get home as he wanted to get through some paperwork as his plan had finally taken shape.

He took a short cut and drove through the back streets that were filled with the smoke of cars, buses, and scooters. He noticed that on the side if the street were the ruins that had once been warehouses but were now being used for graffiti by some budding artists, who, he was sure was not getting a break to pursue the arts.

After having admired some of the graffiti which he thought was colourful and brightened the derelict warehouse, he quickly turned into a tree lined avenue leading to his house.

He had already phoned Sameera to tell her that he would like to talk to her and Khusboo in the evening to discuss his plans after which he rang Aadrika to tell her that, much to his surprise, William had agreed to his application of leave and to let her know that he was leaving in two days' time

"Oh Anil, I was hoping that you would not get leave for I will miss you so" Aadrika choked "But you must do what you think is best. How long will you be gone for?"

"A month Aadrika, which I am sure will fly past and I will be here before you know it!" He blew her a kiss over the phone before switching it off and parking his car in the garage. Anil felt relaxed for the day had started with a delicious breakfast with Sameera, and. he had enjoyed the honest and leisurely pace of having breakfast calmly rather than rushing off to Aadrika.

And after his return from India, he was looking forward to working for 'Jago' the name of Reyansh's organisation that he thought was aptly named for it meant 'awake' and that is what Reyansh was doing; raising awareness not only of racism but other issues that affected the minorities.

After locking the car, Anil walked towards his house when he had a brainwave and wondered why he had not thought of it before. Reyansh had mentioned his organisation was always looking for volunteers, and Sameera, after his departure, would have a lot of time on her hands. She was a woman who liked to help others, and as she too had experienced discrimination and knew how traumatic it could be, especially for Asian women, he was sure they would be glad to confide in her.

Khushboo as a professional lawyer, was also facing these problems, and she too would, with her legal expertise, be glad to help. He made a mental note of mentioning it to them in the evening when he told them about his travel plans, and if Sameera agreed, he would let Reyansh know before he left for India.

As soon as he entered the house, he heard Sameera call out from the kitchen.

"Is that you Khusboo?" She appeared rubbing her hands on her apron, with a smile on her face which turned to one of surprise as she saw Anil. "Anil, you are home early!"

"I do live here you know, Sameera, and can come any time I want!" Anil smiled mischievously. "And you know I had not gone into work today, anyway, what are you making for dinner? Whatever it is it smells delicious! I am going to change then am starving!"

He raced up the steps asking over his shoulder. "Did you ask Khushboo to be here, I need to talk to both of you after dinner."

"Yes, she will be here." Sameera replied, re-entering the kitchen and wondering what Anil wanted to talk about. As Anil disappeared into the bedroom. Sameera smiled for she had not seen her husband looking so relaxed, in fact since they had first moved into the house.

At that moment, Khushboo entered, threw her coat on the banister, washed her hands and entered the kitchen. "Mum, I am starving!" Khushboo said as she pulled out a chair.

"Dinner is ready, Khushboo, your father has gone up to change, Ah, there he is now."

"Hello Khushboo," Anil smiled as he entered the kitchen.

He was feeling fresh having bathed and changed into his track suit, and quickly pulled up a chair and sat rubbing his hands in anticipation

Sameera had already laid out the cutlery and small bowls that were crowding the table. and in the centre, she had placed a large bowl of basmati rice that that she had cooked with nuts and onions and the usual chutney (Indian) and pickle that went with every meal.

Also on the table were Naan (Indian bread). Sameera had decided she would cook chicken, so had marinated it in yoghurt and spices, left it overnight in a fridge, then cooked it till tender and before serving, she had cut coriander leaves and sprinkled them on it.

"Mum that smells and looks delicious! I am going to start, I am starving!" Khushboo put some rice on her plate, but instead of putting the chicken in a bowl, she put the chicken on them. "Dad this is nice, having a meal with you for a change, I think you work too hard!" then between mouthful added "you wanted to talk to us?"

"Yes, I did but that can wait, Khushboo." Anil replied. "We can have it over a cup of your famous tea, in the meantime let us enjoy the lovely meal your mother has prepared."

"Anil, I did not know you knew our daily routine, I make the dinner and Khusboo makes her special tea which we have in the front room!"

"Not forgetting our chats, Mum!" Khushboo retorted.

They finished their dinner in silence and after they had finished, Khushboo picked the plates from the table and stalked them in the dishwasher.

"Mum why don't you go ahead to the front room, and I will bring in the tea."

"Don't be long Khusboo I am parched!" I cannot digest my food till I follow it with a cup to tea!" Sameera called out over her shoulder as she followed Anil into the lounge. Khushboo put on the kettle laid out the mugs on a tray then went quickly went up to her room to change.

"My God, I had forgotten how comfortable and cosy this room is!" Anil remarked as he switched on the lamp and sat on the sofa.

Sameera was wearing a pale blue saree and in the glow of the light, she looked beautiful and elegant with her hair in a bun at the nape of her neck.

"Is everything all right Anil? What did you want to talk to us about?" she looked at him with concern.

"I'll wait for Khushboo, Sameera, but it is about the conversation I had with you earlier at breakfast."

Khushboo meanwhile had changed into leggings and a loose top and ran downstairs just as the kettle was boiling/She quickly poured the boiling water in the mugs, put them on a tray and went to lounge, handed the mugs to her parents, then placed the tray on the coffee table at the centre of the room.

She sat on the sofa and fluffed out the cushion before placing it behind on the sofa her then picked up the mug from the table.

" That was quick, Khushboo, I see you have changed into something comfortable."

"Yes, Dad sounded serious so thought I would make myself comfortable in preparation! Now dad, what is so important you wanted to talk to us about?"

Her dad had sounded so serious that Khusboo had thought her father was going to tell them that he was leaving them!

Chapter 23

"I know you don't like me smoking, Sameera, but I could do with one.!" Anil cleared his throat and when Sameera nodded, took out a packet from his pocket and after taking out one, lit it and exhaled.

"Khusboo, your mother is right, the tea is delicious!" Anil exclaimed taking a sip, then explained, starting with the conversation he had with his mother earlier in the day and as he spoke, he would lean forward smoking and darting forward every now and then to tap his cigarette into an ashtray that was lying on a side table that was just out of his reach.

"Here, I think you better keep this near you." Sameera handed him the ashtray.

"Thank you Sameera! Anyway, finally, I thought I would speak to William late in the evening before office closed and to my surprise he agreed to my leave, so before coming here decided I would pay a visit to the travel agent who, again to my surprise, had a seat on a flight leaving for India in two days, which I confirmed." He put the mug on the table with a self-satisfied smile.

"Anil, I know you had mentioned earlier that you would be going alone, but I had hoped thought that we, or at least I, would accompany you" Sameera said unhappily, "In fact, I have been looking forward to going back home."

Although Anil had spoken to her in the morning, she felt hurt that he got his leave and booked his flight without consulting her.

"Sameera, I thought I had made it clear that my visit is not for holiday purposes and that I would be going alone! I am only going because I am worried about my parents and to see that they are safe for the protest is getting to be intense and there is fear of violence erupting at any time. Plus, I, having worked on the farms and do not agree with the bills so want to join the protesters too."

"Dad, I don't think there is any fear of that for I have seen their interviews and they seem to be a peaceful lot. It is the Government who is provoking them by putting nails around the site of their location and of course, the media tis doing its utmost in trying to discredit the farmers."

"I agree Khushboo, they are all sincere poor people who are fighting for their and their children's livelihood.! Sameera retorted vehemently." But, Anil, although it is a nice thought that you would want to take part in the rally, I do not want anything to happen to you, maybe if you just called and talked to your parents, I am sure they will do as you ask and return home?"

Anil started to light another cigarette, but when he saw there was already one burning in the ashtray, he put it back in the packet and picked the one from the ashtray.

"Sameera, you know how stubborn they are, Aarev has tried to talk to them and as for calling them, their internet has been cut off as well as their water!"

"I tried too but thought the signal was back on. Anil, you really must quit smoking! It is not good for health." Sameera admonished. "but I would like to go with you and see that my parents are safe for they are joining the protesters too!"

However, Khushboo thought that her parents were putting too much emphasis on the protest because of which they felt defeated in a conflict that they thought was predictable and by doing so ensured that they created a conflict where there was none.

Khushboo saw the annoyance on her father's face and had sensed the tension in the air, but could not quite put her finger on it, thinking it maybe had to do with the fact that they rarely sat down as a family to talk? But now she finally put a finger on the atmosphere that was causing tension, as usual, her mother was being quietly manipulated by her father, but this time her mother stood her ground.

"Sameera, I have booked my ticket." Anil replied firmly. "I will only be gone a month and besides which I don't think Khushboo should stay here alone."

"Dad, I am not a child!" Khushboo replied indignantly. She knew the value of independence and looked slightly perturbed but did not want to hurt her mother so kept quiet and shrugged her shoulders.

In a way she could appreciate her father wanting to go alone. for although she loved her mother very much, she knew her to be a needy woman who she thought would not be exciting enough for her father; she did not possess the capability to stimulate him; however, what she could do was to help him survive by catering to his basic needs. Khusboo hoped that this was not the case, for that very weakness could draw him to an assertive woman who was strong, good at solving problems and one who would also have the knack to embellish their conversation with gossip and talk of recent fascinating events!

Khusboo had been lost in her thoughts but was bought back to the present to find that her parents were still arguing over her decision to stay single.

"There is no argument…I will look for a decent boy for Khushboo and…" Anil declared firmly pushing back the hair that had fallen on his forehead.

"Huh? What? Oh my God! Dad, how can you arrange my marriage without my knowing anything about it?! This is the first time in I do not know long that we have sat down together as a family! If you knew me you would know that I do not want to get married, and Mum knows it, as would you if you had spent time with us!" Khushboo wiped the tears from her eyes.

Khushboo looked at her Sameera's rounded shoulder, the curve of her back and word defeated came to mind.

"Anyway, it is not about me, it is about Mum, she is stuck in the house and now would have been a good chance as any for a holiday and you are depriving her of that! You have never taken her out, not even for a drive!" Khushboo waved her hands in front of her as it to clear the air of cigarette smoke then got up to open the window.

"Khushboo! That is enough, if your dad feels it is for the best he should go alone, I will happily stay back."

Sameera, faced with a choice made a conscious effort to calm her voice and.as always, felt she had to support her husband. She sat with her hands folded in her lap, looking calm for she had, by now accepted the fact that was shackled to Anil and that he controlled her, however, her whole body tingled with resentment, but no way was she going to show her feelings especially in front of Khushboo and Anil,

"Mum why can't you be a bit more assertive and tell Dad what you would really like to do instead of always letting him decide for you?" Khushboo was astonished at how the problems in her parents' marriage went unseen by her mother, or was she deliberately closing her eyes to them?

"Khushboo, you don't have to protect me, I know what I am doing, as does your dad. We need to respect that."

Anil, however, had been taken aback at the intensity of Khushboo's accusations, however true... He had not been around for either her or Sameera for he had been enamoured with Aadrika, who had shown him that he no longer needed Sameera; she was a nice and sweet woman who was only there to look after him and cook his favourite dishes,

In a flash, Anil's plan further unfolded and became clearer, and he knew what he was going to do.

Chapter 24

"Thank you Sameera, for your support, but she is right, and I apologise, but now we have to think ahead to the future." Anil wiped his face and lit another cigarette. "Sameera, there is an organisation called 'Jago' which raises awareness about ethnic and cultural differences we face in this country. It is run by a man named Reyansh whom I went to see today. During our conversation, he mentioned that they are always looking for volunteers who have been have experienced racism to reach out to our people. So Sameera, whilst driving home, I thought that since you like to help people you might like to volunteer for them, in fact, after my return, I am changing my job and will work for them too."

"I have never done anything like this before, Anil, I don't think I will feel confident I hardly ever go out." Sameera arched her back but buried her hands deep in her lap in uncertainty.

"That is exactly the reason why you will be ideal, for your stories of human interest will be based on personal experience which I think will be invaluable, and as for confidence, all the people you will deal with will be Asian women, and Reyansh, he is the founder, is a very nice man and will help you."

Khushboo looked at her father in astonishment for she knew that her father thought that the women of importance were only those who realised their place, which is home, so why was he suddenly encouraging her mother to undertake a job as a volunteer which would mean leaving the house? Or was her father e trying to control her mother by giving her an illusion of control?

"You mean Reyansh from 'Jago'?" Khushboo asked wide eyed.

"Yes, that is right, Khushboo you know him?" Anil asked in surprise.

"Yes, I do, I get invitations to meet different community groups, and I have found that it to be a good idea to meet them as they have good media connections which makes my job easier, and he too sometimes calls me when he needs legal advice."

"Well, that is wonderful, because that is exactly what I was going to suggest to you too.! They do wonderful work in raising awareness."

"Anil, apart from the experiences we had at the newsagent, I don't think I can be of much help. I mean I don't have any legal knowledge and I would not want to misguide anyone." Sameera said faintly.

"Don't worry about that, just the fact that you are aware of it shows you will be right kind of person. If you agree, I will ring Reyansh tomorrow to expect a call from you Khusboo, and the fact that he already knows you will make it much easier. He will see to it that your mother is assigned in the right branch for they also have a sister organisation that help in housing for those fleeing domestic violence or provide moral support to women."

"Yes, I deal with them too, the name of the organisation is 'Raksha' and gives shelter to abused women."

"What an appropriate name, 'Raksha 'it means protection!" Sameera exclaimed. "Yes, I would love to help the women if I can, because most of our women are afraid to speak out about what they are going through in their marriage and even families. It would mean a lot to them to know they have someone they can talk to openly without being judged."

She thought of the women back home who met at least once a week; a meeting that afforded a respite from their daily duties, and their get togethers was not only to share light gossip, but also to offer moral support and advice to each other, especially to the women who were having to deal with a tricky situation at home.

"Dad, we should have thought of volunteering before for Mum and anyway, my friend Aishya will be arriving from Dubai so there will be three ladies here."

Khushboo rubbed her neck with her delicate hand for she had had a tiring day at the office.

"Yes, your mum told me, you were together at university. "Anil stated.

"Yes, we were, she is a very nice girl, but she changed to journalism whilst I did law, but we have kept in touch."

"Does she live in Dubai and is she only coming for a holiday?"

"Actually, her sister lives in Dubai, but she was covering a very hot story about the daughter of a very aristocratic family in Dubai, who, it is alleged, is kept locked up by her parents." Khushboo replied.

"I am sure the govt did not like her poking around, especially if she is a journalist and might expose their secrets, if they have any!!" Anil remarked. "I hope she is not in any danger because of it, for I don't want it to follow her here!"

"Dad! Of course not!" Khusboo replied angrily. Her father had not shown any concern about them before, nor met any of her friends and now he was showing love and concern? And although she had agreed with her father that her mother would make a good volunteer, what advice or guidance could she give when she herself was suppressed and, not even aware of it? She was so passive and docile that her father walked all over her!

On the other hand, when she saw another woman in a situation like hers, that might just be what she needed to show her that she was being manipulated by her husband? However, she wondered as to why her father was thinking of her mother now; was it only to pacify his guilt at going alone for a holiday? She gave a start as she realised her father was talking to her.

"Khusboo, will you take care of it? I will ring Reyansh tomorrow anyway to tell him to expect a call from you."

"Yes, I will, it is always nice talking to him, he seems a nice man who is selflessly doing such good work, but Dad, how long will you be gone for?"

"My flight leaves day after tomorrow and I will stay there for a month during which time I will, hopefully, be able to talk some sense into your grandparents! But I know how stubborn they are, that is going to be very difficult, so I might have to stay longer."

"Oh, I hope not!" Sameera exclaimed as she put her hand over hand mouth.

"Don't worry Sameera, I am sure it will not come to that, oh and, another thing, I spoke to Aarev, my brother, I think he will be coming with me. He does not have a job, and knowing the situation there and the opportunities here, I suggested he come. He refused initially, but finally I managed to talk him into it. If he does not like it here, he can always return. I trust Aishya is only here for a few weeks?"

"Yes, she will be long gone before you return, and it will be nice to meet uncle Aarev Mum has told me a lot about him and how very kind and gentle he is"

"Yes, he is Khusboo, but Anil, have you spoken to your parents about his coming here?" Sameera asked. "You know how your mother dotes on him and he does look after them."

"Yes, I know Sameera, but it is about time Aarev broke away from them. Anyway, nothing is cut in stone, if he is not happy here, he can always go back."

At that moment Khushboo's mobile phone vibrated and she saw there was a text from Aishya giving her flight details.

Chapter 25

"Mum I have just received a text from Aishya, and she is arriving on the same day that Dad will be leaving." Khushboo said excitedly. "We will go the airport to see dad off, in fact we will make a day of it, I love spending time at the airport, all the people coming and going to different destinations of the world and to browse in all the shops! And then whilst having coffee, see the planes lights dimly shining through the clouds and then see them dip downwards, land and race down the runaway of the airport before finally stopping in front of the allocated gate!"

"How very poetic that sounds, Khushboo, but it will just depress me;" Sameera sighed. "Seeing all the people travelling makes me wish I was one of them."

Khushboo was mortified when she saw the sad expression her mother's face and was mortified that she had just reminded her of it,

"Dad, I did not think of this before, but you will be careful, corona virus and all?

"Yes, I will, but you know the virus has died down here, also in India where I believe there are very few Covid cases, and most people do not even wear mask! Anyway, we have a lot to do tomorrow, so I am off to bed, but I have some paperwork to do before so…."

He got up and stretched his arms than helped Sameera to her feet." Sameera are you okay with this? And don't worry, I will find out about your parents and ring to tell you how they are and Khushboo you don't have to come to the airport to see me off."

"We have to go to the airport to receive Aishya anyway, and it is a good thing it is Saturday, so I do not have a problem with taking a day off."

However, Anil, as usual, was not being thoughtful, he did not want them at the airport because Aadrika had insisted that she see him off.

'I will not be seeing you for a month, Anil and I want to make the most of your company' And nothing he could say would dissuade her, so, they had compromised, if Aadrika saw him with Sameera and Khushboo, should they decide to come to the airport, she would keep her distance, and Anil trusted her to do just that.

"Thank you, Anil"

Sameera took his hand to help her up, and once on her feet, patted her sari pleats in place, a sad and thoughtful look on her face for she knew that, although Anil had promised that he would visit her parents to keep her informed, he would not do so, for he did not like them; her parents had sensed it and felt hurt and disappointed.

They walked out to the landing followed by Khusboo, who, although happy seeing her parents talking and making plans, did not trust her father's sudden change of attitude. Maybe it was the thought of his leaving that had reduced the stress which may be the cause of him expressing and talking to them so effortlessly? Or maybe he was relaxed because not only was he going to meet his parents, but he would also not be working for William, who, from what her father had told them, was a bigot and a bully.

"Goodnight, Dad, Mum I am going to make myself another hot cup of tea, I am too tired! Can I make you some?" She rubbed her forehead wearily.

"No thanks, Khushboo, not for us, but have green tea, that will help you sleep" Sameera called over her shoulder as she followed Anil into the bedroom.

"Thanks Mum, I think I will do that."

As Khushboo waited for the kettle to boil, she faintly heard the voice of her father telling her mother that he was going into his study. After she had made her green tea with honey, she went to her bedroom, excited at not only the prospect of meeting her friend who she had not met for a long time, but also at the chance of talking to Reyansh.

Chapter 26

The following day Anil planned to have a quick lunch with Aadrika to discourage her from coming to the airport and then have a follow up meeting with Reyansh.

There was an aroma of Sameera's cooking emitting from the kitchen as he came and sat at the kitchen table. He too out his mobile and began texting as Sameera placed the stuffed chapatis on the table with a pot of tea and some mugs.

Khushboo entered the kitchen looking smart and professional in a black suit, pearl studs in her ears and her hair tied back with a white scarf.

"Good morning, Dad, Mum, I will have a quick cup of tea before leaving for work, in fact I might have one there!"

"My, my, Khushboo you are looking very nice." Anil commented, for he had never seen his daughter so in a professionally dressed for he since he left early, they never met in the mornings.

"Khusboo you are not leaving without a proper breakfast!" Sameera admonished.

Khusboo looked at her watch and as she was early, decided to join her parents.

"Sameera, this looks delicious, but you shouldn't have, gone to all this trouble," Anil said, but took a stuffed chapati and placed it on his plate as Sameera poured out the tea in a cup and handed it to him." After breakfast I need to run some errands, most important, I need to have a covid test done which is required before departure. I think I know a pharmacist who does this, so will do my packing later on. I don't think we need a suitcase, Sameera can you check and let me know so I can buy it?"

"We have a suitcase, no need to worry, and as for your packing I can do that for you." Sameera offered.

"No Sameera you don't have to; I will do it in the evening." "In that case, I will lay out the clothes you will need." Sameera said as she took put some curd in a bowl then saw that Khusboo was nibbling at her food. "Khushboo, why aren't you eating? I thought you liked this 'Indian breakfast'?

"Oh, I love it, but only on weekends, when I can sleep it off afterwards! And Mum we also must have a room ready for Aishya. Anyway, I must rush off now, and dad I will be talking to Reyansh about one of his cases so will tell him about Mother. I am sure he will be delighted that somebody is willing to volunteer for a worthy cause."

Khusboo quickly pushed back her chair, grabbed her bag, wore her coat and gloves and slammed the door behind her.

It was drizzling so Khushboo tipped her head back and felt the light drizzle fall on her cheeks as she ran to her car, wishing she was going to India so she could escape this horrid weather, which, although she was born and brought up here, she could not get used to. However, she felt better when she remembered that Aishya was coming and in that context, she wondered if her office would let her take a few days off…it was last minute notice but…

With all the talk of travelling and airports, she wished she could take a break from her job too, for lately it had become too depressing. It was satisfying and rewarding when she guided and helped women, but the other side of her work was different, it meant she occasionally had to deal with youths, who, sometimes being high on drugs, without thinking, killed without fully understanding the consequences of doing so, but luckily, she was not given many of these cases.

As was her norm, she stopped at a patisserie, queuing with office workers to buy croissants that was a cheering start of the day and which she shared with Stella, her para legal, over a mug of freshly brewed coffee that Stella would have ready.

After getting the croissants, she drove to her office, quickly parked her car at her office building car park then ran inside clutching the hot croissants in her hand, impatient to apply for leave. As soon as she reached her office, she hung up her coat on the coat stand then put her head around the door to say good morning to Stella and to invite her for their usual coffee

Stella smiled with a 'good morning; and came in wearing a business-like grey skirt with grey silk shirt. She was pretty and funny with frizzy ginger hair and Khusboo liked her for not only was she smart and efficient but was a single mum looking after a young child.

She held two cups of coffee in her hand which she placed on the desk; then quickly ran over paperwork she had sorted with Khusboo

Khushboo explained to Stella her idea for taking leave, and how she needed to put in an application as soon as possible. So, after they had finished their coffee and croissants and Stella had left the room, Khushboo pulled her laptop towards her and emailed James, her boss, requesting and attaching her application leave starting from the coming Monday. She explained it was needed because her father had to leave suddenly for India, and she had to look after her mother who was not well.

To her surprise, James called her, agreeing to her leave which he would confirm via email, starting from coming Monday for a week as requested but was willing to grant her an extra day, so she need not come in Friday.

As today was Thursday, she buzzed Stella and told her the good news and if there was anything urgent. In her excitement and hoping to get as much work done as possible, the morning flew past, with her trying to tie up pending cases, shuffling through all the paperwork to see if there was anything that required her urgent attention

She was deep in paperwork when she heard a knock on the door and as soon as she said 'come in' saw with surprise that it was James.

James was a distinguished and smart looking man wearing a three-piece suit. He had a thick head of hair with a touch of silver and a black and white beard that was neatly trimmed.

He was accompanied by a young short blonde woman with big blue eyes and hair that shone and cut in page boy style framing her piquant face. She was wearing a full-length coat that was open and revealed a grey pencil skirt over denier tights and pair of black snakeskin heels. Her makeup was subtly and flawlessly applied, with the colour of lipstick that was appropriate for the office.

"Ah, Khushboo, you seem to be busy, but I thought I would introduce you to Isabella, who will be joining us." James smiled as he propelled her in front. "In fact, she will be looking after your work whilst you are away."

Khusboo rose from her chair and came around the desk to shake hands but could see from the way Isabella spoke to James and the brightness in her eyes when she did that their relationship might be just more than professional, she hoped not for it could have a very disruptive effect on professional judgement. and, wondered if Isabella was the reason her leave had been approved so quickly by James?

This was followed by a disturbing thought; would she have a job when she returned, or would she be gradually phased out?

Chapter 27

"I thought it would be a good idea if Isabella spent the afternoon with you so you can update her although I am sure you have everything under control." James smiled genially, then after he had nodded his greeting, brushed an imaginary stray speck of dust from his creased trousers.

"Of course, James, no problem." Khusboo smiled for she had heard about his fixation about cleanliness, and the covid virus was just feeding his obsession!

"Great! Isabella, Khusboo is one of our best and we are lucky to have her as we are to have you with us too, so will leave you two to it!" James smiled cordially, waved, and left the room.

"Make yourself comfortable, Isabella, here let me take your coat." She helped her out of her coat then hung it on the coat stand at the corner of the room next to her coat.

Isabella smiled as she sat on a chair and Khushboo thought that although she looked like a woman of the work, she seemed to be quite young and naïve.

"Would you like some coffee, Isabella? I was going to make some for myself." Khushboo asked.

"Yes, I would love that, may I call you Khushboo?" Isabella smiled shyly.

"Of course, you may," Khushboo said.

She poured out the coffee from the coffee maker into two mugs, handed her one than went round the desk to sit on her chair after setting her mug on it.

"Now Isabella, you will find that I have sorted out the current cases priority wise and have made notes on the ones that are urgent. In fact, that is what I was going to do this afternoon, ring them and tell them the course of action when I return. But now that you are here you can take care of all that. In fact, you can have a quick read and ask me anything whilst I am here? Though I am sure you are more than capable in handling them. Any questions you can ask Stella, in fact she knows more than I do! She takes care of filling and Administrative work."

As she spoke, Stella came into the room to ask if she needed anything and Khusboo quickly made the introductions.

"Stella, I won't be in from tomorrow and Isabella will be filling in for me whilst I am away."

Stella smiled uncertainly, for she liked Khusboo, and they worked well together, and as she closed the door behind her, only hoped Isabella was not going to be too demanding as some of her bosses before Khushboo had been.

"Before we start the paperwork, Isabella, I am waiting for a call from one of the clients to tell me how and when the next drugs shipment is going to be delivered" She quickly gave a brief background of the case.

"Thankfully, I don't have many of those kinds of cases, it is very depressing to see teenagers as addicts who one cannot help because they don't want to help themselves!"

At that moment the red light on her phone flashed, and after Stella had put the call that she was waiting for through, Khusboo spent some time on the phone occasionally making notes.

"Now at last we can concentrate on the work at hand!" Khushboo put down the pen and turned towards Isabella. They spent the afternoon going through the cases, and at one-point Khusboo was so tired she wondered if all this was worth it for just for being on leave for a week. Once again it crossed her mind that maybe James was preparing Isabella to take over her job permanently? She knew he could not do it legally so maybe would make things so difficult that she would have no choice but to leave? However, she thought James to be a decent man, not like William, her father's boss, then remembered she had to call Reyansh.

"Let's take a break and leave the rest for later Isabella, there is a phone call I need to make".

"Yes, I think I can do with one! James was right, you are very efficient, I don't know how you get through all the work alone! "Isabella stood up and arched her back before going to make herself a cup of coffee. "Shall I make one for you?"

Yes, that is kind of you, Isabella, I'll have it after I have made the call, as to the work, it helps to feel I am helping someone."

Khusboo excused herself and left the room to call Reyansh and as soon as he answered, told her that he had just that minute spoken to her father who had filled him in, and as she had expected, he was glad to have her mother as volunteer. And when she had told him about her mother's concerns, he had assured her that he would take care of her personally. Khusboo sighed with relief and went back to her office to find that Isabella was standing by the window looking out at the rain.

However, she turned with a smile as soon as Khusboo entered the room, and they took their former positions of going through the caseloads.

At around 6 p.m. Khushboo arranged the piles of papers tidily across the desk, took a sip of coffee from her mug but found it had gone cold.

"Isabella, I think we should call it a day." Khushboo said as she rose and put on her coat ang gloves. "Oh, and if you get stuck, which I am sure you won't, Stella can help or else she has my mobile number, and I can be contacted anytime."

"Yes, I am tired too, it has been a lot to take in!" Isabella remarked as she too put on her coat. "But thank you, there won't be any need for that we will manage, you just forget about everything and enjoy your leave."

"Bye Stella, and don't stay too late."

"Bye Khushboo, and don't worry, just enjoy your leave, you deserve it."

"Thank you, Stella," Khusboo handed back some of her files and letters that she had signed to her, after which' Khushboo decided to see James before leaving for home. All her cups of coffee had got cold so as she was feeling thirsty, first went to the canteen for a takeaway coffee and carried it to James' office, grasping the lid between finger and thumb because the cup was too hot.

She knocked on the door and as soon as James said 'come in' entered and found that he too, like Isabella, was standing at the window looking out at the rain

"Come in, ah Khushboo, everything okay?" James walked back to his desk, sat down then tilted back in his leather chair, hands steepled in front of him

"Yes thanks, James, Isabella seems a nice girl and very efficient, we have been through a lot of work. I just dropped in to thank you for agreeing to my last-minute leave application, my father has to..." Sat placing her coffee cup down on a coaster.

"Don't worry about it, Khushboo, you take care of your mother, and we will see you in a week." James eyes narrowed as he looked at her. "Thank you again, James, I will see you then, I have left my number with Isabella and Stella in any case."

"You don't worry, Khushboo, we will manage." James gave her a friendly and assuring smile.

But as Khusboo closed the door behind her, she wondered if she had imagined the look of alarm on James' face when she mentioned that she had given her number to Isabella, then thought she was being too suspicious and smiled as she thought of the week head with Aishya.

Chapter 28

It was late when she reached home so went straight to her room to take a hot shower to wash away her tiredness. After changing into black leggings and a pink sweatshirt, she felt better and after brushing her damp hair, she ran downstairs to the kitchen.

To her surprise she saw her father seated at the table whilst Sameera was bustling around the kitchen preparing dinner with a smile on her lips. Every two minutes she would look at Anil, as if trying to reassure herself that he really was at home.

Over dinner, Anil explained that everything on his part had gone smoothly, that he had done the required, mainly he had his PCR covid test which was negative and which he was required to show at the airport.

"Did you call Reyansh Khusboo?" Anil asked as took the bowl of lentils from the table and with a spoon, covered the rice on his plate with it. "If you didn't have time, never mind, I did."

"Anil! I have kept some small bowls for, so you need not put it all in the plate!" Sameera handed him a bowl, but Anil shook his head.

"Don't worry about it, Sameera, I like it this way. Now, Khushboo, did you have time to call Reyansh?" he repeated.

"Yes, dad I did, I spoke to him just after you had, and of course he was delighted. Not only that, Mum, I am going to be home with you for a week!" When she saw the look of worry on her parent's face, quickly explained" On the drive to work, I thought that there was some leave due to me too, and what better time than to take it now? My only worry was that James, my boss might refuse because he might think it was too sudden, but anyway, he agreed to it and not only that but had found someone to take over my duties for the week I will be away."

Anil saw the look on his daughter's face "Khushboo, you don't seem to be very happy about that?" Anil asked uneasily, for that would spoil his plans.

"No Dad, I am not, I am only going to be away for a week, and I don't have a back log of work to catch up on, and I thought, for a moment, that maybe he might want to replace me? After all I am the only Indian in our office and he seemed extremely comfortable with Isabella, the woman who will look after my work. But must be my imagination, for he did not have time to recruit anyone. It must be all this talk about raising awareness of discrimination that the minorities have to face."

At that moment, her mobile vibrated and she saw that there was a text from Aishya. She picked up her mobile quickly, hoping she was not cancelling her plans, however, having read the text, she turned to her mother with a smile.

"Mum, Aishya is not coming alone but with her elder sister, Ekta, I met her once when she came to see Aishya and found her to be a very nice woman, but can we accommodate her too?"

"Of course, we can Khushboo, they can stay in our room, and I will move into your room. In fact, I am glad she is coming for you two young girls will have a lot to talk about and at least I will have someone to talk to too!!"

The following day passed quickly and uneventfully, and it seemed to be in no time they were having dinner, which they finished quickly. Khushboo and her mother were talking excitedly making plans for the following week.

"Sorry to interrupt ladies, I am going up as I still have to finish my packing as we leave early tomorrow. Sameera and Khusboo are you sure you want to see me off? I will be leaving early as I have to meet a friend and you can go to the airport later to meet your friends flight?"

"No, Anil, we will see you off," Sameera said firmly as she cleared the table and asked Khusboo if she would make tea. "I think we will take it up to our room."

Having cleaned the kitchen, Sameera laid the table ready for breakfast for the following morning as they would be leaving early

. "Mum, you are already thinking of the next meal! Honestly don't worry! A cup of tea would do...and I meant to ask, has Olga been coming regularly to do the housework?"

"Yes, she is right, a cup of tea is all I need." Anil said impatiently. "We shall see," Sameera replied. I know in the morning you will think differently for it is going to be a long day and, Anil, I don't know what time they will serve a meal on the flight. And yes, Olga has been coming regularly."

Both knew it was useless to argue with her so were silent knowing full well that Sameera would have an answer to any of their objection. Khusboo, having made the tea, placed the mugs on the tray then, after Sameera had switched of the lights climbed the stairs where Khusboo took a mug for herself and gave the tray to her mother.

"Good night mum!" She kissed her lightly on the cheek before opening the door to her bedroom glad her mother had confirmed that Olga was coming regularly. She had not met her, so hoped that she would during the time she was home.

"Thank you and good night Khushboo!" Sameera took the tray and entered her bedroom, where she found Anil talking on the phone. But as soon as he saw her, he quickly ended the call and as Sameera handed him the mug, wondered why he looked so guilty and secretive.

She quickly changed into her night suite then got into bed to have her tea. "You go to sleep, Sameera, there is still some paperwork I need to cover."

"You don't have to, worry Anil, Khusboo will take care of them and anyway, you will only be gone a month."

"No, there are some things only I can take care of." Anil replied curtly as he slammed the bedroom door behind him.

The tears suddenly welled up in Sameera's eyes at his tone, but as was her nature, tried to excuse it so as she had her tea propped up in bed and listened to him moving around the room. She sighed as she finished her tea and put the mug on nightstand before tucking herself in bed and closed her eyes.

However, she could not sleep, so saw with half closed eyes, that it was quite late when he returned with a bunch of papers in his hand, switched on the light then collect his passport and close the suitcase,

After which he struggled out of his tight jeans whilst grabbing the side of the wardrobe to keep his balance then pulled off his sweater so that his black curly hair stuck up. He changed into his pyjama threw back the quilt on his side of the bed and switched on the bedside lamp before he turned off the light of the room and got into bed.

Just as Sameera drifted off to sleep, she thought about the startled look on Anil's face and put it down to the stress of travelling and making the arrangements for his arrival.

Chapter 29

The following morning, Khusboo threw back her quilt, swung her feet on the floor than ran to the window. She pushed back the net curtain and looked out and saw that it had clouded over during the night with the result that a thick mist hung in the air.

She quickly had a bath, donned her jeans, a denim blouse over a jumper and tied her hair into a ponytail, which she covered it with a sports cap before running downstairs in her sneakers.

Her father was dressed in jeans and reading the newspaper in the kitchen whilst her mother made tea for them, smiling as she greeted her over her half-moon glasses that dangled on a chain around her neck preparing to make breakfast.

"Mum! I thought we said no breakfast?"

Anil looked at Khusboo and shrugged his shoulders. "I tried telling her, Khusboo, now it is your turn!"

"Dad why are you in such a hurry anyway?! Your flight is not till late in the afternoon!"

"I told you yesterday Khusboo, I have to meet a friend!" Anil replied impatiently as he threw the paper down with a thump. "And you can have breakfast at the airport whilst you wait for your friends flight, I hear there are some good restaurants at the airport."

Sameera hurriedly took of her reading glasses. "Alright Anil, tea is on the table and as soon as you have finished, we will be ready to leave. Would any of you like some toast with it? I will wear my coat in the meantime."

Seeing the tears in her eyes, Khusboo stopped her. "No Mum, Dad did not mean immediately, I am sure he would like a cup to tea before he leaves." She looked at her father who nodded but did not say anything.

"Don't worry about Dad, Mum, he is just stressed." She quickly hugged her mother, angry at her father for hurting her mother when all she did was care for him and see that he was well fed before a long journey. They finished their tea in silence, Khusboo glaring at her father who ignored her.

"Right, shall we make a move then? Or do you want to wait till tomorrow?" Anil asked sarcastically.

Khusboo was going to answer back when Sameera put her fingers on lips and shook her head. "We are ready, all we need to do is put on out coats. Oh, and Khusboo, it would be wise to take something warm for Aiysha and Ekta; they are coming from a warm country."

Anil started to put his luggage in the boot of the car whilst Khusboo and Sameera wore their coats

"I have taken a scarf and gloves for Aishya but that is very thoughtful of you Mum."

"And I have got a shawl for Ekta if she needs it, now let us go before your father loses his temper. I don't know what has come over him, he has been touchy the whole morning."

"Maybe mother, because he will miss you?"

"I doubt that Khusboo, your dad has changed over the years, not at all like the kind man I married." Sameera sighed as they reached the car and as they neared Anil said tersely.

"I will drive, Khushboo, you can drive back in the car with your friend."

"Anil, have you got your passport and all the other documents you will need to show at the airport?" Sameera asked

"Sameera stop fussing so, we went through this last night and again this morning and then the breakfast! One would think you are making sure that I leave!" Ani replied in exasperation."

Sameera looked at him, her eyes sparkling with tears, then stood still, trying to compose herself, feeling confused as to the reason of Anil's behaviour, for he had been abrupt the whole morning. She had tried to ask what was bothering him, but the only answer she got was 'it is none of your business' Her head was paining for she had been unable to sleep and felt there to be an unbearable pressure building up at temples of her head. She rubbed them then got in the front of the car,

Anil started the car and drove out of the driveway whilst Khusboo sat quietly at the back, angry at the way father had talked to her mother, even blaming her for letting him walk all over her! She wanted her mother to stand up for herself, or at very least show some form of resistance, for this was not the first time he had snapped at her and thought of the countless times he had humiliated her mother.

But whichever way her mother reacted, it would always be she, the woman, who paid the price, whether she stayed in her marriage or broke free. And that would never happen, for her mother, like most Indian women of her generation, had been taught from an early age to be subservient, patient, and to endure their husband's moods and tantrums.

It was emphasised that their destiny was to accept the unloading of the emotion of one half of the population (men/husband) on to them; as if they were emotional dumping grounds whilst the men, having done so, steered clear of any kind of emotion!

She knew her mother was hurt so tried to distract her by trying to lighten the tension in the car as they passed central London.

"Mum, look at all the tourists, I don't think I have been to all the places they have been to in London!" Khushboo remarked

She pointed to the tourists, some of whom were prodding their partners as they pointed to something of interest, all were laughing, delighted at what they saw. They passed a red double decker tourist bus with tourists sitting at the top, pointing, and listening as the guide explained the history behind the buildings, at the same time, informing them about British customs. She was sure that there would be other tourists who would be tramping through streets that took them to museums parks etc.

"That may be because you know that you have plenty of time to do so as you live here whereas the tourists only have a couple of weeks to see as much as possible." Sameera answered, glad of the distraction. "And neither have I been to see the many places I have heard of."

"True Mum, now that gives me an idea, I think next week that is what we will do, explore all the places we have not seen. And, of course, Aishya and Ekta would love it too, for this is just the right season to go for walks in the parks!"

Anil had been driving thoughtfully, but as soon as he heard Khushboo talking excitedly he, turned his head briefly.

"Hey, steady on Khushboo, I thought your mother was volunteering? She will be too busy so you can go on your own with your friend." Anil remarked, his jaw set tightly.

It was then that Khushboo realised it had not been from the kindness of his heart that he had suggested volunteering for her mother, but only because he wanted to make sure he would know where she was, working and no free time for herself!

Khushboo trembled at the extent to which her father would go to control her mother with his cunning manipulation.

Chapter 30

"Oh, that is no problem, Dad, "Khushboo said cheerfully, only too glad to puncture her father's sly move, "When I spoke to Reyansh, I told him that Mum would start the following week, which means she will be free next week!"

Khusboo was pleased to see her father looking stumped and perplexed for he was sure that his plan had been fool proof, but before Anil could find a way to counter it, they reached the airport,

"Khusboo, I will drop you off with the luggage at the area reserved for that purpose and park the car in the car park after which I will meet you at the flight counter." Anil said sulkily

"That will be fine, Dad." Khusboo and Sameera quickly got off the car and between them, unloaded their father's luggage on to the pavement.

The clouds were still oppressively low, and Sameera felt as if they were trying to suffocate her under their thick grey duvet. So, as it was windy, she wrapped the coat tightly around her whilst Khushboo went to get a trolley, passing a lady wearing a hat shaking hands with a man in a suit, with one hand shaking his hand and with other, trying to hold on to her hat as if it was in danger of being blown away in the wind.

She returned with a trolley and after they had placed the suitcases onto it, walked towards the entrance of the airport.

"I didn't know Dad had so many clothes mum, he is only going for a month," Khushboo exclaimed pushing the trolley.

"I am surprised too for he was busy with some paperwork last night and saw him put some in the suitcase, maybe that is why they are so bulky."

"But you did tell him that he needn't worry and the bills and all, I will look after everything here? In fact, I was waiting for him to call and explain everything to me."

"I did mention it to him, but he said he has left everything in order so as not to worry you."

As soon as they entered the airport building, Khushboo crinkled her nose in distaste for people were walking in and out of airport, smelling of sweat from their journey.

They walked over to the departure flight counter where they found Anil waiting, pacing nervously, then sighed with relief when he saw them and although there was time till his flight departed, was adamant that he completes the formalities quickly.

"You never know, there might be some delay due to the latest covid rules." He said as he checked in his luggage, showed his negative covid test and got the boarding pass he had been assigned.

Sameera and Khushboo, whilst waiting for Anil to complete the paperwork, saw a couple of girls walking past, wearing denim jeans that were too tight. They were speaking into mobiles and Khushboo admired their nail that were decorated with stars and crystals that created a sort of arc as they held the mobiles to their faces.

At that moment Anil walked towards them, having completed the formalities and the required paperwork in his hand.

"Dad, will there be someone to meet you at the other end, I mean, won't they all be at the protest?" Khushboo asked. She was voicing what her mother was concerned about, for, after being belittled earlier, Sameera was afraid of being snubbed again.

"Khushboo, I know my way around India if no one comes!" Anil retorted irritably "Now I better hurry and go through security to enter the duty-free shop for I have arranged to meet my friend there. He is also travelling to India on the same flight, bye and look after your mother."

Anil abruptly turned and disappeared into the crowd of people who were all waiting to be given the' all clear' by security.

Khushboo and Sameera were both surprised and stunned at Anils abrupt and rude attitude, and Khushboo saw the tears well up in her mother's eyes. She had not realised how sensitive her mother was so quickly tried to reassure her. She had seen how he always treated her mother before, but he was going away, yet he did not even have the decency to say goodbye to her properly! One would not even behave like that with a stranger!

However, she put her feelings aside and tried to distract her mother, who, was unsuccessfully trying to conceal her disappointment and hurt for she her eyes were bright with unshed tears...

"Right, Mum we have about three hours before Aishya and Ekta arrive. Shall we look around the shops before sitting down in a café? I am starving and that breakfast Dad mentioned sounds tempting!"

When Sameera nodded, she took her arm and steered her past the retail shops, still seething at her father's behaviour.

"That sounds delightful, Khusboo, I haven't been out for coffee for I don't know how long! And the breakfast sounds tempting too."

"Mum, you have never been out, though that is partly my fault too. I always felt you would like Dad to do that, and with me you would find it boring."

"Khushboo, how can you think that! Of course, I would prefer your father to take me out, but I do not find your company boring! Why, the highlight of my day was our talk in the evening!" She squeezed her daughter's arm affectionately.

They finally found a small coffee shop that had comfortable looking armchairs. Khushboo sat her mother on one of the tables and went to order coffee and breakfast.

As she walked back, she noticed that there were cups of half-filled coffee and remains of pastries and sandwiches on some of the tables

'Yuk" Most probably in a hurry to catch their flight!' she thought as she plonked herself opposite her mother.

Her mother had taken out her reading glasses and was going through a paper that had been left behind on one of the chairs whilst Khushboo looked at the framed photos and paintings hanging on the wall of the restaurant.

On the table next to them were an elderly couple who looked as if they had come from a pleasant holiday for, they were laughing at what she thought must be memorable moments of their trip whilst awaiting their order. The man looked to be a kind man with innocent blue eyes and a quivering white moustache, and his wife was a middle-aged plump woman with pale freckly face and coppery hair wearing blue cowl neck sweater.

"Mum, you are engrossed in the paper, anything interesting?" Khushboo asked, feeling bored.

"Yes, well I have been following the story of what happened to the aristocratic family from Dubai, apparently the family is involved and..."

"Don't worry Mum, Aishya will fill us in for she is coming from Dubai and in her line of work, knows what is often hidden from the public.

Apparently, her paper convers most high-profile cases."

At that moment the waiter arrived with their order, and they ate in silence, each engrossed in their thoughts.

"Dad was right, the breakfast is delicious, as is the coffee!" Khushboo remarked, finishing the last of her breakfast.

"I enjoyed it too, food tastes better if one does not have to cook it!"

However, under her light-heartedness, her heart was heavy although she was used to it for, at the rare times he did talk to her the tone of his voice was either terse, rude, or sounded too hearty and loud, and Sameera wondered why he could not talk to her like a normal person?

Chapter 31

Aadrika had been waiting at the corner of the duty-free building when she saw Anil disappear in the crowd, and as soon as Sameera and Khusboo had vanished from sight she quickly took out her mobile and called Anil.

"Anil, I have just seen both your daughter and wife walk away so it is safe to meet, I am waiting at the corner of duty shop."

"Hi Aadrika, thanks for coming to see me off and your consideration in staying in the background, I am outside the duty-free shop too, so am walking towards the crowd." Anil said into his mobile" but I cannot see you, oh there you are"

However, Aadrika although his voice had sounded lively, she sensed that it was forced. She waved as she saw him walk towards her wearing alack pullover under a white shirt and jeans. He looked pale and the lines of tiredness made him. look a few years older. His hair, Aadrika noticed, was beginning to grey and recede slightly at the temples, which she thought only made him look distinguished and attractive

She ran and threw her arms around him however, when she felt his body stiffen, put her hand on his forearm, but as soon as she became aware of his rigid attitude, took a step back. She looked up at him in confusion and her heart sank as she looked up into his face sensing that he was gradually building up to break his big news, whatever it was.

"Oh, I am so glad I could get to see you before you left." She cried as she put her had on her arm and looked at him with bright eyes.

"Hey, steady on old girl! Sameera and Khushboo might still be here you know!" Anil said, and Aadrika again felt he was trying to forcibly be trying to inject a breeziness into his voice.

"Anil, I don't want you to go, I hate being on my own!" Aadrika cried. "I met you soon after Dhruv left and with you I felt safe and protected, something that only Dhruv made me feel!".

"I have to go Aadrika, and anyway you have Aarush, but look here I can only stay for a few minutes, I will have to go in soon for I have to meet a friend." Anil said. "Look after yourself, and when I get a chance, I will call you from India."

He pulled her into a corner and slid the other around the back of her neck Aadrika looked at him sadly from under her long lashes as he pulled her closer to him.

"Oh, don't worry, I will call to see how you are, it would be nice to hear your voice at least." Aadrika said as she pulled away and put her fingers on her lips.

"Oh no don't do that Aadrika, I don't know where I will be., and it will be difficult to explain who you are!" Anil replied much too quickly,

"Never mind, we can catch up on your return, at least you can text me your return flight details?" Aadrika asked

"Sure, but nothing is confirmed as yes, but Aadrika, can I borrow your card please? In all the rush, I forgot to keep some cash on me, and my card is packed in my bag, for safety!"

"Of course, Anil," Aadrika took rustled in her bag for the card, and having found it, handed it to Anil.

"Thanks, Aadrika, you are a life saver! Wait here, I will bring it back to you." He hurried of into the building and came back a few minutes later, gave her the card and a quick peck on her cheek

"Oh, that reminds me, Aadrika, my brother will be returning with me so as things are going to change, I will not be able to spend time with you." Anil said in a matter-of-fact tone as he looked approvingly at a tall blonde beautiful woman with her ponytail falling jauntily over her bare shoulder.

Aadrika looked at him in panic "Anil you know that I have not demanded much of your time but am content with the little time we had. Are you telling me that I won't even have that?"

"Yes, Aadrika I think we should not meet any more, anyway, look after yourself." He said abruptly as he turned and went into the duty-free shop, leaving Aadrika stunned.

Although the thought had occurred to her that one day their affair would end, and was surprised that it had lasted for as long as it had, nonetheless, she felt sad at how at how easily Anil had switched of his feelings of desire and tenderness for he had announced the end of their affair in a very cruel and brusque manner, However, she reluctantly accepted that maybe he was right for the vibrancy and passion of their affair had run its course and was now like a faded photograph or negative.

She sighed as she walked towards the exit passing a young blonde in a fur collared anorak sitting at a café. Her throat felt dry, and it was a long journey home, so she decided to have a cup of coffee before she left for home. She quickly entered a café, saw an empty chair, and quickly hung her coat at the back before she went to get a coffee.

Luckily, there wasn't a long queue so after paying for the coffee in cash, she carried the cup back to the table, where she sat sipping her coffee, trying to organise her thoughts at the sudden turnoff events,

Anil had always treated her with respect, but today, she felt that he had been cold and distant. Their affair had been so exciting in the beginning, but gradually that had turned to comfort and routine so she had not thought about its end, but he on the other hand, must have, Aadrika wondered when the actual moment was when he had thought about breaking with her, and if he had been with her at that time, how could she have missed the sign?

But thinking back, she too had been feeling trapped in a net that society had first weaved around her then labelled her as being 'the other woman'. And with it came that thought that had she stayed with Anil any longer, she would have been unable to free herself and would be tied and labelled forever to its rules.

Had they continued, she would have become an emotional coward, afraid to face the world, a 'scarlet woman' who was branded, forbidden to emerge in society's social order, and as such, Aadrika would have no rights, she would be a woman to be concealed, to resurface only to serve Anil's desire. And if by chance, Anil was to acknowledge they were an item, the information would cause ripples of gossip, it would not only damage him it would come to his wife's attention. And Aadrika had no desire to break up a family, for she had just seen his wife and daughter and his wife looked like a nice and kind woman.

And being trapped in the affair, she would have been constantly looking for someone to blame, be it Sameera, Anil or even Khushboo; when, there would have been no one but herself to blame. Their affairr had started with Anil saving her from hooligans, developed into a casual friendship with sharing lunches and coffee, which then became intimate, and they had become romantically involved,

It had been a pleasant time for Aadrika, having someone to talk to confide in, a friend who did not judge.

There was a faint smile on her lips as she recalled that from then on, she had begun to feel like a woman, something she had not felt since Dhruv left, nay, even before that, and she had begun to pay attention to how she looked, to take care of what clothes she wore, even adding perfume behind her ears and wrists to work!

Then with a pang of guilt and sadness she remembered his furtive calls on days he could not meet her, and the last-minute aborted arrangements when Aadrika had to spend lonely afternoons on her own, But over time, both had acknowledged the fact that their past/present was imbedded in the limitations of their circumstances, for Aadrika still loved Dhruv, who she was still legally married to, and Anil would not, under any circumstance, leave his wife. Therefore, as they could not annul the past, they tried to control it, had succeeded for a time than in the end succumbed to desire and excitement. But, Aadrika thought, had the affair continued, it would surely have led to arguments and resentments, so maybe it was better to end the affair whilst her memory of it was still warm and rich.?

Aadrika wiped her eyes and decided that as soon as she reached home, she would call her friend Anika to come and stay with her, then remembered that she was staying with her mother. Anika had all along advised her against continuing her friendship with Anil, for that, she had said, would ultimately hurt her, which it had.

She blew her nose with a tissue, took out her compact from her purse and powdered her face, trying to cover the tiny flecks of mascara on her eyelids and the purplish marks under her streaming eyes. After finishing, she put back the compact in her purse and slinging it over her shoulder, walked out of the café.

As she moved towards the exit, she looked wistfully at a middle-aged couple who were sitting in comfortable silence, a silence, that Aadrika thought, could only come from years of marriage. They knew each other so well that they did not feel the need to talk. They communicated with each other by the raising of eyebrows, or tiny twists of mouth when they wanted to convey range of emotions that ranged from amusement, delight, or pity.

As she left the café, Aadrika sighed and thought that maybe she was not destined to have a loving partner?

Chapter 32

Aadrika's eyes were bright as she walked towards the exit of the airport building, this was not the first she had been hurt, and over the years, she wore her own scars and bruises! They had been accumulated from years of not only being bullied but having had to tolerate racist people who had not missed an opportunity to demean her: Most of the bullying she suffered under an institution that was supposed to protect and see to her welfare!

It was only now that Aadrika recognised that what had happened to her then was direct discrimination, for it was only because she was Indian that she was bullied and picked on. Her ethnicity was the reason she was neither fostered nor adopted, because she had seen other white children leaving the home into caring homes.

She passed some girls wearing colourful scarfs that they had looped across their necks, wearing tight skinny jeans and wearing such high heeled boots that Aadrika wondered how the girls could walk in them!

Aadrika strolled past some shops, one of which had some very colourful clothes hanging in the window so stopped to admire them, however, it was not long before her thoughts drifted back to Anil who, till today, she had thought of as being a decent man. But his recent conduct had shown him to be a petty and selfish man, maybe not born so, like all men, but one whose prejudices had been nurtured.by his mother and grandma till their indulges and mollycoddling turned him int a male chauvinist and finally, Sameer too maintained Anil's sexist attitude by catering to his every need,

However, she was hurt and disappointed that Anil had made her feel guilty by implying that to maintain the furtiveness and secrecy around the affair was her responsibility alone! She felt a fresh pang of sadness as she recalled Anil's face before he had gone back into the duty-free shop; when he had turned and looked at her, there had been an expression of pity and sadness on his face.

She took a deep breath, for although she had felt sad at the end of their affair, and would miss him, she felt free, although worried at how she would cope for there had always been someone to help her, first it had been Dhruv, and after he had left, her friend Anika had stayed with her, and after she had left, she had met Anil.

She had been strolling in the building, as if by staying in the airport building, she was close to Anil when a man bumped into her.

He was wearing a black leather jacket. black hair which was tied in a ponytail and had a stud in one ear. Aadrika looked at him angrily.

"Hey, watch where you are going!"

"Oh sorry," She turned to continue to cover the gap to the exit when the man stopped her.

"Hey, wait Aadrika it is me. Dhruv!"

Aadrika turned indignantly, sure that someone was playing a trick on her, but when she looked closely at the man, saw that it was indeed Dhruv, a very changed man to her childhood sweetheart. In her astonishment at seeing him, she bumped into a tourist who was hurrying past and nearly fell over.

"Dhruv! Oh my god! You look so different I did not recognize you.!" Aadrika exclaimed, trying to find her footing. "What are you doing here?".

"Aadrika, it is good to see you., you look beautiful, as usual" he put out his arms to steady her and as she fell into them, felt his hand on her back move upwards over her back to touch her hair lightly.

She put her arm on Dhruv's forearm to steady herself and blushed when she felt the knotted muscles of his arm and the warmth of his body. She squeezed her body intuitively and gently into the curve of his body and breathed deeply, thinking of another time, different and happier times and the feeling was familiar and comfortable. That was not surprising for she had been married to Dhruv for a year, and before that they had been at the orphanage at the same time and spent most of their time together

Aadrika blinked and looked at him again in surprise, for he did not look like the gentle Dhruv she knew, loved and married. But when Dhruv came close and looked down at her, she saw the familiar striking brown eyes that twinkled with kindness and mischief, eyes that she had once loved.

But suddenly a mask of wariness crossed her face as she remembered his temper. She glanced at him from under her long lashes. thought he was like a chameleon, always changing his colours. He had been so loving and protective in the care home, but after they were married and the birth of Aarush, he had changed from the kind gentle man to an angry one...She had discovered that during their marriage Dhruv tended to store grudges than accuse her with them in an argument.

Aadrika had not seen that side of him and had not known how to handle the situation. It felt like Dhruv was destroying her love for him with his cruel words and they felt that with his words, he was pouring stinking water over her, water that was left when the flowers had wilted and died! Her only fault then had been the time and love she devoted to Aarush, which Dhruv had resented.

Maybe it was always her fault for she put the men in her life on a pedestal, first Dhruv then Anil. Aadrika had made them into one-sided people, one who was without spite or malice men who, had brought safety and joy into her life, not pain. To her they had been men of beauty with no ugliness surrounding them, men with generous hearts who did not seek any kind of repayment. Maybe men with those kinds of qualities could not be shifted from mere casual involvement to one of a relationship and then to one of marriage and commitment?

Aadrika had understood Dhruv, knew that he had an immense capacity of energy that would never be used if he stayed in the marriage, and that would have been painful to her. It would have been like seeing Dhruv with his feet tied or having a painful cramp continuously till he became mentally crippled! Added to that was the fact that although she wanted the best for Dhruv, she had becoming increasingly afraid of his temper, afraid of what he would do to Aarush.

Ultimately, they had separated because he was always grumbling that she was paying more attention to Aarush than to him. And when she asked him to choose between Aarush and himself, he had chosen to ignore Aarush, so she had quietly told him to leave her house.

Chapter 33

Dhruv saw the uncertainty in Aadrika eyes and smiled gently. Aadrika was relieved to see that he seemed like the Dhruv she had first known and as she was still smarting at Anil's treatment of her, felt she needed a friend. But at that point, she began questioning her feelings and if it was normal to be afraid of a friend or if one could want and not want something at the same time?

"Are you all right Aadrika?" Dhruv asked and Aadrika saw the kindness in his eyes, "Sorry about bumping into you the way I did, I have just arrived from abroad and am still disoriented from the flight!"

He leant forward to give her a light kiss, the whiff of her favourite light scent took him to earlier happier times. He looked affectionately into her eyes, her big bright intelligent brown eyes that usually twinkled with merriment but now looked sad.

Aadrika smiled faintly. "I am fine Dhruv but, what are you doing here, I thought you were travelling the world?" "

She felt confused, unsure of what was true and what was not, so much so that her hand balled into a fist so that her nails bit into the soft flesh of her palm.

"Well, it started of that way, but look here Aad, I am feeling a bit faint, do you have time to have a cup of coffee with me?" When she did not answer, he added softly, his eyes tender. "Aad, I am so very sorry for behaving the way I did and abandoning you to cope on your own…please, pretty please?"

Dhruv smiled mischievously and as usual Aadrika could not resist his charm, but before she answered, weighed her feelings, not sure whether she was willing to go down the rollercoaster of emotions of hurt guilt and remorse!

Dhruv looked at her, his eyes probing hers, knowing that the silence would linger unless she answered so smiled and nodded her head, He had always been there to protect her from others and sometimes even from herself, and today too, she was sure, was no chance meeting but destiny's way of protecting her again? She was a romantic and idealist and liked to believe that he had been unconsciously drawn to save her yet again and bring joy into her life again, be it for a little while?

What Aadrika was unaware of was that actually, like she originally thought, Dhruv was like a chameleon and hand many layers to his character, one of them being his ability to influence and charm the women he wanted to control. It would have shocked her had she known that this was no accidental meeting, but that he had been living in London all along and had orchestrated the casual reunion! Similarly, he had had his friends stalk and frighten her into Anil's arms whom he had come to know him through his shady friends.

His friends, who followed Aadrika, had told him that she had finally started an affair with Anil, whom he had gone to meet to find out his intentions, and when he was satisfied it was not serious, came to a financial agreement with him and had even given his blessing! Unbeknown to Aadrika he had lied all through not only their childhood, but also the brief time they had been married.

Being deceitful and dishonest with Aadrika had been effortless, for Aadrika had been innocent and trusting, attributes that made her an easy target for him to control, thereby making him feel powerful. And it was him that Anil had phoned the day before, explaining the situation and his plan and suggested they meet at the airport.

Aadrika would be there too and should Dhruv want to get to know his son, this would be the ideal time to right time to meet her, for she would be feeling needy and vulnerable.

Dhruv looked at Aadrika anxiously, wondering that, if in the time they had been apart, she had become unaffected by his charm. However, he smiled with relief as he saw Aadrika smile and nod her head.

Aadrika was not impervious to his charm and deep in her heart she felt she would like to replace that which had been taken from her, first by him then by Ani, However, she had expected more from Anil, that their affair would limp to a halt with a polite goodbye by him and a vague promise to speak again sometime in the future. That would have given her closure, but what Anil had done was slam the past in her face, consequently her past would slam shut in her face again, maybe for ever?

"Oh, alright, you do look tired, actually I have just had a cup, but it will be nice to catch up." Aadrika replied.

However, as soon as she had agreed, she wondered if she, instead to succumbing to his charm should have concentrated on what really happened when their marriage ended; how Dhruv had abandoned her to create new experiences for himself without including her in them.

However, she could not help wondering if she should she try to revive the love they once shared, or was it too late and the avenues of invasion and occupation were now closed to her? And if so, was she only considering it because Anil's departure had left a gap in her life?

Chapter 34

"Thanks, Aadrika, it is kind of you to even talk to me after what I have done, but that is what I love about you, your sincerity and of course not holding a grudge."

Aadrika's heart skipped a beat when he said 'love about you' in the present tense; the sentence and the way he said it filled her in equal parts of pleasure coupled with nervousness.

Dhruv smiled, shoved one hand in the pocket of his jacket, smiled down at her with his brown eyes, then reached for her hand with the other. "Come let us find a café." He said as, holding her soft hand, he looked around for one.

They passed one and as the smell of fresh coffee reached their nostrils, Dhruv steered her towards it.

Outside the café stood a blonde woman with frizzy curls and lips that were smeared in bright red and wearing a blue sleeveless velvet dress that she was a size too small for her! And with her bare arms she was drinking what Dhruv thought looked like cider, out of a bottle and impatiently looking at the man standing beside her who had his mobile phone pressed to his ear

"I love the aroma of fresh coffee, nothing like it." Dhruv said as he passed them and found an empty table. "Wait here, Aad, I will get the coffees., you know we are lucky to have found a table, the café is packed."

He sat Aadrika on the empty chair beside it, pulled out another, took of his jacket and hung it on its back. Looking at him, Aadrika thought she could not remember a time when Dhruv was without that particular jacket and to her it had become his logo!

"Yes, we are," Aadrika placed her purse on the table and clutched a tissue in her wet palm, hoping it would absorb her sweat as she saw Dhruv talking to the man at the counter.

Whilst waiting for his order, Dhruv looked across at Aadrika and noticed how beautiful she looked in slim black fitting trousers, a jacket on top of a red blouse that was open at the neck Her thick hair, which he had loved, fell softly down her shoulders. Suddenly, he was physically attracted to her so casually opened the top button of his shirt, showing his hairy and manly chest.

Aadrika became aware of his masculinity and chose to remember only the good times they had shared. As far back as she could remember, Dhruv had looked after her and warned her about certain pair of people that she should avoid, movements and meetings she should dodge if possible...

Suddenly the warmth and love she had suppressed for so long suddenly erupted and she felt secure and warm in Dhruv's presence again. However, she was not sure that he loved her still, and if so, would he be willing to commit and acknowledge that he would have to share her love with Aarush who still needed her care and attention, or would he still want to move on to pastures new?

Although uncertain of Dhruv's intentions, she looked affectionately at him as he carried over 2 cups of coffees and scones on a tray, admiring his broad shoulders and chest.

"I thought we would treat ourselves to a mini breakfast, Aad!" Dhruv smiled as he saw the look in her eyes, and thought that, after all, he had not lost Aadrika and hoped, that if he played his cards right, would once again, be able to control and manipulate her to his way of thinking.

He placed the tray on the table than tucked a strand of Aadrika's hair around her ears and smiled. He winked at her and Aadrika's heart again beat fast as she heard him call her Aad tenderly for it had always been his special nickname for her.

He sat down with a "Oh boy, I need a caffeine boost or else I will start getting withdrawal symptoms!!"

Aadrika giggled as she pushed a cup towards him and took a sip from hers, glad that he still retained his sense of humour.

"Thanks, Aad." Dhruv took a sip and closed his eyes feeling energised.

He reached into his pocket and pulled out a rumpled packet of cigarettes, flipped it open, took out one and put it between his lips. After he had lit it, he puffed on it, wondering as to what his next move should be. One that would not frighten Aadrika and at the same time, one that would appeal to her good heart at the same time showing him to be the injured party, maybe?

"Ah that is better" Dhruv put down his cup and pushed his hair from his forehead.

They sat facing each other. Aadrika on edge, waiting for Dhruv to speak, unsure of what was happening and how much significance their meeting had, if any.

Dhruv too looked uncertain but when his face softened, Aadrika could see how difficult he was finding this conversation and it showed in the hesitancy in his voice, slowly picking up possibilities and deciding the best thing to say and then, how to say it.

"Aad, whilst travelling I have been doing a lot of thinking. I, we were happy till Aarush arrived and you became so engrossed in motherhood You looked after him when he was so tiny and helpless, but I could not do anything right, and I think you did not trust me with him for you would not even let me hold him! It was then that I began to feel that maybe I had the potential to do something with my life but could not because, one I did not know what and secondly, I was not skilled enough anyway, I felt tied down. I think you know that."

"I do, Dhruv, you made it quite clear before you left." Aadrika said drily.

"Yes, sorry about the way I put it, but I never got to spend time with Aarush, but you knew what he was feeling, he did not have to tell you what he needed, you knew it intuitively. It was then that I saw another side to you that I had not seen before and one that I, no men do not have."

"Come on Dhruv, he was only a baby!"

"Yes, I know, but you kept him from me, and, to keep you happy, I did not insist otherwise, we would have bonded. I mean, kids are cute, but it is difficult to spend hours with them! I could not for the life of me understand your attachment with Aarush and began to miss the excitement of being free, especially after the constraints of the orphanage, I wanted to get out but to stay with you seemed the decent thing to do. But after some time, I am sorry, but I had to get away! If I had had you to talk to, I could have handled the situation, but you were always locked in the room with Aarush! And, just to clear the air, Aadrika, I was not running away from you, but you held up a mirror of what my future would be like had I stayed., a future that was dull and boring."

Chapter 35

" I am so sorry you felt like that, Dhruv, and you know, I have been doing a lot of thinking too, and it was not all your fault, I should have spent time with you too, but I was so afraid of getting it wrong with Aarush that…" Tears welled in Aadrika's eyes, thinking that she had been right in predicting that the meeting with Dhruv would involve guilt and remorse, for that is exactly what Dhruv had succeeded in making her feel.. "And I did not tell you this because you might have thought me to be a bad mother, but there were times when I shook him, why I nearly dropped him once!"

"So now I know why you felt you had to protect him! I wish you had spoken to me, I understand now, but at that time, if I had stayed, it would put limitations on my freedom, and I am not proud of this, but I got scared. We had only been out of the orphanage for a few months and were beginning to enjoy the freedom that entailed."

His voice wandered off and he looked at the floor wondering if he was doing the right thing by bringing up their past, and that if by doing so he had scared her and consequently any hope for a future with her? When he raised his eyes and looked at her his eyes were moist and Aadrika could not resist the lost little boy look

"Aad, I wanted a life with goals, ambitions and achievements and I was sure I had abilities that were as yet not trained, lying dormant, and that maybe I should create my own opportunities and therefore destiny. Most children's ambitions are shaped whilst they are growing up, but we never got a chance, and I strongly felt that I could not explore them if I had responsibilities that would surely hold me back"

He reached out and stroked her hand which he held for a moment, but the electricity that passed through them was enough to disrupt the rhythm of conversation, the thread of which Aadrika continued.

"I too had ambition to live," Aadrika exclaimed "to have a career have fun and enjoy the sense of freedom that came from being out of that institution. I wanted to live a normal life like everybody else, but did not know how, for you had always been there to protect me. Therefore, I had to option but to accept what life had dealt me and live through my experience successfully so that they would, hopefully shape my sons." Aadrika said in a thick voice.

"Look Aadrika, I did not want to bring up the past... anyway, let me get some more coffee."

Dhruv got up quickly and went to stand in the queue and again cursed himself for bringing up their history and his feelings. However, he had done so hoping to convince Aadrika of his remorse and regret at leaving her which might pave the way for the future. He returned with the coffees and a packet of crisps and placed them on the table.

Aadrika added some sugar in her cup and as she stirred it, said. "I don't want to bring it up either, but it is good to clear the air. Anyway, how are you feeling now, still disorientated?"

"No Aad, I am feeling much better thanks, getting all that of my chest and also getting a chance to apologise." Dhruv replied, relieved that their conversation had not alarmed her.

"And I agree with you that it is better to clear the air! Anyway, the man at the counter asked how long we will be staying as we had been occupying the table for a long time and I told him that our flight had been delayed!" He added winking mischievously. "Now, where were we? I am sorry I was talking about myself all the time, telling how I felt when you too must have felt hurt. But let's not talk about the past."

"No, I would like to talk about it, too clear the air, Dhruv, I was terribly hurt when you left because I had always had you by my side protecting me. But we are both wiser now, you explained clearly today the reasons why you felt you had to leave. Then, you were angry most of the time, begrudging me my time with Aarush., and when you did explain it was like you were accusing me, and, to top it all you asked me to make a choice between Aarush and yourself! How could I do that for you are my husband and he is my son. You did not understand how I felt, for I was very young when I pregnant and it terrified me. And the one thing that held me together was having you by my side!" Aadrika said in a lacklustre voice, her eyes full, blurry and burning.

She wiped them with the back of her hand then lifted her head as if trying to breathe in air.

Dhruv felt the hurt in her voice for Aadrika had not bothered to mask it. He took her hand and moved his thumb gently across her knuckles.

"I am so sorry, Aad." He whispered." You did not even let me see Aarush, and he is my son!"

Aadrika, having offloaded her concerns, continued.

"You had always saved me from bad people in the orphanage, that it never occurred to me that your feelings would change. And yes, maybe I was too engrossed with being a mother, but there was no one to give me any advice and I was so afraid I would do something wrong and hurt Aarush like Darpan. And when you told me that day how you truly felt., it was awful.!" Aadrika trembled.

Dhruv sat listening to her, realising how deeply he had hurt her.

"If you had only talked to me sooner, I myself would have suggested you take a holiday, but you just told me that we were suffocating you!" Aadrika choked on her coffee. "And worse than that was that after you left, you never bothered to find out how we were, for we had no money and…as if that was not enough, seeing a single woman people began making comments about that, my race and background".

"I am so sorry, Aad, that you had to face that alone.!"

"But it was enough that you left, you never bothered to find out how I was managing with Aarush."

"What can I say but that I am sorry Aadrika? I have missed so much with Aarush; I have no memories of him and he none of me." Dhruv took both her hands stroking them "but do I have a chance to form new memories? That is if you will let me?" he brushed the hard band of the wedding ring that Aadrika still wore "Look, I am also wearing my wedding ring, I have always worn it, for it made me feel close to you."

"I don't mind that you meet him, Dhruv, but even I rarely get to see him. He spends all his time at school then with his friends, he comes home late and then goes straight to bed."

"Isn't he too young to be out alone at night?" Dhruv asked.

"He is, but he has been cooped up with me during the lockdown in the flat and I don't have the heart to tell him not to see his friends, especially when he is so excited about meeting them."

However, Aadrika resented him questioning her parenting skills, and felt she could not go through the motions and pretend everything was as it had been before they broke up, yet, deep in her heart she knew she loved him unconditionally, but should she show him that she did?

Dhruv saw the confusion on her face and how conflicted Aadrika felt by her emotions.

"Words are not enough, Aad, but I truly am sorry" Dhruv searched Aadrika's face for any sign of bitterness but saw only pain and disappointment.

Chapter 36

He bought a note of tenderness in his voice and eyes, hoping that would tip Aadrika's reactions in his favour as he rested his hand on her slim delicate hand, the one that still had his wedding ring.

"I know I should have contacted you after I left. but I felt so ashamed of the way I treated you that I could not think of a way to make it better. and the more I put it off, the more difficult it became! But you and Aarush were always in my thoughts so after some time, even the excitement of travelling wore of, as did the feeling of being free" He spoke thoughtfully occasionally scratching his chin. "And anyway, I can tell you, it is no fun travelling alone! In short, I am so fed up with it that I am ready to settle, anyway tell me, how is Aarush? And are you with someone?" he narrowed his eyes.

Aadrika's eyes widened in surprise and shook her head. Dhruv brought her hand to his lips and when she did not object, looked pleased and after taking in a long breadth, let it out in a long sigh of relief.

A young man wearing jeans and t-shirt with a backpack. Passed them holding a cup of coffee in a cup, glanced at them briefly than sat at the next table. After placing the cup on the table, he took out his mobile and made himself comfortable and began texting, after which, Aadrika thought, he would start playing a game on his mobile.

Aadrika took a sip of coffee than put it down on the saucer, thinking that she had had enough coffee today to last her a month! Dhruv, together with the packet of crisps, had bought a carrot cake, which he remembered she loved. Aadrika had noticed the thoughtful gesture which had bought a slight smile to her lips, for and it were these little bits of thoughtfulness that had endeared him to her.

"Dhruv, Aarush is growing up and is beginning to look a lot like you and has a lot of your mannerisms, and no I am not with anyone." Aadrika confirmed feeling pleased.

"That means, Aad, he is a very handsome boy!" Dhruv winked and the impish smile that had so endeared him to Aadrika spread across his face. "When can I see him, does he know I am his father?"

"Dhruv, like I said, these days I rarely get to see him for he is too busy with his friends and no, he does not know about you, he was very young when you left, and later on how could I tell him that his father had walked out on him? No, I told him that his father had business that took him abroad and occasionally I told him that I had received a postcard from you, and that you had sent you your love. But now he has grown up and I cannot lie to him anymore, I had meant to tell him the truth soon,"

Dhruv looked at her tenderly. "Aad, that was very considerate of you, you are always thinking of others, I am surprised that you alone, for you are very beautiful! Surely there must have been somebody?! Anyway, now that I am here, we can tell him together?" Dhruv asked softly.

The look in Dhruv's eyes caused Aadrika knees to feel week and was angry at herself for falling prey to his charm when she should feel angry at the way he had treated them! She wondered what Anika's reaction would be, for it was she who had picked up the pieces of Aadrika's broken heart when Dhruv had left, even if she had only stayed one night.

"Thank you, Dhruv, but I don't think so, but tell me, are you seeing someone?" Aadrika asked "I mean, you must have met some exotic woman during your travels who plucked at your heartstrings?"

Dhruv laughed heartily. "No there hasn't and nor will there be," Dhruv replied, his face becoming serious as he put his hand over Aadrika's that was lying idly on the table. "If I have to be with anyone, it will be with you."

Aadrika was flustered yet flattered by Dhruv's compliments, "So how long are you in London for?" she asked in a shaky voice.

"Hopefully permanently." Dhruv replied. "But I have not even found a place to stay so that is the first thing I must do."

"Still leaving things till the last minute Dhruv?"

"No Aad, but you don't have a good opinion of me, have you? Anyway, I do have a friend who is willing to put me up, but I have not been able to get in touch with him, I hope he is okay, I think I should try again and hopefully this time get through!"

He took out his mobile and dialled but, when it went to voicemail again, put it back in his pocket with a frown." I do hope he is all right, this is a scary time, and one tends to think the worst."

"I am sure he will be okay like you said, these are scary times for nearly every family has some sad news around the virus."

"Tell me about it! Anyway, I think we better leave Aadrika for the café is becoming too crowded for my liking and I also I need to find a hotel. Anyway, that is not your problem, but do give me your number, I would like to see you again and of course my son. Better still, this is my mobile, give me a missed call and I will save your number.

He took out a pen and wrote his number on the napkin,

"Yes of course." Aadrika took out her mobile, looked at the napkin and rang his number from it so he could save which he did.

Suddenly Aadrika had an idea, one which she hoped she would not later regret. At the moment, she felt she could not go back to an empty flat for Aarush was once again staying with his friend.

"Dhruv, why don't you come home with me? Aarush is staying over at a friend's; my flat is not big but if you don't mind sleeping on the couch?"

"Oh Aad, that would be nice, it would solve my problem for the time being, I will ring him again tomorrow,"

He got up from the chair, put on his jacket, then put out his hand to help Aadrika.

"Is it the same flat, oh and it would be best if we tell Aarush immediately that you came to the airport to receive me and..."

Aadrika looked up startled and her eyes darkened and narrowed. "Thank you, Dhruv, no it is not the same flat, anyway Aarush will not be home, we will tell Aarush that you are a friend, again, that might be confusing, so let me think about it on the way home."

"Don't worry Aad, I will not interfere, so will leave it to you to handle Aarush."

Dhruv grinned as he pulled his luggage trolley behind him and followed Aadrika, admiring her slim figure and her soft hair cascading down her waist and again thought what a fool he had been to leave her and the wasted moments and nights...all because of Aarush! However, he knew better this time...

Aadrika felt the circumstances in her life were changing too quickly and drastically for she preferred people from her past to remain there, but she felt that destiny was rewriting history. Aadrika wondered as to whether it was doing so to make things easier for her, maybe even to make them fit in with her perfect version of past and/or future events? And maybe, like Dhruv said, by giving them a chance to invent new memories?

They took the underground back home and again Aadrika was glad of Dhruv's company for he was so charming that she put Anil and their affair behind her.

The weather had been fine when they left the airport, but just before they reached the flat it began pouring so they decided to take a cab from the under-ground to her flat., which was not far...

Luckily, they did not have long to wait for one and as soon as it had arrived and they had climbed in, Aadrika gave her address.to the driver who looked at her surprise.

"I know that place, it is not too far from here, but I must say it is a very secluded place, sorry it is not my place to say anything." With that he turned the taxi and drove off. Dhruv and Aadrika looked at each other in surprise

He steered the cab towards Aadrika's flat and turned into a lane, at the end of which was a yard with a row of sheds, and at the corner of them was a block of flats. The building of the flats had originally been painted in yellow, but the paint had faded, and wall of the building were overgrown with ivy that needed pruning.

The taxi stopped outside the building, Dhruv looked around and remarked, "Aad, this does seem a very dark and isolated place, is it safe?"

"Well, I had to move to a new place and the rent is cheaper here." Aadrika replied. "I have had a few problems with some thugs, but all in all in is okay."

"What about Aarush? You said he comes late at night?"

"I make sure that the parents of his friend drop him." Aadrika answered as she paid the cab.

As they walked towards the flat, Dhruv noticed a couple wearing matching trench coats holding hands walking slowly, but the woman was struggling with one hand to put up an umbrella that would protect them from the rain. At the corner of the square Dhruv noticed a few boys loitering around idly; and Dhruv again thought it did not seem a safe place but did not want to bring up the subject again.

As they entered the flat, Aadrika could not but help recall the words of her friend Anika

'One day you will remember me Aadrika for I can tell you from experience that most men will knock at your door and once you let them in, they will be nice in the beginning, they will be kind and considerate and put you first but, gradually, they will make themselves at home. They will plunder first your fridge, then bed and then take over your space in life, just like that! They will take over you rights however much you protest, till finally they will take over your life and tuck you into their pocket where they assume you will be happy!'

Aadrika looked at Dhruv who was coming up behind her and for a moment, doubted her decision, then assured herself that Anika had Anil in mind when she said that and not Dhruv, who she was becoming increasingly sure, would not treat her that way again. Aadrika heaved a sigh of relief and threw her coat on the banister and went to the kitchen calling out to Dhruv over her shoulder.

"Dhruv, can you wait in the lounge whilst I make us something to eat after which I will set up your bed. You must be tired."

"Thank you, Aadrika, that will be nice, but no coffee please!" Dhruv replied with a twinkle in his eye as he followed her into the kitchen.

"I see what you mean! There is coffee coming out of my ears too!" Dhruv stood in the doorway, admiring Aadrika as she moved around the kitchen, her eyes darting and constantly changing expression, her soft black hair hanging halfway down her waist. Her face looked calm and composed, showing nothing of the inner turmoil she felt, for Dhruv had always had that effect on her.

In fact, such was Dhruv's effect on her that her affair with Anil now became meaningless, leaving no trace of it in her mind and it was as if it had never happened. And, if by chance, she did remember, she immediately tried to erase it from her mind, for she realised that had the relationship continued, she would have become invisible to society, and that Its rules would not apply to her in as much that it would first shun then forget her.

Therefore, she decided to take took control of her life by forgetting Anil, when she suddenly remembered that he had not returned the control of her finances back to her, so till that was sorted, she was still going to be tied to him, at least financially.

Chapter 37

After finishing the coffee and breakfast, which both had enjoyed, Khusboo and Sameera strolled through the airport shops, and as soon as it was announced that the flight from Dubai had landed, Khusboo and Sameera stood at the arrivals gate with the rest of the crowd, Khushboo pushing her way through than tapping her foot impatiently when she did not see Aiysha and Ekta.

The arrival hall was crowded with faces that were whitened by the glare of the lights of the arrival hall. Some of the people waiting were drivers holding name cards of people they had had come to receive, others were backpackers in shorts and t shirt. There were extended families of Asian and African descent that had come to receive their relatives, dressed in a blaze of different dresses that were bright with colour, and in doing so, implying to their relatives that they had not forgotten their roots! Everyone eagerly watched the automatic door from which only a few people were trickling through.

"What is taking them so long?" Khushboo exclaimed in exasperation.

"Maybe because everybody is following and getting used to the new Covid testing and guidelines?" Sameera replied, trying to calm her daughter. "Remember your father had to go through them as well and those rules apply not only to Departure but Arrivals too, don't worry, they will be out soon."

At that moment, Khushboo spotted her friend with a woman who she presumed must be her sister Ekta, both wearing masks and dragging trolleys behind them.

Khushboo waved frantically trying to catch Aiysha's attention and when she saw her, Aiysha rushed over and hugged her then drew back as she suddenly realised that maybe she should adhere to social distancing. Aishya was wearing jeans, t shirt and a casual suede jacket. with sunglasses that were resting high on her forehead and carrying a beige hessian bag that was slung over her shoulder.

Khushboo was surprised to see that now her hair was cut shoulder length, for she recalled admiring her long thick hair, Aishya had a cute slightly upturned nose with twinkling brown eyes that were fringed with long lashes and flawless coffee coloured skin. But what had not changed about her was her love of jewellery, for as always, she wore bracelets on the wrists of both her hands and long loop earring and if she could rings on her fingers.

"Wow, it so good to see you Khusboo.! It is nice of you to come to receive us; but you shouldn't have bothered, we would have got a taxi" Aishya laughed.

"Gosh, Aishya, I have looking forward to seeing you too." Khusboo smiled, showing her dimples.

"Oh, by the way, Khusboo, this is my sister, Ekta, I told you that she would be coming with me? Maybe you might have met? Hello aunty." Aishya spoke quickly as she turned towards Sameera.

"Hello Khusboo, Sameera, I think we did meet but it was a long time ago and that too for a very short time." Ekta said in a soft voice.

She looked very elegant and chic in a pale blue blouse over navy blue trousers with not a crease out of place. She had nicely shaped lips under a pert nose that had a tiny nose stud perched on it, and her thick black hair was plaited then knotted into a bun at the nape of her long neck. She had flawless skin under the long sweep of her lashes that fringed almond shaped eyes. Sameera and Khushboo looked at her in admiration for although she had spent the last 8 hours or more on a plane, she looked cool and poised.

"Dad has left for India today, so thought we would see him off and welcome you to London at the same time." Khusboo grinned as she took Aiysha's arm and both began talking at once again, Sameera smiled when she saw that Aishya and Ekta were talking fast and getting impatient if either Ekta or Sameera tried to interrupt.

With the result that both Sameera and Ekta stood apart, Ekta silently standing watching her sister fondly, admiring her sister's easy-going nature. Ekta was a quiet reserved woman who often wished she was like her sister, more of an extrovert, go to parties and be able to make friends as easily as her sister, In fact she was so shy that she was mortified and ashamed of it, as if it were an awkward illness that she had to hide, unaware that it was this very trait that endeared her to everyone who met her, including Sameera and Khushboo who thought that she was beautiful and exotic.

Sameera took Ekta's by the arm and called out to her daughter.

"I know you two have lots to talk about, Khusboo and Aishya, but I think we should make a move home." Sameera smiled. "Khusboo, you are not being considerate, they must be tired after their long flight, and you can continue talking over a nice cup of tea."

"Sorry Aishya, Ekta," Khusboo apologised. "Mum is right, we should make a move.".

"Don't worry about it, Khushboo, I am so excited that I do not feel tired!" Aishya said as they walked towards the exit.

"Hey Aishya, do you think we should help those gentlemen?" Khusboo asked as she saw a party of German tourists looking confused.

"Khushboo, now is not the time! I am sure there will be somebody to help them," Sameera said in exasperation, wondering how Khusboo had noticed him them for the girls were walking, arm in arm, talking. ceaselessly.

They left the airport building and as they went out the ice-cold air numbed their faces.

"I had not expected it would be so cold at this time of the year!" Aishya remarked, rubbing her face with hands that felt cold and were beginning to turn blue." But you look warm and prepared for any kind of weather."

She looked at Khushboo who was wearing her trench coat over her legging, a few strands of hair escaping from out of her ponytail, which even her sports cup could not conceal.

"Although you need to brush your hair, you never know, Mr Right might be around the corner!" Aishya said cheerfully, her eyes twinkling.

"Okay Miss know it all! And you are cold because you are wearing cotton pair of turned up jean and you don't have gloves scarf or hat." Khusboo said. "But I thought you might not have, so I, no we, got some gloves and a scarf." she rummaged in her bag and handed her a scarf and gloves then turned towards Ekta. "Mum has got something for you Ekta."

"I have I brought a shawl for you Ekta, which I think should keep you safe from the wind. If not, I can give you mine too, for I am wearing a very warm cardigan." Sameera replied.

"Oh, thank you, I had forgotten how thoughtful you are!" Aishya smiled and as she put the scarf around her neck and pulled the matching gloves over her hands.

"Maybe you are feeling the cold because you have from Dubai where the weather is warm! But actually, you know it is not as cold as it was, it had snowed a couple of weeks ago, which, at this time of the year is unusual, but the weather is unpredictable! Anyway, there is a hot cup of tea at home. Ladies, can you wait here whilst I get the car...it will be easier." Khushboo remarked.

As soon as they nodded, Khusboo hurried to the car park whilst the three women stood waiting, standing in a circle watching people entering and leaving the airport, departing, and arriving from various destinations and listening to the traffic of the planes that were flying overhead, whilst Aiysha rubbed her hands and stamped her feet.

Chapter 38

"Oh, come on Aishya, it is not as cold as all that!" Ekta reproached her sister.

"You have a nice woollen shawl which you have wrapped around you to keep warm'!" Aishya retorted, rubbing her hands. "Oh, I have just remembered, I have to make a call,"

After pulling off her gloves, she fumbled in her beige hessian bag and eventually managed to find her mobile and both Ekta and Sameera watched her first frowning then, jabbing at the mobile with her cold and glittery nails, trying to send a text and when she could not, frowned as they heard her swear silently under her breadth.

"Aishya!" Ekta scolded "where are your manners? I am sure the call can wait; you can phone once we get home."

"Yes, Ekta, you are right., but let me try again." Aishya muttered.

She jabbed on her phone, the bracelets on her wrists jingling till she finally managed to send a text, then quickly dropped her mobile back into her bag.

"Aishya, you have been finding it difficult to use the mobile because I saw you stumbling around, trying to find your balance and you know why? Not only are you feeling the jetlag, but you were far too occupied in trying to sling your bag over your shoulder and keep it there, because it keeps slipping off your shoulder, and of course the bracelets that you never take off were getting in the way! I remember telling you that your choice of bag was not practical for travel!"

"All right, all right, Ekta, you are right, but actually the bad is very practical and..." however when she saw her sisters face did not finish her sentence.

There were other people with luggage standing alongside them, all waiting impatiently for friends or relatives to pick them up. Amongst them was a small plump woman with heavy rimmed glasses under white bushy eyebrows standing beside a girl wearing a black baseball cap black and windcheater over black jeans who Aishya assumed to be her daughter for she was glaring at the woman under her baseball cap.

"Mum, we should have gone with Dad, you know how long it takes for him to walk!" the girl said to her mother, her voice loud and rude...

"Young girl you should be thankful he has come to pick us up at all! And you know how long it would have taken me to walk, you know very well that I suffer from arthritis!"

The girl mumbled under her breadth, took out her mobile, turned her back on her mother and began texting.

"That girl is being so rude to her mother, children nowadays! "Sameera exclaimed. Aishya and Ekta too had heard for the girl had not bothered to keep her voice down.

"Aishya, you do look tired, Khusboo will be coming soon, she told me that Anil had not parked the car too far inside the car park."

She had barely finished her sentence when Khushboo drove up and after parking the car in front of them, got out and she and Aishya started loading their luggage into the boot of car. Once all the luggage was in the car, they hurriedly got into it, Sameera sitting in front with Khusboo whilst Aishya and Ekta sat at the back.

Khushboo started the car, twisted around her seat to make sure that there were no cars approaching from behind, waved her hand, then pulled out into the road that led to the main road.

It had started raining when they started, but it had not been an outburst but a shower that looked like a silver sprinkle of dust that had drifted across the city and slowly trickled down the side windows of Khushboo's car.

But once she turned into the carriageway the drizzle stopped and the curling grey clouds unfolded slightly as if consenting to let the faint yellow/orange coloured light of the evening pass through them.

As she steered her car, Khushboo glanced sideways quickly and noticed that the hedges at the side of the roads were glistening and the road surface up ahead of her was wet and quite luminous...Khushboo was a careful driver, checking her mirror frequently and slowing at the merest hint of approaching risk.

"Mum, Aishya and Ekta are nearly asleep at the back they must be tired, can you put on some music on please, there are some CD's there, you can choose the music."

"Sure Khushboo, as long as it does not disturb them."

"We'll keep the volume low."

Sameera took a CD, and the car was enveloped by the background classic music Khusboo sometimes listened to when stuck in a traffic jam.

"Hey Aishya, will this music put you to sleep or wake you!"

Khusboo adjusted the mirror and grinned at Aishya, who she saw with surprise, was busy on her mobile

When she came across traffic lights Khusboo tapped her fingers on wheel impatiently, in time to the music from stereo and when she looked in her mirror trying to catch Aisha's eyes, saw she was still busy on her mobile so looked at her windscreen, fascinated to see that the raindrops from the earlier downpour were still clinging on to the windscreen holding for a moment midway, before losing their hold and starting to glide down the windscreen.

"Is it far to go?" Aishya asked yawning.

"No, we are nearly there. I thought you were not tired, and I also did not talk to you so as to give you a chance for a nap!"

"No, you didn't!" Aishya retorted. "I saw you through the mirror, you were trying to catch my eye!"

"Well, it seems I did, but you were too busy on your mobile!"

"Girls, girls" Sameera looked worried for they had not even reached home, and they were fighting. Ekta had seen the anxious look on Sameera's face.

"It is what they do, Sameera, bantering is part and parcel of their friendship and I think what keeps it alive."

"Mum, before I turn into our road shall I stop and get some take away?"

"No don't worry, Khushboo, I had cooked something yesterday so, don't worry."

"Wow mum you are efficient." Khushboo said as they arrived outside terraced house with a well-tended garden, Khusboo parked the car outside and opened the door. "Mum you and Ekta better go in whilst Aishya and me will bring in the luggage."

After they had placed the luggage in the landing, Sameera turned to Khushboo.

"Khushboo, you two go in the lounge I will bring the tea." She smiled "Dinner is ready, all I have to do is heat it up, so anytime you are ready please let me know, and Ekta, if you need to freshen up, I will show you to the bedroom."

"Thanks Mum, Aishya if you wait for me in the lounge, unless you too want to freshen up?"

Chapter 39

"No, I am fine, Khushboo, thanks, all I need is a hot cup of tea." Aishya took off her jacket.

"Yes, that goes for me too," Ekta said as she too off her shawl and jacket and handed them to Khusboo.

"Thanks, Ekta, here, Aishya, give me your jacket and I will hang it up" Khushboo opened a cupboard door and took out a hangar then hung it back in the cupboard.

"I can help you make the tea, Sameera," Ekta said softly.

"No, thanks, Ekta, but you can sit with me whilst I make it and we can get acquainted." Ekta nodded and as they entered kitchen Ekta saw with appreciation that the evening light was pouring in through windows.

As she sat on the kitchen table, she watched Sameera move about in the kitchen efficiently First, she put on the kettle and then opened the unit door to take out some sups, plates and tea coffee and a bowl of sugar which she laid on the worktop after which she turned to Ekta.

"It might be too early for dinner, Ekta, but I have got some snacks, Samosas, so whilst the kettle is boiling, I will fry them. I hope you like them."

"Oh yes, I love them, I have not had a chance to eat Indian food in Dubai."

"I thought there were a lot of Indians there so assumed there would be lots of Indian restaurants there too." Sameera asked

"Oh yes, but I lived alone there and oh... it is a long story."

"Well then, you can have your fill for I love cooking and it gives me immense pleasure to feed others." Sameera said.

She put some oil in a frying pan, then took out some frozen samosas from the freezer which, after defrosting whilst the oil heated, she put gently in the hot oil.

Ekta had been watching Sameera in fascination... "Although I love them, as does Aiysha, you don't have to do all that work, Sameera, all we need is hot cup of tea! You must be tired too, for you made dinner for us than saw your husband off in the morning then waited to receive us."

"I am not tired, and this is no problem, for I love cooking, Ekta we will have dinner later on, I don't think the girls are going to sleep tonight.!"

Sameera stood over the sizzling fryer as she put each samosa in it and Ekta watched fascinated as the Samosas floated to the surface before Sameera turned them as they turned brown and sank back into oil. After both sides were brown, she shook the wire basket shook it, then placed them on a plate covered with a piece of kitchen roll to soak the oil from the samosas, after which she wiped her hands on the apron around her waist, undid it and hung it in its usual place behind the door.

Ekta, meanwhile thought that perhaps one of the reasons her marriage to Aryan, her husband, had not worked was because of her lack of domesticity, which Aryan had pointed out. To please him she had learnt to cook but he was unable to resist taking the moral high ground by spitefully pointing out her faults however minor.

Khushboo and Aishya meanwhile had left them and gone into the lounge.

"Oh, this is nice!" Aishya exclaimed as Khushboo switched on the light. "Very comfy" she said as she placed her dark glasses on the centre table, sat on the sofa and stretched out her legs.

"Yes, it is my favourite room too, but look here, if after tea you want to rest, we can talk tomorrow. I have taken the week off and have bought tickets for concerts, ballets and plays and we will see any movie you like and afterwards try out all the restaurants in London! Since lockdown has been lifted and we are free to move about, still with masks of course, if the day is nice, we can go for walks in the park and...."

"Hey steady on Khusboo!" Aishya tried to curb her excitement but found that she too looked forward to everything for her last assignment had been difficult.

At that moment Sameera walked in with a tray of tea and samosas on the tray.

"That looks nice.!" Aishya said as Sameera handed her a cup then placed the tray on the coffee table at the centre of the room and turned to leave the room.

"Hey, where is your cup Mum? Come and sit with us"

"Ekta and myself decided to have it her room, she wants to show me something. And I am sure you have loads to talk about!" Sameera smiled, patted Khusboo on the head and left the room.

"Your Mum is really nice," Aishya commented

"She is the best; but I wish my father thought so too! Anyway, tell my about yourself, you sounded distressed when I spoke to you. What were you doing in Dubai anyway?"

"Give me minute and I will explain, I need to phone my office." Aishya took out her mobile and went out of the room whilst Khushboo sipped her tea and wondered that although they had been close and kept in touch, there was very little about her personal like she knew, all she knew was that Aishya was a highly paid journalist which meant she covered high profile cases.

Aishya finished her call and returned to the seat she had vacated earlier looking thoughtful.

"Everything all right Aishya? You know I have been worried for you sounded very upset when we spoke on the phone. Anyway, what were you doing in Dubai, your parents live here don't they?"

"No, they are in India, and I was in Dubai because the paper I work for sent me there to cover an important story. And of course, I jumped at the opportunity, for my sister had got married and moved to Dubai and that gave me a chance to catchup with her."

"I knew you had done journalism but did not know you had made that a career?" Khusboo picked up the plate of Samosas and offered it to Aishya."

"Yes, I did, when I saw there are so many hidden stories that need to be uncovered and told to the world."

"It does sound interesting, Aishya!" Khushboo placed the plate back on the table then took one. "But tell me, actually, it is Mum who bought it to my attention, she is following what is happening to a Princess in Dubai, did your assignment by any chance have to do with her and her family? If it was, I hope you were careful." Khushboo asked with a frown.

Aishya nodded, but avoided elaborating on it, so, Khusboo tactfully kept quiet.

However, Aishya tied to explain about her job, talking fast and switching from one case to another, without providing any clear background, so Khushboo had to interrupt occasionally to ask questions. "But about the story in the paper, yes, the family is involved, but how no one knows,"

"But that is dangerous, for obviously they would not want any of their secrets to be out in the open.?" Khushboo asked worriedly. She had been sitting with the teacup in her hand, listening to Aishya attentively.

"One has to It doesn't do to get angry in that country, people hold it against you and also stops them from opening up. Oh, by the way, when I spoke to my office, they said they had another assignment for me so I can only stay for a couple of days before I move on. I wish I hadn't phoned my office; it could have waited till morning and is now only spoiling the small time I have with you." Aishya sighed as she finished her tea and placed the mug on the coaster on the table.

"I hope nothing as dangerous as the last one Aishya! You need to get a safer job! Anyway, I am sorry I shouldn't be talking shop, you should chill."

"No actually Dubai was a piece of cake, but they are sending me to Mayapur and cover all the violence there and then there is Afghanistan too, I believe the Taliban will be taking over soon so my paper would need someone there at some point…"

"Oh, my you are right, that is dangerous! There is so much violence in Mayapur, I don't even think at the moment they know if it is against the protesters. I heard that people are being taken from their home and not being heard of again! Look, you don't have to take this you know,"

"I have already accepted and there is no way I can refuse now. There are just three jobs lined up now, they will give details soon."

Although Aiysha's makeup was a mess, she still but looked pretty with wide apart brown eyes upturned cute nose and full pouted lips. Her hair too looked messy and there were dark shadows under her eyes which she had been massaging in little circles, which showed, in spite of what she had said, that she was tired. Adding to her weariness was the stress she was under in having to cut short her holiday to go into a dangerous country.

"Would you like to freshen up Aishya?" Khushboo asked. You look tired."

"Khushboo, don't beat about the bush, you mean I look awful! Well, I am too tired to go to the bathroom, but I will just powder my nose here if you don't mind."

She took out her compact from the bag, quickly powdered her nose, retouched her lipstick and gently brushed her hair in place.

"There, I am done, I do feel better!" Aishya said with a whoop as she put her brush and makeup back in her back.

"And you look better!" Khusboo grinned as they began gossiping happily about old times they had and every bit of news since they had last met.

At that moment Sameera entered and smiled when she saw the two friends eagerly chatting.

"Sorry to interrupt, but dinner is ready! Girls you can continue your chit-chat tomorrow!"

"Come to think of it, I am starving!" Aishya exclaimed as she rose from the sofa.

Chapter 40

Sameera ushered them out of the lounge into the dining room that had a black ebony table in the middle of the room with chairs. The table was covered with a tablecloth of white lace and a vase of fresh flowers at the centre.

In one bowl at the centre of the table she had put Kidney beans with cream and coriander leaves sprinkled on it. In the other Sameera had cooked her famous basmati rice seasoned with spices. Also on the table were all the other side dishes that went with Indian food, salad, Naan (Indian bread) pickles and yoghurt.

"Wow! That looks delicious Aunty! How did you manage to do that is such a short time?"

"Your sister helped and actually it is nothing."

As they seated themselves around the table Aishya remarked. "I have been living in a hotel for such a long time that I missed home cooked meals "

"I am sorry, but usually I make at least 2 dishes but today I have got Kidney beans, but don't worry there is some Indian dessert to follow!"

"Wow! This is a feast for us Sameera!" Ekta exclaimed as she dished out some rice on her plate.

"Thank you, girls" Sameera smiled as she looked around the table. "I thought you were staying with Ekta in Dubai?"

"Ekta had got a job there, so yes I was staying with her but as both of us do not like cooking, we either we got take away or went out."

"So Ekta, you are only here for a holiday and will be going back to Dubai?" Sameera asked.

"No Sameera, my contract with the firm finished so I will be looking for a job in London, Aishya I think will be staying on here."

"That was the plan Ekta, but I got an email from my office, and they are sending me on another assignment, in fact, I was telling Khushboo that I will only be here for a couple of days before I move on, But Khushboo, will it be possible for Ekta to stay with you till she figures out what she what she wants to do?"

"Of course!" Sameera exclaimed. "It will be nice to have some company when Khusboo goes back to work."

"Thank you, Sameera, but where is your office sending you this time Aishya?"

"Myanmar, to cover the violence there and how the government is ignoring basic rights of their citizens, in fact, they have given me three assignments, the last of which is Afghanistan, I think they are expecting some trouble there so want someone there to cover it..."

"But that is too dangerous, Aishya," Ekta exclaimed."

"Exactly what I said, but would she listen...noo." Khushboo stated

"There is a lot of problem there, people being killed, each side hiding evidence using weapons false propaganda, spread. In short, somebody needs to find out what the truth is because there is so much censorship there one doesn't really know what is happening. Innocent people being killed each affixing blame on the other."

"But can't they find someone else for that assignment?" Ekta asked. "You have just come back having completed one; I am sure they will want to know what you have uncovered."

"Technology these days, Ekta, I emailed my boss immediately as and when I discovered any relevant new piece of information. There are many countries around the world in turmoil because of people protesting, but someone has to uncover the truth. Villages in some parts of the world are being wiped out by Government because of their thinking."

However, what Aishya did not tell her was the previous journalist, who had been a friend of hers and who had been covering the story in Myanmar had been beaten by the police and was still in hospital.

"That is true, Aishya, but why should it be you? Anyway, I know you are very stubborn so will not listen to us. So, when will you be leaving?" Ekta asked miserably. "You know I was looking forward to spending some time with you. I think the only time we spent together was in the evening in Dubai for a couple of hours, and I don't know when you will be back."

"Don't worry, Ekta, I will be leaving in a couple of days but will return as soon as possible, in the meantime I am sure you are going to find an amazing job and flat, so that when I return, I can stay with you." She went across to her sister and kissed her on the head.

Ekta and Aishya rose when they thought the meal was over.

"And where do you think you are going? If you, do you will miss the highlight of the evening...Gajar Ka Halwa...Indian carrot cake!" Sameera said triumphantly.

"Oh yummy no way am I going to miss that!!" Aishya sat back promptly in her chair as did Ekta.

"Khushboo can you please clear the table, just leave some bowls and spoons for the carrot cake."

"Here let me help with that." Aiysha got up to help Khushboo clear the table of the used plates and bowls and took them to the kitchen. They returned with Sameera holding the carrot cake in a plate whilst Khushboo carried a carton of cream.

"Sameera, this is delicious, but do you how many calories this has? "Ekta said as she poured some cream on the cake on her bowl.

After they had finished and Khushboo had licked her fingers for this was her favourite dessert Aishya announced she would help again in clearing the table and washing up.

"No don't worry, we have a girl Olga who will come tomorrow. All we need to do is run the plates through hot water from the sink before we stalk them in the dishwasher. Olga will do the rest."

Aishya and Khusboo took the plates into the kitchen and as they did Sameera called out after them. "Khushboo, after you two have cleared up, and thank you Aishya, why don't all of you go to the lounge. I will make the tea, a duty that is usually Khushboo's, and bring it there, sorry that is if is all right with Aishya and Ekta? You must be tired so we can skip that if you want."

"I slept on the plane, Ekta, how do you feel about it?" Aishya asked. "I would certainly do with tea to wash down the delicious dinner and dessert.!"

"I am fine too, for as there were not many people on the plane, I slept too, and Khusboo, I would love to get to know you for Aishya has told me a lot about you! Sameera, would you like some help?"

"No thanks Ekta, you have been a great help with the dinner, especially after your flight!"

"Not at all, Sameera, I am glad I have been of help though you had everything ready, I hardly did anything. Anyway, thanks again for putting us up."

"Our pleasure Ekta." Sameera went into the kitchen and as she put on the kettle thought what a nice woman Ekta was, affectionate yet reserved.

Ekta followed Sameera with the tea into the lounge where Khusboo and her sister were chattering away, and she marvelled at how they could find so much to talk about, even though they had not seen each other for some time.

Ekta walked over to the mantelpiece, admiring the porcelain figures and ornate salvers that were exhibited on it. There was a photo of Khushboo, laughing up at the camera, and another of Anil and Sameera, both in silver frames.

"You know, I was so busy admiring the rest of the décor of the room that I did not see them!" Aishya exclaimed as she sauntered over to the mantelpiece to join her sister... "and this photo of yours is nice."

"I was surprised about that for none of my photos are usually flattering, mostly like passport photos!" Khushboo's infectious laughter rang ou as Ekta and Aishya made themselves comfortable,

Chapter 41

Once everybody had a mug of tea in their hand, Sameera turned to Aishya.

"Aishya, when are you leaving, you mentioned in a couple of days, is there no way you can persuade your boss so you could go a week later? I mean Khusboo has been looking forward to meeting you for so long and has made a lot of plans... I mean not only Khushboo I too would love you to stay too!"

"And when you talk to him you can tell there are other protests that are happening around the world that you can cover!" Khusboo exclaimed! "I mean, my father has only gone to India because of the farmers protests being held there. My grandparents are involved in it, so he has gone to reassure himself that they are safe. And then there is Minnesota and the trial being held there about the murder of George Floyd"

"I cannot choose my assignments Khushboo. and you are right, there is so much injustice there, racism has become rooted into a country's structures of power, culture and education, in short, all institutions that effect the identity of ethnic minorities who report incidents of racial abuse – both verbal and physical – with many experiencing attacks regularly. In Minnesota, I believe the people are waiting to see the sentence handed to the policemen responsible for George Floyd's death, and you are right Khushboo, the situation there is just simmering and will erupt in violence at any time."

"So, isn't it just as important for you to cover that rather than go to Myanmar?"

"If I could get out of this I would, but come on, the violence in Myanmar has to be priority. We should be ashamed of ourselves that it took a 45-year-old nun to stand between the protesters and the police!" There was clink of spoon against cup as she added sugar into tea. "And actually, I have already been given an assignment following that, they want me to cover the situation in Afghanistan and…"

"Oh, come on Aishya, don't they have other people in your office." Ekta cried in exasperation.

"Calm down Ekta, of course there are. It just that because of Covid they are being extra careful and asking employees to isolate at the smallest hint of any symptom for our job is to travel around and the risk of infection and carrying variants is high."

"And that is another reason why you should find yourself a stable job, one that does not involve you travelling abroad." Ekta said, for once her poise shaken.

"I too would like that Ekta, but how could I live with myself knowing that facts in the politics of some countries are constantly being either changed or buried by their governments. And they do this so that the writing of history is made easier, to make details of realities fit into their chosen accounts of events, and to create memories to fit with their version of movements and actions! And eventually, these recollections, as we all know, if imposed upon people often, would gradually be perceived to be true!"

"But what does all this have to do your job Aishya?" Khusboo asked, confused.

"Through my job I hope to make a difference by helping to uncover the truth. Khusboo, I have seen something akin to madness in the pain of minds that have been shattered by circumstances that have been created by falsehoods and it was when I saw their raw pain that I wanted to stay in political journalism. But, however tempting a normal life sound, I will not be able live with myself knowing that I ignored their pain, or that I had a chance to expose the truth had I remained in my career. Also. I feel I have to unearth facts as they are and not as shadows in the dark, I need to expose policies, governments, theories and facts that appear obscure to the public."

"That is very noble of you," Khushboo said. "But don't forget the times we are living in. This is the covid 19 age where the virus controls every aspect of a person's life, and because of that travel is going to be made more difficult, what with travel permits, covid guidelines, not forgetting the restrictions that Brexit will put on us. And you will be vulnerable to catching corona for not all countries are doing well with vaccinating their people. That reminds me, Mum, cases in India I believe, are rising, I hope Dad is okay?"

"I have tried to call him, but he is not answering, must be busy with the protest or being looked after by his mother!"."

"There is not much danger of contracting Corona, Khushboo, I have had my vaccinations but actually they have given me choice of two jobs, Afghanistan and the case you were talking about earlier, officer has been found guilty of killing George Floyd and who is actually appealing, so and not only will the United States be on high alert, but the eyes of the whole world be on the whether the courts are going to allow him to appeal. It has been the first time that a policeman is prosecuted for the death of a black person, and if found guilty, is bound to change attitude to racism. They have also offered the same to another colleague, so it depends on the one he/she refuses."

"Whatever makes you happy, talking about raising awareness, Mum will be volunteering for an organisation whilst Dad is away." She briefly gave a background of Reyansh's work." And that gives me an idea, would your sister like to accompany my mother? He could do with some confidence, and I think they have hit it off."

"That does sound like a good idea, Khushboo, I will ask her, she too has had a horrible life."

let's not talk shop, Aishya, in fact, let's not talk about it whilst you are here, let us enjoy the time we have together, like I was saying I have made lots of plans, but I don't think we will have time to complete them all!"

"Oh yes we will, Khusboo, we will cram as much as we can in a day and after I leave, Ekta will be with you and she enjoys ballet, theatre and walks too.!"

"No, Aishya, you know I do not, I am more of a homely person; just an occasional movie dinner at a restaurant and I am happy! I don't know about you, but I am beginning to feel tired!" She yawned as she got up and stretched her arms.

"Actually, come to think of it, so am I, though I would love to sit and chat some more, Khusboo." Aishya agreed and rose.

"Sorry, our fault for keeping you up so late," Sameera said apologetically. "Come I will show you to your room and once you are settled, will bring up a jug of water, or would you like another cup of tea?" "Oh no thank you, Sameera, water would be fine and no need for you to bring it up, we will take it up now with us."

"You go ahead Ekta, I will bring the water." Aishya said as she turned towards the kitchen.

"Nice to see you are making yourself at home Aishya and if there is anything you need, we will be in the bedroom next to yours."

As they went upstairs, Khusboo showed her the bathroom before they said goodnight and turned into her room where Sameera was busy fluffy up the pillows on her bed.

As Aishya changed and got ready for bed, she thought how nice Khushboo, and her mother were. They had made them feel at home and she liked the feeling so much that she mulled over what Khusboo had said. Maybe she should consider getting another job, for in her present job she did not have a social life, and the pleasures in Aiysha's life would be limited time because her job, was built on quicksand that changed from one day to the next in which any kind of entertainment would be measured in spoonsful.

After she had got into bed, Aiysha turned towards Ekta to wish her goodnight but saw that she was already asleep, her long lashes resting on her cheeks.

Aishya sighed and turned on her side, but unable to sleep, thought how, after spending one normal evening with Khushboo, she desired a solid life, something real that she needed to hold on to, and on that note, she finally drifted off to sleep.

Since Khusboo and Sameer had not shared a bedroom, they talked late into the night before finally switching off their night lamps...

Chapter 42

As Khusboo got up the next morning the sunlight was streaming through her window, and as she felt the sun on face, thought it was going to be a beautiful day

She quickly wore her gown over her pyjamas and went down, and as she did, she could smell fresh coffee brewing and knew that her mother was already up and would be making breakfast!

"Good morning, Mum, you did not have to get up early you know! You too are on holiday too!" Khushboo said hugging her affectionally.

"You call this early? Buy this time usually half my day is gone!" Sameera smiled.

"Well, you don't have to worry now, Dad is not here and none of us are going to get angry if something is not done or not done on time. Is Olga coming today?" Khushboo asked as she poured herself a mug of coffee.

"Yes, she is but you don't have to worry, if she doesn't, you won't have to do the work!"

"That is not I meant Mum!" Khushboo replied indignantly as she sat on a chair beside the kitchen table. "I see Aiysha and Ekta are not up, they really must be tired, I think we kept them up too late."

At that moment Ekta and Aishya walked in, also still in their nightwear.

"Good morning, Aiysha and Ekta, I hope you slept well, you know there was no need for you to get up! You are on holiday!"

"And dying to start it, I don't want a minute longer wasted in bed!" Aishya grinned.

"Hey, Aishya, I hope we were not making too much noise, you know you can sleep as late as you like. Good morning Ekta, I hope you slept well? Can I get you some coffee?"

"We did, thank you, and don't worry, we will help ourselves." Ekta poured two mugs of coffee, for herself and Aishya and placed them on the table. "Would you like a mug Sameera?

"Don't worry about me I woke early so had my coffee, now I am going to make some breakfast for us whilst Khushboo tells you what she has planned for us!"

Khushboo smiled affectionately at them just as her mobile vibrated, and as it was an unknown number, she excused herself and left the kitchen to take it.

To her surprise the caller identified himself as being a manager from a bank and briefly explained that he was trying to get touch with her father. And as he could not, he had rung her as Anil had given this as the number to be contacted in case of emergency.

Khushboo was puzzled, and when asked him the reason for his call, was told that he needed was some information urgently and if she would be kind enough to collect it for him?

"Sure of course." Khushboo answered, then, after noting down the information required walked back into the kitchen with a frown on her face.

"Right, Mum, you wanted to know what I had planned for today, well…." Khushboo explained what she thought would be ideal way to spend the day since it was a sunny day.

Sameera meanwhile was busying cooking breakfast, and they could hear the noise of her crack open the eggs before placing them into the heated oil in the frying pan, followed by the screech of metal as she pulled out the grill tray to turn the sausages.

"Sameera, are you sure I cannot help?" Ekta asked.

"No thank you Ekta, you must still be feeling the jetlag. Khushboo, you can help by making toast?"

"Of course, mum." Khusboo got up sheepishly and put the slices of bread in the toaster whilst Sameera put a plate of fried eggs and sausages in front of Ekta and Aishya.

As soon as the toasts were done, she brought them over to the bible together with marmalade, jam and butter that she had placed on a tray.

Ekta buttered a piece of toast and gingerly put it in her mouth.

"Sameera after yesterday's dinner, I had planned on skipping breakfast!"

"Me too, but this looks good, I have never had the luxury of sitting down for a proper breakfast." Aiysha agreed.

"Would you believe it neither have I." Khushboo replied as she walked went to refill their coffee mugs. As she bought them back and sat down, she explained what she and Aishya had planned for the next couple of days, with Khusboo trying to get through the list of entertainment that she had planned.

"One thing is for sure. Mum you will not be cooking, we will end each day by going to a nice restaurant."

"I agree, Khusboo and we will try different foods. For Ekta needs a change, has been stuck in the house looking after her husband and working at the same time."

"I would like the same for Mum. Aishya, father has been so busy working he never had the time to take mum out.!"

"Khusboo, we are still quite tired so won't have the energy to be out the whole day, so what you were talking about earlier sounds ideal." Aishya pushed the hair back with her hand. "We haven't even had a bath as yet."

"And to be honest, I would prefer to sit and talk." Ekta added "we don't have to go out".

"But Ekta, after being cooped up in the plane for 8 hours I thought you might like some fresh air. The day is bright, and I believe that is going to be quite warm, so we can go to the park nearby and then to a Chinese restaurant I have wanting to try. That is if it is okay with everybody?" Aishya and Ekta nodded their heads.

"And we will pack a picnic lunch with sandwiches and…" Sameera said but was interrupted by the others.

"Oh no! No more food please!"

"Hey, you are bound to get hungry in the fresh air and…"

"No Mum, "Khushboo said firmly, "If we do get hungry, we will get some snacks from the shops nearby, I would rather stay hungry until evening for the Chinese food, I have heard it is delicious."

"Right, you better get ready, and I will clear up here." Sameera began clearing the table.

"There is no need for that Mum, Olga should be here, ah that must be her." she said as the doorbell rang.

"We'll go up for a bath." Ekta and Aishya said as she went to answer the door, and she did, called over her shoulder.

"Oh, and wear something casual for the park, for as it is close, we will come back home to dress for the evening.".

She opened the door and gasped for Olga was standing outside, her blonde hair tousled, a black eye and a swollen cheek.

"Olga come in what has happened, oh my God, mum we need some frozen peas. to put on her eye!"

"I am sorry, mam, I don't want to be a bother, I will just do my work and go." Olga cried as Sameera came hurrying with a bag of frozen peas and gave a cry when she saw Olga.

"What nonsense Olga, you are going to sit down, put the frozen peas over the eye whilst I make you a cup of tea. Then you are going to tell me what happened!" And as Olga sipped the tea and put the frozen peas on her eye, she felt a little calmer so rose from her seat.

"Thank you very much, man, you are very kind, now I will do my work and…"

"Sit down Olga, you will do nothing of the kind, now tell me, who did this to you, did Alexei follow you here?"

At the mention of his name, Olga broke down and started sobbing.

"Yes mam, he did, I am not sure know how he knew where I was. Now he insists he is going to live with me, and every time he drinks, he starts beating me."

"Olga, look I can help you with getting a restraining order and…"

"Oh no mam, he says if I go to police, he will kill me and anyone who tries to help me..."

"Ok no police, but you don't have to go back home either." She thought of Reyansh "We will keep you safe, now we have to go out, promise that you will stay here till we come back?"

At that moment Aishya and Ekta walked in wearing jeans and trainers. Aishya pivoted before Khushboo

"Dressed in casual as requested. Hey how come you are not ready?" Aishya turned towards Khusboo, but when saw her with her arm around Olga who was crying, was taken aback. "Sorry," she muttered.

Khushboo tried to reassure Olga again that she would be safe and not to worry about the housework.

"Won't be a second, Aishya" Khushboo ran upstairs wiping the tears from her eyes for she was very fond of Olga.

Her mother too liked her a lot for Olga was extremely loyal and she was happy, settled and making a life for herself, but it looked like Alexei had got his claws into her again and was not letting her go.

She quickly changed into her jeans shirt and sneakers then quickly took out a leather jacket from her wardrobe and ran downstairs, where she saw, Olga had begun doing her chores.

"Mum why is Olga working?" Khushboo cried,

"I tried telling her not to, but she is such a sweet girl she insisted, and I thought it might take her mind of her problem and pain."

"Maybe your right, Mum now are we all set to go? Now Olga you can work but just as soon as you feel it is too much, please rest."

"Thank you, mam," Olga smiled through the tear in one eye

They all went out, deciding whether they should walk to the park or take the car, when Khusboo ran back into the house to reassure Olga and remind her that she was not ton leave the house, nor was she to open the door to anyone but to wait in the house till they returned.

"Don't worry, Olga, we will sort something out." Khushboo hugged her but quickly pulled away when Olga gave a cry.

Chapter 43

As soon as they had left, Olga cleared the table and started putting the dishes in the dishwasher, then caught her breadth for her ribs hurt. Alexie had repeatedly been kicking her, however, by now, she was used to the pain. She had come to London to escape from him, and her sister had helped her to do so, and was puzzled as to how he had tracked her whereabouts.

However, when she had spoken to her sister, she had filled her in, apparently one of his friends had met her in London, and when she revealed the name of Alexei's friend, Olga was astonished, for it was the person she had been dating, a man she thought had been so nice and decent. He had told Alexei where she lived, even though he knew how Alexei had treated her and how she had just barely escaped from him. she had told him what she had been through and how she had escaped him.

Her sister had warned her to move as quickly as possible, apparently it had not been quick enough for one day, Alexei was on her doorstep, a cruel grin on his face as he saw her surprised face, and since that day, had not left her flat.

Olga cried out as she clutched her ribs and thought that if Khushboo had known about her bruised and broken ribs, she would have insisted she take her to hospital! But Olga did not want her to do that for she was frightened, not for herself as much as for her sister and her children and Khushboo too. if she went to the police! She knew that Alexei was a ruthless man, who belonged to a gang whose comrades were more than ready to do favours for any one of their members.

Olga cleaned the kitchen, resting every five minutes, then when the pain became unbearable, thought she would take make some tea, have some painkillers that Khushboo had so thoughtfully left for her, then continue cleaning the rest of the house later.

She had the painkillers with a glass of water, then made herself some tea, and as Khushboo had told her to make herself at home and take it easy, she went to the sitting room and gingerly sat in one of the armchairs, closed her eyes and slowly put up her legs.

At that moment her mobile vibrated and she trembled in fear for she thought it to be Alexei, calling to check up on her, however, saw that it was Khushboo. Olga told her that she was not feeling well and was resting and would come in another day to make up for the time. Khushboo reassured her not to worry but rest.

As Olga put her mobile back in her bag, she again thought how lucky she was in having a friend like Khushboo., and the circumstances that had brought her here.

She closed her eyes, thinking that this was all her fault, and that it was only because of her stubbornness that she was in this state, for her father had warned her about Alexei and recalled their conversation.

"Olga, I have heard about him, one of my friends knows about him. My friend told me that he belongs to some gang, I think it has something to do with skinheads. Please Olga, don't have anything to do with that man for men like him do not respect women!!"

But Olga was deeply in love with Alexei and thought he was very handsome, and when her father told her that he belonged to a gang, thought that just added, to his masculinity!

Alexei had sandy eyebrows were over pale green eyes with blonde eyelashes, but what Olga had not noticed was that the expression in his eyes was always lifeless, He had a squashed nose, which he proudly told her had happened in a fight. His cheeks were red and laced with broken veins, which Olga now knew was because of his drinking. His hair was shaved close to his scalp and on his large hairy arms were tattoos that went up to his elbow and he wore ring on the fingers of each hand.

Her mind again wandered off to the past, how nice Alexei had been at first and how blissfully happy she had been, then how he had changed specially in the company of his unsavoury friends who she had not liked. Alexei would bring them home sometime and they would sit around in the house, lounging and drinking beer whilst some of whom looked at her lecherously.

When she had mentioned this to Alexei, he had told her that he was flattered they thought her desirable because he did not! Olga was stunned, for she had sincerely believed that he loved her, and after that day he became cold and indifferent, making unnecessary demands and criticising her; and however, much she tried to please him, he was sure to find fault!

Nevertheless, she gave in to Alexei's cruel behaviour, hoping that it was temporary, and only caused by his friends, so one day had plucked up her courage and bought up the subject again.

Although it was morning Alexei was drunk and was sitting in the living room of their small flat in the same shirt jeans that he had worn for a week. He had not shaved and was staring at the tv with its volume turned on high. In his right hand was a burning cigarette and with the other he held a bottle of vodka.

"Alexei, I do not like your friends, you have changed, and I think it is because of their company, maybe you should not see them anymore and…Alexei?"

But Alexei just sat there, fiddling with his rings, twisting them around and around as if he was doing everything to keep his temper bottled up. How dare anyone speak to him and tell him what to do, let alone a woman, his wife who was only supposed to be meek and docile! She was telling him how to behave with his friends? Hah!

He quickly threw his cigarette across the room, put the bottle of vodka on the table, jumped out of the armchair and seized her wrists and stared at her with blood shot red eyes.

"Olga, don't you dare talk to me about them; they are like my brothers, and we are willing to give our lives for each other! And if you ever bring up the subject again I will...!" He raised his hand.

That was the first time she had seen his anger and had cringed with fear, so had not brought up the subject again, but seeing the tension between Alexei and Olga, Alexei's friends became bold, and their visits became more and more frequent. And as Alexi did not object, some of them even began making a pass at her under the leering eyes of the others who looked at them and licked their lips.

This went on in front of Alexei who was aware if but chose to ignore it by turning his head towards the television. He would turn the volume at his highest with the remote and by doing so, it was as if he was giving permission to his friends to do what they liked with Olga

By this time, Olga had recognized the lengths he would go to keep his gang brothers happy so, terrified, had fled into her room and when Alexei had followed her, had turned to him angrily...

"Alexei, I promised I would not bring up the behaviour of your friends again, but I am your wife, how can you let them disrespect me? That man was trying to grope me whilst the others were egging him on!" Olga spluttered. "I was afraid they were going to rape me.!"

"Don't flatter yourself, Olga! Nobody would touch with you with a barge pole, but we want some beer so come down or else!" Alexei snarled raising his hand.

"No, I don't want to go down!"

Chapter 44

Olga remembered that she had said that there was no reaction from him, so she had closed her eyes and tried to stay calm, hoping that when she opened them, he would be gone, but when she had, saw that he had come close to her and gripped her wrists with his large, tattooed arms, looking down at her angrily.

Abruptly Alexei let go of her hands and punched her on the cheek, and when Olga fell abruptly on the bed, he picked her up and punched her first on the breast then in her stomach.

"Now will you do what I say, or do you want more to that? Now, I want you downstairs!" Alexei roared." And if you don't, I will tell the others to come to our bedroom and do what they want with you."

Olga was lying whimpering, her eyes swollen and black and in pain, but knew with certainty that he could and would do just that! She looked at him from where she was lying, wondering what she had seen in him? He was a monster, and had she seen this side of him, she would not have married him.

"Olga and if you ever think of going to police or run away, I will follow you, for you belong to me, a true Russian, and I can do what I want with you because you are not a true and pure Russian!"

Olga attempted twice to get up he from the bed, but Alexei shoved her back down, holding her by the throat and raising his left hand to show her that he was prepared to hit her again.

"I will see you downstairs, now.!"

Saying that he strode out of the room leaving Olga with no choice but to go down and face the consequences. So, was it because of that? He was mistreating her because of her ethnicity, just because she was from a different part of Russia.

Olga tried opening her eyes slowly and as the fog gradually dispersed and she began to make out shapes and outlines. She blinked and saw the cream-coloured window curtains on one window and on the other a blind was drawn right down to the windowsill. She could barely see the door and brown chest of drawers and when looked above her head and saw what seemed to be a lamp suspended from the ceiling so thought she must be dreaming.

However, after some time everything fell back into its original place and she got up slowly, one hand massaging her head, as she heard loud noises drifting up from downstairs.

But before going down, she went into the bathroom to wash her face then applied some foundation under her eyes and cheeked in the mirror that it had covered all the bruises. She brushed her hair which Alexie had pulled so hard that it looked. like a nest of snakes. That was the first time he had been so violent towards her but what had followed was even more terrible.

She had gone straight to the kitchen but one of the men, who she had heard Alexei call Dimitri, followed her...

Dimitri was a large man wearing a maroon jacket that was open, showing his hairy chest that had a thick necklace dangling around it, and like the others, his head was closely shaven, and he had a stud in his ear and earrings through his eyebrows.

"Hello darling." He said eying her up and down with a half-smoked cigarette between his thick lips.

His manner was making Olga uncomfortable, so she put her hand behind her back and pulled her dress around her tightly for Dimitri was looking at her with red eyes that were full of desire and lust. "

Alexei, can you come here please?" Olga let out a cry followed by a deep lung wrenching sob as Dimitri laughed and came closer.

"He will not come; in fact, he is the one who told me I can do anything I want with you. I see the way he treats you, you are beautiful, now if you were my wife.!" He came so close that Olga could smell the vodka in his mouth.

Dimitri bent down and caught her under her arms and lifted her up. Olga struggled and tried to free herself, but he gripped her dress and twisted it in his hands and pulled it above her knees, then with his fist slapped her across face.

"Please, let me go…! "Olga tried to get past him, but he caught hold of her and hit her so hard that she fainted.

When she came too, she was lying naked on her bed, and when she tried to get up found her arms were fastened tightly to the bed and saw Dimitri first pull up his trousers then zip them. Olga looked around the room and saw with horror that there were other men in the room who were also pulling up their trousers whilst Alexie stood in the doorway, saying 'hurry up hurry up! She is coming to' and as they passed him, they winked and put some money into his outstretched hand.

Olga was aching and sore and now she knew why; she had been gang raped! And it had been organised by none other than her husband! Olga cried in panic and struggled to free her arms so that at least she could cover herself but found she was fastened to the bed so securely she could do nothing but lie back and call Alexei for help.

Alexie counted the money then strolled over to the bed and calmly undid the ropes that were tightly bound around Olga's wrists and with a" Well done Olga! I told you we brothers share everything and everyone" walked out of the room leaving Olga terrified with just one thought, how was she going to escape from him, but just then Alexei came back into the room.

"Don't ever think of going to the police, go to the hospital or run away from me, I will find you. But tonight, as it has been your first time, you can get to Katrina, your sister, she will look after you for the boys really had a good time with you. Hurry up and get dressed and I will drop you at her house and pick you up in a couple of hours, now, hurry up, we are all going to Dimitri house. I will wait for you."

Olga got up from the bed gingerly holding the sheet around her then walked slowly to the bathroom for she was so sore that she could feel the blood trickle down her thighs.

Somehow, she managed to clean herself, got dressed and walked to the door where Alexei was waiting, his mobile pressed to his ear.

Olga sat in the car gingerly for she was still very sore. Alexei drove so fast that Olga cried out in pain, but Alexei continued driving recklessly till he reached her sister's where he braked, again so hard she clutched her stomach and cried out in pain.

Olga opened her eyes and looked around at Khushboo's room in surprise, for she had become so absorbed in the past that she had forgotten where she was. She began to cry when she remembered her sister, for she missed he. She got up slowly to make herself another cup of tea, then walked back to the lounge, and relived at how frightened she had been, not for herself but for her sister and her family.

Olga took a sip of her tea, placed the mug on the side table, closed her eyes and recalled the events after Alexei had dropped her at her sister's house.

As soon as Katrina had opened the door, Alexei had driven off and Olga had fallen into her arms sobbing.

Katrina was a slim woman who had thick blonde hair that was usually tied either in a bun or a ponytail. Today, her hair was tied back in a ponytail and her eyes that were always bright and alive, filled with tears as she saw the bruises on her sister and her black eye.

"Olga did Alexei do this to you!" she exclaimed in anger as she looked at the taillights of his disappearing car...

"Yes, he did, Katrina" Olga said as she slowly walked into the room holding her sides.

"What a brute, you are not going back Olga!" Katina said. "Did he rape you?"

"It is worse, Katrina, they tied me, and his friends raped me, one after another!" Olga trembled in fear. "And he let them!"

"How awful, he is not a brute but a monster! Don't worry, I have a friend who deals with these kinds of situations, I will call her now, then I will make you a cup of tea."

She dialled on her mobile and when her friend answered, spoke quickly explaining the situation After she had finished, she turned to her sister.

"She says, and I agree with her, that the police won't help, Olga, they think it is the right of the husband to do whatever he wants with his wife" Katrina said as she deftly applied lotion than bandaged Olga's wounds, but not before she took a few photographs.

After she had made her a cup of tea, Katrina handed it to her then sat down beside her.

Chapter 45

"Olga, this is what we must do now, my friends name is Khristina, and she helps women who are victims of domestic violence and when I explained how you had been raped by his friends too, and that he will be coming to pick you up in a few hours, that on no account should you return. She is a good friend for when I told her that happened to my sister, she is dropping everything to come here to see and guide us what to do, now did Alexei say what time he was going to pick you up tonight?"

Olga shook her head miserably, "I think he said in a couple of hours." then flinched for the slightest movement was causing her pain.

"Okay, give me his number and I will tell him that you are in no condition to go home so will stay with me tonight."

"Katrina, he won't believe that he will only get angry, and he has already made threats against you, I don't trust him."

"Don't worry Olga, my husband is a lawyer, and we can think of ways to deal with him. I will tell him I have to check your wounds every hour for you have been hurt internally."

Once Olga had got Alexei on the phone, she told him firmly that Olga needed to be seen to, and if he did not let her stay with her, she would have to take her to hospital, so Alexei reluctantly agreed that she could stay, but only for one night.

"Whew! That is one problem dealt with! I am so sorry what happened to you., Olga, but father did warn you that he was not a nice man."

Katrina kissed Olga on the head and when the bell rang, went to open the door. She smiled when she saw Khristina.

Khristina was a tall and slim woman with shoulder length blonde hair. She was an unusual looking woman with a pointed nose and grey eyes that were kind and thoughtful. She was wearing tight jeans and she was so thin that her belt was done up to the last hole.

"Hi Khristina, thank you for coming so quickly! Katina hugged her friend." We were waiting for you,"

"How could I not help another woman, especially your sister... Don't worry, Katrina, I will look after her" Khristina said kindly as she followed her friend.

Khristina took one look at Olga and taken matters in hand. She explained that she knew a woman, Khushboo, who would help her, but she needed to get to London as soon as possible, She suggested that Olga come immediately and stay with her till the documentation was sorted.

"But I cannot do that!" Olga explained. "Alexei told me that if I did not go back home, he would hurt Katrina and her children, and I don't want any harm to come to them because of me!"

"Don't worry about me, you are not going back Olga, now that Khristina is here we will think of something. I am going to make some more tea." Katina said firmly as she disappeared into the kitchen.

"She is right, there is no way you can go back to him, that will show him you are dependent on him, and he and his friends will do the same thing to you again!" Khristina said as she took Olga's hand.

After a few minutes, Katina came in with a tray, handed a mug to Khristina and then to Olga who took it with difficulty for her hands and wrists hurt, as she had been tied so tightly to the bed with ropes.

"I have had an idea, Khristina, when Alexei comes in the morning, I'll tell him that I found a letter by Olga saying she is leaving, and that she would rather be homeless or die than put me in danger or go back to Alexei."

"That is a very good idea, Katrina, and we can leave as soon after we have had tea. The sooner we start on the documentation the better."

"Yes, I guess that would work for it would show him that it is not your fault but mine" Olga said. I only hope he will believe it".

"Yes, you can show him Olga's letter and that will protect you from him too."

Olga had, in the meantime quickly started writing on a piece of paper that she was leaving Katrina' house, not coming back and not to try and find her, after she had completed and signed her name on the letter, she and Khristina had left, after a tearful goodbye with her sister,

"I will miss you Katrina, give my love to the children and papa, and tell them I love them." Olga said as she hugged her sister carefully.

"Goodbye my little sister. Take care of yourself." Katrina wiped her eyes with the back of her hand as Khristina carefully led Olga to her car.

Katrina was still standing in the doorway when Olga waved to her through the window.

She had shown Olga's letter to Alexei the following day and as expected, he was angry at first, but as Katrina had said, the letter confirmed that she had left of her own accord, so he had left, muttering under his breadth than slamming the door behind him

Olga had stayed with Khristina for a few days, days that were spent in recovering from the bruises and getting the documentation ready. The day before the flight, Khristina informed her that she would be travelling as an asylum seeker, escaping her husband and country which could not afford her protection for their rules favoured the husband.

She handed her the photos that Katrina had so thoughtfully taken after being gang raped and that were so important in validating her case.

And once she had landed in London, Khushboo had taken control and guided her in all aspects of her life, Olga was only one of the many women who had being victimised by their husbands with no hope of getting justice, but who had been referred by Khristina to her

And when Khushboo had met the petite frail girl, her heart had gone out to her, and she had vowed she would do everything possible to help her.

Olga was grateful to Khushboo's help and felt guilty so got up slowly from the armchair to finish at much work as she could before she returned.

Chapter 46

It was a beautiful day with a blue sky and puffy ball clouds were floating in the sky, so Khushboo and the others, after she had told Olga to stay at home until they returned, decided that they should walk down to the park which was nearby.

As they sauntered down the road towards the park Khushboo noticed that the trees that in winter had looked dead, now looked alive with their branches full of leaves.

"What was all that about Khushboo? Poor girl, I presume that was Olga?" Aiysha asked.

"Yes, it was, she is such a lovely girl" Khushboo briefly explained how her husband had followed her to London from Russia. "I don't how he came to know that she lived in London."

They turned into the park where the daffodils blew in the wind along with other colourful yellow wildflowers that were scattered on the grass.

"This was a good idea of yours Khusboo, "Aishya said taking a deep breadth.

"Yes, everybody has been in lockdown for so long that it is nice to be out; in the fresh air. and I see that a lot of people had the same idea"

Khushboo looked at the crowded park, with children running and playing. There was a suntanned man in jeans shirt amongst the crowd whilst a young woman was standing beside a pram, then knelt and opened her arms to a toddler who ran into her arms, his face a picture of joy as his mother held him tenderly in her arms.

"That is so sweet." Sameera commented as she saw the mother's face as they looked for a bench to sit.

"Mum you are missing the point of being in the park; it is good for health being out in in the fresh air and walk barefoot in the grass."

"I agree Khushboo." Aishya looked around for an appropriate place. then pointed to a tree whose huge trunk and big leaves on its branches could protect them from the sun.

"Come on, sitting under the shade of that tree, I think, that will do!" and when everyone agreed, they walked over to it.

Khushboo and Aishya threw their bags and sat down on the grass.

The branches of the tree were just budding into tiny green nodules on each branch that was casting a green haze in air giving a lovely aura in the shade.

"Ohh, this is an ideal spot, days like this are very rare so everybody tries to make the most of it!" Khusboo lumped her sweater into a ball lay then lay her head on sweater on it.

She cocked her head as she listened to the gentle noises of the trembling and gentle brushing of the leaves as the breeze rustled them gently.

"Sitting on the floor is okay for you young girls but not for me!"

Sameera took out a sheet she had folded in her bag, spread it on the floor then sat gingerly on it.

"Same here, I love the outdoors, but I do prefer being at home reading or watching Television."

Ekta sat beside her then hurriedly added "Not that this is not a good idea, Khushboo, this is just what we needed, after being cooped up in the flight for 8 hours, and before that the restrictions placed on us and the jet lag to top it all,"

"And we will round up the day with good Chinese food in the evening!" Khusboo stated as she looked up at the blue sky and, with her hand, she plucked some wildflowers from the grass.

"Oh, look at that bird!" she pointed towards a tree where a bird was sitting, trying to settle down by tucking its head under its wing. But although the branch was thin, he sat perfectly poised with no fear of falling.

"Yes, that is cute, I am looking forward to dinner too, but in the meantime, I see an Ice cream truck, who is in for some ice-cream?" Aishya rose, brushing her jeans that were streaked with grass and dirt with her hands.

"Maybe later, Aishya?" Khushboo replied and when the others nodded Aishya lay back on the grass and looked at Khusboo.

"So, tell me Khushboo what are you going to do about Olga?"

"I don't know Aishya, you should cover this in your newspaper, how abused women in Russia cannot expect any help from the government for whilst most countries reported an increase of domestic violence during pandemic and toughened their laws, Russia did not. But even before the pandemic, they had brought about a law saying that if the person did not end up in hospital, dead or alive, it was to be classified as an administrative offence and the accused person io be let off lightly! They don't, for example, understand the idea of rape in a marriage, and because of that, the men feel they can get away with anything, and most often do, as in Olga's case Alexei and his friends did what they did because they knew they would get away with it!

"That does sound awful." Aiysha remarked horrified, though she had heard about it.

"It gets worse, the victim also has to prove everything themselves and often the police don't respond or even come to investigate a call. But that happens here too, too, the police force think that a crime is not a crime till the victim is near death's door or is drenched in blood! Or has left behind fingerprints, clothes, photograph, anything that would make the job of the police easier."

"I don't think they want an easy job, more like the job should be done for them so they can just come in and take credit for it! Anyway, how did you come to know Olga?" Ekta asked.

"Through Khristina who is Katrina, Olga's sister's friend. she herself had been a victim of Domestic violence too, but somehow, she escaped and now devotes her time in helping and rescuing women in similar positions. She sends the women to London as asylum seekers, but I can tell you, Olga's case is the worst of them all."

She briefly explained how Olga had been gang raped by her husband's friends, but luckily her sister, Katrina, was Khristina's friend, so had managed to escape leaving behind a note that she was leaving her sister's house, destination unknown.

"So how did he find her here? Sameera asked frowning.

"I have no idea though I think Olga knows, I am sure she will tell me once we have had the chance to talk." Khusboo got up and brushed her clothes with her hands. "Now, I am ready for some ice cream for it is quite warm, Mum Ekta?" She asked and when both nodded, she picked up her bag, followed by Aishya.

As they walked towards the ice cream truck, a dog tore across them to fetch his ball that was thrown by his owner, and with pure uncomplicated enjoyment he snatched it from the air and brought it back to the man who repeated the activity.

"You are not going to send that sweet delicate girl back to the monster, Khusboo, are you?" Aishya asked as they walked back, trying to balance the scones in her hand.

"No of course not, Aishya!" Khusboo replied, handing a cone to her mother "But I have to handle this very delicately as Alexei is here and he will hurt not only Olga, but anyone who tries to help her."

"Khushboo, what about the organisation you told me about, the one that your mother will volunteer for? They deal with women who have been abused, don't they?"

"Yes, they do and, that is a good idea, but Alexei knows that she comes to work for us, if Reyansh helps, as I am sure he will, Alexei will hurt us, no this has to be done slowly. Now, shall we make our way back home?"

"That will give us some time to have tea freshen up and go the restaurant!"

"Yes, good idea, it is getting cold, and I could do with some tea!" Sameera got up and began folding the sheet which had come in handy. Most of the people in the crowd too had started leaving as it was beginning to turn chilly.

Chapter 47

As they strolled back, the thin chilly wind blowing gently caused the grass by the roadside sway gently. and Sameera trembled slightly, wrapping her arms around her.

"Brrr, it is cold, maybe we should have driven down in the car."

"Mum never mind now anyway we are nearly there." Khushboo pulled at Aiysha's arm and whispered, "I need your advice, walk with me."

They kept back as Sameera and Ekta walked ahead.

"What is the problem Khushboo?"

"It is about Olga; I have thought the best and safest way to handle this is to send her back home and…"

Aishya stopped suddenly and turned towards Khusboo, "No you cannot do that, Khushboo, you know what he is capable of!"

"I know but I cannot see any other way and when I said back home, it will only be for a few days. If we send her to a shelter or the police now, he knows she works here so will know that we have helped her. And from what Khristina told me, not only will we be in danger but her sister too for he is a member of a gang, the ones who raped her, and who, I am sure, had a hand in finding her."

"But what if he does something to hurt her again? "

I will explain to Olga what I have just told you and since he is at home the entire day, I will suggest we have increased her working hours from a few hours a week to the whole day for the week, of course with increased pay and the reason for that will be we have guests which is true, that way she will be out of his reach, at least during during the day!"

"But will he agree to it?" Aishya asked as they entered their house.

"Oh, he will because he does not work and is feeding off Olga, and that will give up time to think of what to do next,"

Sameera had gone straight to the kitchen where she put the kettle and set out the mugs and as everybody followed her remarked

"Olga is not here Khushboo, I hope she is all right?"

"She said she will wait for me, hang on let me check the front room, she did mention she mentioned if I would mind if she did not work the afternoon? She is so sweet..."

Aishya and Ekta went to freshen up, and Ekta quickly changed into a frilly blouse with black trousers whilst Aishya changed into a casual grey trouser and jacket.

Whilst Sameera made the tea, Khushboo hurried into the lounge and found Olga lying on the sofa, eyes closed but as soon as she heard her, she opened her them sleepily.

"Mam, I hope you don't mind but I was hurting so could not work anymore."

"Olga, don't worry about it, tell me, how did Alexei find out where you were?" Khushboo said down beside her.

"It was through my boyfriend, I thought he was so nice and decent, but his ex was also raped by Dimitri, and when he threatened to have her gang-raped, in desperation she said something like 'I wish I was as lucky as Olga who escaped from you and Alexei and is now safe in London...' And of course, Dimitri told Alexei who went to Khristina and tortured her into telling him your address. Khristina had not told her about my address at first for just this reason, but Katrina somehow managed to get it from her. If it had not been for that woman...! At first Katrina did not tell me the whole story only that it was my boyfriend who told him, Anyway, all that does not matter now, Alexei s here." Olga groaned

"I don't think it was intentional, Olga, just bad luck." Khusboo too Olgas' hand. "Look I have thought of a way to help you and..."

"No mam, thank you but no one can help me, he is a very dangerous man and when I am with him, I feel I can't breathe!"

"I know Olga, but there are organisations that help women like you, you were doing fine till now, so I did not mention them. The only problem is that can't happen immediately for we don't want to put your sister in danger and my mother too for he knows where you work and that she might have helped you. No, I suggest that you call to tell him that we have changed your working hours and now want you for the whole day, at least till our guests are her, and don't 'forget to tell him that we will pay you extra!"

At that moment Sameera entered with a tray on which were 4 mugs and some biscuits.

"Here let me mam," Olga got up, then gave a gasp and clutched her stomach.

Oh my God, Olga, you did not tell me Alexei had hurt your ribs too?"

"He kicked me, but I am okay, I am used to it, sorry I could not do any work…"

"Don't be silly Olga! Here, has some tea."

"Thank you, I will go to the kitchen and call Alexei about the change of my working hours…"

"Tell him that we will drop you home later." Khushboo called after her "And if he does not permit you to work the extra hours, I will speak to him."

At that moment Ekta and Aishya entered the room, looking refreshed. and after taking a mug made themselves comfortable in the armchairs.

"We don't have to go out you know, Khushboo, you need to sort this problem." Aishya said.

"Yes, I agree," Sameera added" I can cook something here."

"No Mum, we will stick to our plan, but I just need to make sure that Olga goes to a shelter, but there is no way that Alexei should link her escape with us. For now, she needs to spend as little time as possible with Alexei. Now, Aishya Ekta, I see you have already changed and looking very nice too!"

"Yes, we have, thought that would save time, today it is only casual dress but from tomorrow we will get ready properly! But Khushboo, you have been so busy trying to sort out Olga's problem you have had no time to freshen up."

"Which we will do now, come Mum, see you in a bit, Aishya."

Before going to her room, Khushboo went into the kitchen just as Olga was ending her call and when she saw Khusboo, gave her a thumbs up. Khusboo, relieved that all was well, at least for the time being, quickly went straight to her bathroom to splash her face with cold water.

She came back into the room and opened her wardrobe, took out a grey sweater and black jeans, quickly picked up her black patent shoulder bag. She brushed her hair before applying light make up, pouting at herself in front of the mirror to apply fresh lipstick, then slung the bag over her shoulder as she left her room just as Sameera came out and of her room. Sameera had changed into a beige shalwar kameez that was adorned with little mirrors along the neckline and sleeves.

"Mum you should try wearing trousers, they are very comfortable you know," Khusboo said as they walked down the stairs. "I will meet you all outside, I want to talk to Olga first"

After she had told Olga that she would drop her home, they left and arrived quickly at the Chinese restaurant for it was nearby, its neon sign blazing and as soon as Khushboo had parked the car they walked towards it.

"I am starving." Aishya said as they entered, "I am glad it is not too crowded".

"It will get crowded later, now that covid rules are relaxed and people have been vaccinated, everything is going back to normal. That is why I thought we should come early, for I was sure to get a table, not forgetting that we did not have lunch, so everyone, I am sure must be starving I know I am!"

As soon as they entered, the aroma of wok fried vegetables and garlic. wafted up to their nostrils.

"I second that, I am hungry too and that smells delicious!"

They were shown to their table by a Chinese waitress wearing the restaurants uniform, a red top in Chinese Silk with Chinese collar and a black skirt.

There were Chinese lanterns and scrolls spread out in the restaurant in a proper location of the valuable objects to create an optimal effect for the Chinese restaurant interior.

"It is beautiful here," Aishya commented as she pulled out a chair and looked around her.

"Yes, one of my clients was a Chinese woman and she told me that a Chinese restaurants design and layout should be eye pleasing and painted in exotic picture to stimulate appetite!" Khushboo said as she made herself comfortable.

"It is indeed pleasing to the eye." Ekta said as she seated herself.

Chapter 48

"Yes, the design is supposed to emit something spiritual with the seating layout, though I do not know what is meant by 'spiritual.'" Khushboo opened the menu and turned the pages. "I am only going to have their speciality which I have heard is the best!"

"I am going to have their Yangchow fried rice which sounds nice with shrimp, diced ham, carrot, mushroom, baby bamboo shoots, crumbled egg, and corn with sweet and sour pork."

"That sounds lovely, the same for me too." Ekta added. "Khusboo, what did you say their speciality was? I will have the same too."

"It is Kung Pao Chicken on the first page, have a look first.

" "Oh yes it looks delicious, main ingredients are diced chicken, dried chili, and fried peanuts...yummy!"

"What about getting a plate of dumplings and fried rice which we can all share and whilst we wait, I think we should order spring rolls till the food arrives?"

When everyone agreed Khusboo gestured to their waitress who came over with a smile and after she had given the order, asked, "

"What about drinks? Do you want something Chinese or some coke?"

"Coke for me please." Sameera said, and the order was seconded by Aishya and Ekta which Khusboo passed on the waitress adding a coke for herself.

The restaurant began to fill up and gradually every table around them was occupied and the conversations became loud and sometimes heated.

"You know, Khushboo, if it had not been for Olga's tragic situation, this was the end to a perfect day!" Aishya remarked as the waitress came with their spring rolls and cokes.

"Yes, you are right, Aishya," Khusboo bit into her spring roll which was hot and crispy.

"Delicious!" Aishya finished her spring toll and wiped her lips with her napkin. "I would love another one but do not want to spoil my appetite!"

"Yes, it is tempting but it is better not to, Khushboo can we take some home?" Sameera asked

"Mother!"

"I meant for Olga, it would save her cooking."

"Good thinking Mum."

"I cannot use these!" Sameera exclaimed as she noticed the chop sticks lying beside the cutlery.

"Neither can I!" Ekta said with a frown,

"You don't have to Mum, Ekta you can use forks and spoons, me, I find the food tastes better with chopsticks!" Khusboo pronounced.

"Me too, ah I see our food is coming!" Aiysha eyed the plate of spring rolls, debating whether she should have another one before the food arrived.

The waitress placed the dishes on the table and after she had left, Khushboo distributed the dishes ordered and Ekta and Sameera watched fascinated as both Khushboo and Aiysha ate with their chopsticks, deftly manoeuvring them into their mouth. Khushboo saw her mother's face and smiled.

"Mum I know it looks confusing and complicated but eating with chopsticks is easy once you know how to hold and manoeuvre the sticks properly. Here, do you want me to show you how?"

"No thank you Khushboo, I am too old for that, I am enjoying the food with a good sold fork and spoon but thank you for the offer."

The rest of the meal was finished in silence with an occasional visit from the waitress asking if they needed anything else.

"Can we have a takeaway for 2 people?" Khushboo requested.

As soon as she had left, Khushboo looked at the table next to theirs for seated on it was a woman who reminded Khusboo of Isabella. She was wearing a smart grey suit with high heels and blonde hair that shone in the dim light of the restaurant. She was throwing back her head, laughing at something her partner had said

"Right, are we ready for Chinese Dessert? I have heard their banana fritters are very good or would you like to end the meal with their drinks?" Khushboo asked

There was a strong objection to the dessert by all, so Khushboo quickly read out the Chinese drinks,

"They have Jiuniang. Jiuniang, Pearl Milk tea, Xinjiang Black beer, Suanmeitant, Soybean Milk, Yunnan Coffee or Coconut milk!"

"I would prefer to have my Indian spice tea any day!" Sameera declared.

"As would I" chorused Aishya and Ekta.

"In that case I will pay the bill and collect the takeaway, we also have the problem of Olga to deal with."

"Khushboo, before you do, I want to make one thing clear, no, both of us want to make it clear that this is the only time you pay, next times we go out dining, well, either we go Dutch, or it will be on us. And also, although this has been a wonderful experience and the food had been just as delicious as you said it will be, I would like to try different dining means. I don't even mind trying street foods!"

"Point taken and noted, Aishya."

Khushboo smiled, rose took her purse hurried to the counter, noting that the queue was getting longer. As she stood in the line, she rummaged in her bag, trying to find her wallet when the man in front of her turned and bumped into her and she dropped her purse. She looked angrily at the man who was wearing a black leather jacket, had his hair tied back in a ponytail and had a stud in one earing.

"Excuse me, we are all in a hurry!" She said furiously as she knelt to gather the items that had fallen out of her bag.

"I am very sorry, here let me help." He said apologetically.

He knelt to help her, and as he did, looked into Khushboo's eyes and as Khushboo looked angrily at his striking brown eyes that twinkled with kindness and mischief., she gripped her purse tightly. She stood up unsteadily, and as she looked deep into his eyes, she thought she was falling, the floor seemed to tilt and there was a vacuum yawning at her feet waiting for her to fall into it…

She managed to steady herself, on legs that felt week and there was a fluttering in her stomach. She looked down shyly and her lashes covered her cheeks like wings and a faint tinge of red spread across her face but unbeknown to her, Dhruv too had felt the chemistry between them.

Chapter 49

"Look I am terribly sorry; I am in a bit of a rush and." He looked deep into her big brown eyes that were set apart in a heart shaped face and his heart began to beat faster." There are still two people ahead of us so I would like to introduce myself, my name is Dhruv." He put out his hand. His smile lit up his face as he looked at her with a twinkle in his eye.

Khushboo again felt a fluttering in her stomach but somehow managed to speak.

"Hi, my name is Khushboo," she smiled, and the dimples danced on her cheeks. "This restaurant was highly recommended so I thought I would try it with my mother and friend. How did you find the food, I myself loved it."

"I am taking it home with me, but if you say so, I am sure I will love it!" He smiled and again, Khushboo's legs turned to jelly.

Soon it was his turn, so he collected his meal settled the bill, turned and left.

After Khushboo paid her bill and collected the takeaway food, for Olga, she turned to walk back to her table, but on the way bumped into a man who she saw with surprise was none other than Dhruv, who had been waiting for her.

As she stumbled, Khushboo put out her arm to steady herself, and grasped Dhruv's forearm, making his arm jolt. His heart took off in a gallop and Dhruv felt there was not enough air in the restaurant, but he could not look away from her almond shaped chocolate brown warm eyes.

"We must stop bumping into each other like this." He grinned impishly "Look I hope you don't mind and think me too forward, but I would like to see you again, maybe for a cup of coffee?" he asked and Khusboo again felt his magnetism.

"I would like that too Dhruv. "She smiled and rummaged in her bag, for her business card which she handed to him. "Not now, for my friend is here on holiday for a week, but maybe after a week? That is if you would still want to!" Khushboo added, smiling playfully.

"Oh, I will want to Khusboo!" Dhruv smiled charmingly than waved and walked out of the door, and strangely, for the first time in her life, Khushboo felt that someone's departure had left a void in her life. But theirs had been such a casual and short-lived encounter that she was surprised at the intensity it had stirred within her.

She arrived at the table just as everyone was getting up to leave. "Wow Khusboo who was that dishy man?" Aishya asked with a wink. "Oh, no one, I just met him at the till." Khushboo answered, her voice shaky. She blushed slightly and as could not look anyone directly in the eye, began rummaging in her bag.

As they walked out of the restaurant, Aishya, Sameera and Ekta nudged each other as Aishya whispered "No-one! Right! More like 'the one' Aloud she said "Khusboo thanks again for a lovely evening and my sister joins me our heartfelt gratitude."

"Oh, come on Aishya! What is with all the formality? We also had a lovely time, now, Mum after I drop you and Ekta off, I will take Olga to her home and Aishya, you can come with me, but only if you want to."

"I will come with you Khushboo, as long as we don't have to talk to that hateful man!" Aishya said in disgust. "Because if I see him, I will say something that…"

"No don't worry, Aiysha we will just see that she gets in safely, then come back to the lovely cup of tea that Mum and Ekta will have ready for us!"

Khushboo's voice sounded more controlled than she felt, for would at times she saw Dhruv's twinkling eyes that would result in a fluttering in her stomach, a feeling she was becoming accustomed to, yet it was strange and she wanted to explore it further so wished she had not told him that she would be busy for a week.

She dropped her mother and Ekta off whilst Aishya quickly jumped from the back seat to sit beside Khusboo in the front.

"I will get Olga, Khusboo, and don't worry, there will be a hot cup of tea ready for you. Be careful, girls."

"We will and don't worry Ekta." Aishya replied just as Olga came out of the door and walked gingerly towards the car. Ekta opened the door for her, helped her in the seat, then closed the door and walked back towards the house.

"Now, Olga, you remember what we talked about?" Khushboo asked, handing her the takeaway food. "I don't want you to spend any time that you have in cooking, but we don't want Alexei to go hungry either for that will make him angry, so from today, we are responsible for your meals. Go up to your room as soon as you have given him his food and we will expect you in the morning, as early as possible. Okay?"

"Yes, thank you, mam, that is very kind of you, you do not have to do so much for me. You are like Katina my sister!" Olga wiped her eyes, then directed Khusboo to her house which was at the end of a lane with overgrown bushes on either side

"Olga is this a safe area?" Khusboo looked worried for the further they drove, the narrower the lane became until the leaves of the bushes scraped against wings of her car.

"No need to come any further you can drop me off here and since you cannot turn back, there is a road that leads to the main road." Olga pointed to a road which could easily have been overlooked by Khushboo had she not pointed it out to her.

"Thanks Olga, and you take care, you have my number in case of emergency."

Olga waved and disappeared into her house whilst Khusboo drove down the road pointed out by Olga that led to the main road.

As soon as they were on it, Khushboo putt her foot on the brake and sped down the dual carriage way that led to their house.

"I hope she will be alright Khusboo, hey steady on!" Aishya shouted as she clung to the handle of the car door...

"I hope so to." Khusboo replied grimly. "If he harms her again, I don't know if I could live with myself."

"You did what you thought best, now tomorrow you can talk to this friend of yours and arrange for her to escape and not involve you in any way."

Having arrived at their house, Khushboo quickly parked the car whilst Aiysha rang the bell, and the door was opened by Ekta. Aiysha entered the house followed by Khushboo.

They went directly to the lounge, where they were joined by Sameera with a tray and mugs of tea.

"Is everything all right?" She asked as she handed a mug to everyone.

"Yes, I think so," Khushboo answered dubiously. "From now on, she will come early every morning and Mum, so she doesn't have to face Alexei I told her that she will dine with us, and she can take something back for Alexei."

"Ah the take way food was for them?" Ekta asked

"Yes, it was." Khusboo smiled softly as she recalled the moment that had changed her attitude on men.

Chapter 50

For the next couple of days till Aishya departure they followed a routine where on most days, they would get up late in the mornings, followed by Sameera's delicious breakfast, and then with mugs of tea in hand they would retire to the sitting room to talk for an hour or so before leaving for the day either to a museum or cinema, then in the evening would be back to dress for the evening ahead.

The women would dress casually for the daytime activity, but in the evening took care with their dress. Ekta and Sameera would both dress soberly for the evening, either in saree or in salwar kameez with light make up.

Khushboo on the first evening out, decided on a navy velvet Palazoo outfit she had recently purchased with matching black sandals and bag whilst Aiysha decided on a double-breasted blazer in and trouser suit in green. They then curled their hair and accessorised their outfits with necklace sand matching earrings.

"Oh, Aishya you do look lovely, here I bought this perfume that would give a finishing touch and then we are ready to go." She sprayed the perfume on her wrists then behind her ears before she handed the bottle to Aishya.

"Hmm, good choice, Khusboo." Aishya said as she first sniffed the bottle then sprayed it under the heavy bracelets on her wrists which clattered against each other when she applied the perfume behind her ears

"Khusboo, Aishya we are ready and waiting!" Sameera shouted from the landing and as the ladies walked down the stairs both uttered a "Wow" "both of you, I have never seen you look so beautiful! You should dress up more often! Then maybe we can get you married." She muttered under her breadth, however, not before Khusboo had heard her.

"Oh, Mum not that and so are both of you!" Khusboo exclaimed as she saw her mum wearing a light pink chiffon saree gracefully draped around her slim figure and her hair was tied in a bun.

However, at the mention of the word marriage, Khushboo's heart began to beat fast as she recalled Dhruv's twinkling eyes. Although she loved being with Aishya, she hoped the week would go by quickly so that Dhruv would call her, and if he did not, she would feel that something was lacking in her life, as if there was nothing to do for the rest of it and that she had left something unfinished.

She felt guilty for Aishya was her dear friend whereas she knew nothing about Dhruv. She had, till now, been against the thought of ever getting married, but now, she could picture herself with Dhruv beside her, and when she recalled his kind eyes, felt she would be able to trust him.

Not only did Dhruv seem trustworthy, she could see herself as his partner, sharing his life and responsibilities; e.g Khushboo would help him wash his car, drying it so there would be no water marks on it...When he clipped hedges and roses, she would arrange the roses n vases., when

Khusboo and Dhruv would come after shopping, he would unpack bags whilst she loaded the fridge sorting out the dairy products, vegetable juices and drinks and then meat, fish and vegetables.

She imagined him to be a man who would like to arrange/rearrange the fridge magnets, then smiled softly for had it only been a day ago that she had said that she would not cook for her husband? And what would her mother think at the thoughts were spinning in her head. For she had told her firmly that all her stubborn views on marriage would fly out of the window when the right man came along, Bur was Dhruv the right one? Well, he must be for her ideas on marriage had suddenly changed, but only so long as he was in her life.

"Hey Khushboo, are you with us?" Sameera clicked her fingers in front of Khushboo's face. "I am only looking nice due to Ekta, she leant me her sari and insisted she do my hair too!" Sameera exclaimed. "And Ekta too is looking lovely in that saree for she has a flair of style and fashion not only for herself but others too!"

"Yes, she is!" Khushboo looked approvingly at Ekta who was wearing a beige saree that set off her almond shaped eyes and naturally pouting lips on which she had applied a light shade of brown. "Mum, please don't start the subject of marriage and can we just enjoy ourselves?"

"I agree, Khushboo, my mum and d Ekta here think the same and are always hassling me about it...!" Aishya exclaimed, her bracelets again clattering against each other as she wore her coat.

"I agree with Sameera!" Ekta retorted "Aishya does not bother to dress up either and runs a mile when the subject of marriage is bought up."

"Ekta, you are not one to talk, you are older than me so..."

"That is no excuse Aishya, I have been there done that."

"And look where that got you." Aishya muttered under her breadth as they got into the car,

However, after they had got in the car the subject again, this time by Ekta.

"Aishya, you know that does not count as I am a divorced woman, as such it is difficult to find a man who will be willing to marry me."

"That does not matter these day Ekta, you are young very beautiful and a nice, woman, qualities not many women possess. I don't know why you don't want to marry again, okay, so you were unlucky with Aryan, but that is all in the past, and any man would be lucky to have you! In fact, I am going to tell Mother that that is going to one of my conditions, I will only marry if you do so first!" Aishya sat back and declared triumphantly."

"Aishya, I agree with you, Ekta is indeed very beautiful, but my condition is that the subject is not brought up again whilst you are here with us."

Reluctantly Sameera and Ekta agreed, and they spent the remaining days shopping visiting museums, if it was a nice day, walking in the park, and at the end the evening, go to a movie, opera or ballet followed by dinner at a restaurant, so usually by the time they drove home the streetlights would be shining and although on most days the roads were deserted, on some days they were caught in traffic.

One evening, they were exhausted and exhilarated with their visit to the museum followed by a movie that Khushboo had wanted to see. As soon as they came out, they looked around for a restaurant when Aishya saw a street vendor selling hot dogs and she sniffed the aroma of hot sausages.

"I don't know about all of you, but I would like a change, to our routine, instead of going to a fancy restaurant, why don't we try some street food, I like hot dogs. Ekta Sameera, what do you think" Aishya asked.

As soon as Ekta and Sameer nodded their heads in agreement, they walked over to the street vendor that was selling hot dogs. As soon as they reached the stall, he smiled at them took the fat sausages, their skins hot and shiny which he topped with fried onions and handed to each of them.

"Wow, this is nice!" Aishya exclaimed, taking the wrapper., took a bite on the sausage., and as it was greasy and hot, she wiped her mouth with a napkin.

As soon as Khushboo had paid him, the strolled back to their car.

"I enjoyed it, but I don't think I would have it again." Sameera commented as she got into the front seat of the car.

"Yes, I agree, Sameera, maybe it is food that the young like and..." Ekta said as she opened the back door of the car.

"Ekta, you talk as if you are a hundred years old! You are so beautiful I don't understand why you have given up on marriage! I am sure there is someone nice and kind for you out there.!" Aishya exclaimed as she switched on the radio for some background music.

"I agree with her, Ekta, you are not only beautiful, but a lovely person, but remember my condition? No talk of marriage?"

By the time they arrived home, the evening light had completely faded and dusk was being replaced by night.

On most evenings they would change into leggings /casual comfortable clothes; Khusboo would wear her favourite joggers with a loose t shirt whilst Sameera made some tea and insisted on making snacks, although everyone insisted, they were not hungry. Afterwards they would go the sitting room, turn on the lamp, soft music, and sit and talk about the memorable day they had had.

Chapter 51

"You know, the glow of the shaded blue lamp gives the room a very cosy aura and that in turn is very relaxing. Khushboo, you know, I am having such a wonderful time I don't want to leave!" Aishya sighed "Khusboo, aunty thank you so much for making our stay so enjoyable!"

"Aishya, you know it is a pleasure having you with stay with us, but tell me, I think I mentioned this when you first came, mum has been following the story of the daughter of an aristocratic family in Dubai, she would love to know more about it."

"Yes, that was the story I was assigned to, but, like I said I know no more than the latest in the media, that the woman is not a prisoner but is being treated at home."

"Yes, but it is so strange, except for some photos of her, she is actually hidden away from the public eye, which of course only helps to fuel the public's interest who spin it as an issue that is shady and mysterious." Sameera said

"No, there is nothing like that and according to the family, as soon as she is well enough, she will reappear in public, sorry aunty, that is all I know."

"Okay, I just thought there might be more to it, Khusboo, but I have been having such a nice time I had actually quite forgotten about it!"

"Mum you never go out, this, I hope this week has shown you that there is a world to explore out there, not only at home."

"Hush, Khusboo, Ekta, I think we should leave the girls, anyway I would like to get your opinion on something I bought."

They left the girls listening to music talking about their lives, jobs and aspirations, both avoiding any talk of romance although it did cross Aiysha's mind that maybe Khushboo might need a friend to talk to after what she had witnessed at the Chinese restaurant, however, then thought it best if Khushboo brought it up herself. Nonetheless, she was worried about her friend, for she had been detached and alone for so long that she was liable to fall for the wrong kind of man.

"Khusboo, what did you mean when you said your mother stays at home all the time?" she asked with a frown. "She is such a nice person I am sure she has loads of friends."

"She is very shy and has not got many friends, and to top it all my father ignores her." Khushboo replied indignantly. "H does not understand that she is a woman with feelings, and that he has a duty to look after her should take her to restaurants and cinemas. It makes me so angry at the way she still pampers him, maybe because women of that generation have been culturally brainwashed to feel inferior to men, abut she maintains his selfishness by catering to his needs. According to mother, that is how the equation of power between husband and wife should be, so how can there be equal blame when there is no equal power in the first place?" She shook her head in despair. "Hopefully once she starts volunteering for this organisation 'Raksha' which advises and provides shelter to Asian women. Hopefully, that will also serve to be like looking into a mirror, she will see how she too is like them, being dominated and controlled by my father. I think I told you about that on the first day you arrived."

"Actually, I do not remember much of the conversation, Khushboo, I was tired. But from what I do remember, their organisations seem to be doing a worthy cause, are they the ones you will refer Olga to? Oh, and is he the dishy guy you met at the Chinese restaurant?"

"Nooo." Khushboo answered flustered, the colour creeping from her neck to her cheeks,

'So, Cupid has struck!' Aiysha smiled slightly and mentally wished her friend luck.

"But you know, I just had an idea, my sister will be looking for a job, and I remember vaguely you telling me that your mother would do some volunteering work? It would be a good idea for her to volunteer as well, that is if they need one?"

"Oh yes they do, and I think Ekta would be very good for she seems very tactful and has been through a lot herself. Plus, it shows that the applicant has shown initiative when shown in the CV, which is a quality that employers like their employees to have."

"Thanks, Khusboo, I am pretty sure she will get a job soon but at least I know she will be doing something useful with her time, for she is like me, needs to be doing something!"

"She can accompany Mum who I am sure would like a friendly face talk to for she is not confident in going out. And if Ekta agrees, I will talk to Reyansh tomorrow. I am sure he will be thrilled to have her."

"I hope so, but how long has your father gone for and when was aunty thinking of starting?"

"Dad has gone for a month, but I would not be surprised if he extends his leave, for he has not seen his parents since he came to London." Khusboo replied, "and mum was thinking of starting once I finish my leave, but if Ekta does not want to volunteer, I am sure mum would love to stay back with her!"

"Oh, don't change your plans because of us, I am sure Ekta would love to go with your mum. As you must have noticed, although she was working back in Dubai, she too is very reserved, and it takes time to really know her."

"Aishya, don't worry, we will think of something but come to think of it we have not heard anything from Dad, but then neither did we call him for we have been having such a fun time! I think Mum called him once, you know she is a different person since you and your sister came. I have never seen her look so relaxed and dare I say, happy?"

Aishya got up and stretched her arms.

"I am glad but hey, I would love to sit and chat some more, but I think I better call it a night. Goodnight Khusboo."

"Good night Aishya, and don't forget to ask your sister, I don't want to be nosy, but it seems she has been through a lot so would understand the problems of another woman"

"Yes, will do and, yes, she has had more than her share of prejudice, chauvinism and sexism all rolled into one! Her husband was awful to her." Aishya said from the door. "And by the way you better contact your father for I have heard that Covid cases in India have spiked suddenly."

Chapter 52

The next couple of days flew by, with Olga staying the day at their place and in the evening, as they had decided, however tired Khushboo was, she would drop her home with the takeaway food

And before they knew it, they were at the airport, again, this time to see Aishya off to her next assignment in Minnesota.

"I should be back in a couple of days for the officer has already been found guilty. Khusboo, I have spoken to Ekta, and she thinks it would be a good idea to volunteer for she and your mum have really hit it off.! You will also be returning to office from tomorrow? Hey, my flight has been delayed, and as we have time to kill, why don't we have coffee, look, that café looks nice."

"No, I will be returning to office the day after tomorrow, and yes, we can go that café, But Aiysha, I know why you want to go to a café, it is not because your plane has been delayed but because of that heavy backpack of yours! I could hear you and your sister arguing about it last night!"

They walked to a café nearby, followed by Sameera and Ekta.

"That is Ekta my darling sister! She did not like my travelling baggage when travelling from Dubai and now she is objecting to my backpack! But I love her and would not have it any other way for it just shows that she cares! And, once you return to office, don't forget to take care of Olga's problem" Aiysha reminded her. "I noticed fresh bruises on her arms, and she has black circles under her eyes!"

"Oh yes, of course I remember that is priority and I did notice the fresh bruises and even found her crying. I have assured her that she will be out of there in a few days, she is such a lovely girl that she is willing to put up with Alexei's abuse just so her leaving him does not lead back to me!"

They entered the café followed by Sameera and Ekta, Ekta looking trim and elegant as always. She had taken her mother under her wing and not only was her mother a different person, for being with Ekta had given her confidence a boost, so much so that she has even begun trying new ways of dressing.

Ayisha chose to sit at a table outside the café where they could see the neon sign detailing flight details, Khusboo offered to get Lattes for everyone and, whilst waiting, Aiyesha looked around fascinated by the hustle and bustle of the busy airport, at men in suits and light trolleys. She was specially fascinated by a member of a family holding on to the pillar of luggage on a trolley. The trolley was being steered by a man who could not control it for the wheels just would not cooperate with where the man wanted it to turn!

As she went to get the coffees, Khushboo's heartbeat faster as she remembered that not only had she met Dhruv at a till of a restaurant, but that he would be contacting her once she returned to work. But then again, he might not, and her heart missed a beat at the thought as she returned with Lattes for all of them on a tray.

As soon as Aishya saw her she giggled and pointed at the man who was trying to control the trolley in vain.

"Aishya, don't laugh!" Khushboo reprimanded as she set the tray on the table. "Poor fellow, look, none of the other grown-ups are helping him except the child who is trying to hold the luggage in place with his little hand! Hey mum Ekta, you can talk all you want once we are home!" "Sorry girls!" Sameera and Ekta looked uncomfortable for both found they had many things in common.

They finished their coffee just as Aiysha's flight details flashed on the monitor After a quick goodbye and take care see you soon, Aishya disappeared into the duty-free shop whilst Khusboo Sameera and Ekta walked silently towards the exit, when Ekta suddenly stopped.

"Khusboo, can we wait awhile for the plane to leave? We can sit in the restaurant overlooking the runways?"

"Yes of course Ekta." Khushboo replied taking her arm.

They sat in comfortable armchairs that overlooked the runways through glass windows, and as they watched them landing Ekta looked at them sadly, and Khusboo guessed at what she was thinking. Although she did not show it, Ekta was worried about her little sister going to dangerous places. At least in Dubai she had been with her, and Khushboo believed that nagging at her sister was only a cover of her love and anxiety.

"Don't worry, Ekta, she will be back soon." Sameera said softly as she put her hand on her arm." And in no time at all we will be back here to receive her."

Ekta sighed "Sameera you know what she said, her office is sending her to another dangerous mission after this one."

"Ekta, I understand, don't worry, when she comes back, we will look for a safer and secure job for her." Sameera tried to reassure her.

The problem is that she does not want to leave her job, I have tried many times to convince her to do so, but she feels she is making a difference in this job by reporting all that some governments are trying to hide."

"Don't worry Ekta, we will try again, together, when she returns... Now, shall we leave?"

Ekta reluctantly agreed, wistfully looking out at the planes on the runaway then followed Khushboo and Ekta.

The wind was cold and biting and Ekta pulled her wrap tightly around her as they walked in silence into the car park, and having located their car, opened its doors climbed in,

Khusboo took her seat behind the wheel and tightened her grip on the wheel and left the carpark after checking the mirror.

"Mum shall we pick up a takeaway, I don't think anyone is in the mood for cooking." She asked once she was on the main road.

"I am not hungry at all" Ekta replied miserably. "

"Ekta, you eat something, and Khushboo, what do you mean, no one is in the mood for cooking.!" Sameera said indignantly "You never enter the kitchen, I am the one who does the cooking, anyway there is some food leftover from this morning,"

"Hmm" Ekta said absentmindedly from the back of the car then clutched at the handle of the door as Khushboo swerved to avoid a car that was pulling out without indicating.

"I hate those kinds of drivers; they don't think of anyone their reckless driving might endanger! "Khushboo muttered under her breadth.

"Calm down Khushboo we are nearly home." Sameera said as they drove past the local garage and past the fish and chip shop onto their road.

Chapter 53

After Khushboo had parked the car and they were walking towards the house, Sameera noticed that the wind had caused a lot of damage to their garden and there were heaps of leaves that had fallen from the branches of trees. The wind had been so strong that it had even carried rubbish and sheets of wet newspaper from neighbouring houses!

Instead of ringing the bell and waiting for Olga to open the door Khushboo took her key ring out to open the door then exclaimed

"I will have to get a broom and clear all that! Mum do we have a gardener?"

"No, we don't and Khusboo you know you do not like working so I will end up cleaning the rubbish, as usual. Who do you think looks after the garden, certainly not your dad, and you are too busy in your work! Oh, look at the shopping bags stuck in the branches, I don't how I will get them down," She grumbled as they entered and she hung her coat on the banister, but as she walked towards the kitchen Khusboo stopped her.

"Mum, you do not have to worry, I will help."

"And so will I." Ekta piped in "you have been so nice, both of you, I don't know how I can ever repay you."

"And you don't have too, it has been a pleasure having you, it is nice to be able to talk to someone, you Ekta, are like my sister." Sameera hugged her.

Olga meanwhile had come out of the kitchen and Khusboo noticed that she had been crying. She was still wearing her coat so took her arm.

"Come, Olga, I will drop you but no wait, I will change into something more comfortable, and mum, can you please give the dinner in the fridge for Olga?"

"Yes of course." Sameera replied as she gathered the leftover food from the fridge and packed it for Olga,

But having changed and before going downstairs, she quickly made a note of things she had to do the following day, the most important being to call their mortgage company for she wanted to sort everything out before she resumed work.

She tried her father's phone again so he could advise her about it, however, his phone again went to voicemail. Khusboo began to worry for she had been trying to contact him for the last couple of days. She thought he might have spoken to her mother, so made a mental note to ask her.

She quickly drove Olga to her house and on the way discussed her situation.

"Olga now that my friend has gone, day after tomorrow I will return to work and I am going to see to it that you leave Alexei, I noticed some fresh bruises on your arm, has he been hurting you?"

"Thank you, mam and yes he has, but I can bear it as long as I know that I will be leaving him, and by not having to cook for him has helped, for he does not have to see me or criticise my food!"

Olga wiped her eyes as she got out of the car, clutching the food that Sameera had given her tightly under her arm and running into the house.

As she drove back home, Khushboo made a mental note to contact Reyansh and explain Olga's dilemma as soon as possible, sure that he would be able to find a safe place for her.

As soon as she entered her house, she took off her coat and hung it in the cupboard, and having heard her, Sameera called her in to the kitchen.

"I thought we would have the leftovers from yesterday." Sameera said as she first put some lentils in a bowl and put it in the microwave to heat, and after it had, she did the same with the rice.

"Khushboo, can you put the pickle and curd on the table please? And Ekta, if you like, we can make salad to go with the food, there is nothing much…"

"No thanks, not for me, Sameera, just some light food would do, I would not have minded toast or sandwich with tea."

"Not in my house you will not!" Sameera exclaimed." You will always have a proper meal here."

"Thank you, Sameera, but there is no need for formality."

After dinner, her mother and Ekta cleared the table and whilst Khusboo waited for the kettle to boil, she turned to her mother.,

"Mum have you spoken to Dad, I tried, but his phone keeps going to voicemail.!"

"No, Khusboo, I haven't! Sameera replied as she stacked the dishes in the dishwasher. "Anyway, I am the last person he would want to talk to, it still hurts when I remember the way he snapped at me, even on the day of his departure! He was so rude and abrupt, just so he could meet his friend?" There were tears in her eyes as she finished stacking the dishes in the dishwasher.

"I am sorry to have to remind you of that day, Mum, anyway, not to worry." Khushboo was remembered the call from the bank and the urgency in the manager's voice.

The kettle had boiled and Khusboo poured the boiling water into them for she had already put teabags of green tea in them.

"Mum I will take my tea upstairs for I knew you two will have a lot to talk about."

"Oh no you won't Khusboo," Sameera said firmly. "You will join us, it has been so nice to have you home, this past week and I will miss you when you go back."

She undid her apron which she hung on the hook behind the door than kissed her daughter affectionately.

"I know you are missing your friend as Ekta is missing her sister, so come on." She took Khushboo's hand.

As soon as they were comfortably seated in the lounge, Khusboo turned to her mother.

"Mum, maybe something happened to his phone, or there is no internet where he is? Aiysha, before she left, said that there had been a spike in covid cases in India. Is it possible he could have spoken to somebody…Aadarsh uncle maybe? Or we could try and call his parents?"

"As far as I know, we did not keep in touch with Aadarsh, anyway I do not have his number. As for calling his parents, I have been trying to call them; but due to internet problems I have not been able to get through. I really don't know what is happening, but now you have told me about the cases going up in India, that is really worrying!"

"Okay never mind Mum, I am sure he is fine, but, remember, tomorrow are going to see Reyansh, so if there are any questions you have, we can prepare them now."

"Khusboo, you know I do not go out much, but even though I think I can talk to other women, I think if Ekta had not decided to come with me, I would have refused to see this through. I mean I thought I would not be able to talk to another woman, but Ekta, you have helped me overcome that, thank you" Sameera smiled

"Oh, Sameera thank you too, for even though I was working and independent, the breakup with Aryan left me with no self-esteem and I found it difficult to make friends."

"Is that how you happened to be in Dubai…your husband was working there? Sorry I don't mean to pry." Sameera asked "

Oh, Sameera you are not! But this is the first time I have spoken about it," Ekta wrung her hands in distress. "It hurt too much to talk about it, even to Aishya. I had no friends in Dubai, and there are no support groups there either..."

"Ekta if it hurts to talk about it, don't..."

"No actually I want to, Sameera. Anyway, we got married in India, arranged of course, Aryan my husband was the son of a family friend. And you know how it is, the glamour of living abroad etc, my parents agreed to the marriage, and I was married within a week. The brief time in which the marriage was arranged did not give me a chance to get to really know Aryan, but even if I had and did not like him, my parents were so excited that I would not have had the heart to refuse. And to be fair to my parents, he was charming, handsome, and polite and on the one occasion that I did see him before the wedding, he seemed almost godlike, with his black curly hair and muscular body! And I thought to myself to be a very lucky woman that a man like him would want to marry me!"

Khushboo, who had been listening, got up from her armchair to turn on the fire for it was getting chilly. She came back and sat her on the armchair with her feet tucked up under he,

Both she and Sameera listened in silence for they could see that Ekta was so emotional that she needed to get it off her chest.

"We left for Dubai immediately after marriage," Ekta continued a faraway and sad look in her eyes. "And that for me was a huge change for not only was I leaving my parents but going to a new country, all in a matter of days. And having arrived in Dubai, I felt homesick for as he did not have any Indian friends, so could not befriend their wives. And once in Dubai, Aryan changed. After about a month, he insisted that I start to look for work, as he was not going to, Luckily, I got a job so all he did was stay at home. He became so lazy that he would not do anything around the house, and I was too tired to cook in the evenings so started getting takeaway curries, Anyway, he put on a lot of weight, his face too changed, he had put on so much weigh that he had a double chin, his eyes began to look shifty, like his character!" Ekta shuddered." Nothing at all like the godlike figure I had married!"

"You poor thing!" Sameera exclaimed. "I can understand how you felt for it was the same with me coming to London with a stranger, but Aryan did not support you at all, Ekta?"

"He did, in the beginning and the first month went by without any problem while I tried to adjust to his habits. But now that I think about it, from the beginning he had a habit of undermining me which I did not notice at first, and even when I did, I ignored them! I refused to be like my mother and let my insecurity worry me till my marriage collapsed, because of it, which it did, eventually, regardless of the effort I put into it." She wiped her tears with the tissue that Khusboo had handed to her.

"Oh, Ekta I am so sorry…" Sameera whispered "I wish I had been there for you, did you tell your parents at all about it, I am sure they would have spoken to his parents to sort out his behaviour?"

"No, I did not, for Aryan's parents and mine were good friends, and they would have been so worried and upset that they would have stopped speaking to his parents. Plus, they were of the view that it is up to the girl to make a success of the marriage and I too believed that! I was so confident that I could take my life in my hands and shape it the way I wanted! But how wrong I was, I thought that my life was out of my control; that it was locked behind some kind of glass through which I could see everything but could not reach or touch it! It was awful, for I felt I could not breathe!"

"That is terrible." Sameera walked over to Ekta and put her arms around her. "Ekta, don't worry, that was all in the past, you are safe here."

Chapter 54

"Thank you Sameera!" Ekta clung to her then turned to get a tissue from the tissue box lying on the centre table "You know, you have made feel at home, that I now believe there are nice people in the world!" Ekta squeezed Sameera's hand then continued." But it got worse, for at first, he would only humiliate me when we were alone, then he began to abuse me verbally in the presence of his friends. At times, it was so bad that I thought it best to leave the room, but Aryan would follow me and pull me back into the room saying he was sorry and that he had not meant to say such vile things. More than once, he got physically abusive and hit me, but I endured his cruelty and crazy behaviour, thinking that maybe I could change him with my love..."

"And when he did not, you decided enough was enough?" Khusboo asked, trying to fathom how men's cruel behaviour took shape in different forms, Alexei's physical violent behaviour with Olga and Aryan's mental cruelty.and she knew from the cases she dealt with, that the cruelty could also take the form of financial oppression or exploitation.

"No, I didn't, for I was trying to make the marriage work, but it seemed I was the only one for he told me, often, that he couldn't care less! I always apologised when he got angry, trying to justify his behaviour till finally. Aryan. came to enjoy the power he held over me."

"That is awful, mental cruelty is what it was, which I think is worse than physical abuse, for physical wound heals, but it takes a long time for one's self-esteem and confidence to be re-established, but at least you finally found the courage to leave."

Khusboo was horrified that someone like Ekta, a kind gentle beautiful woman should be treated that way. Aryan must be a monster and she even began to think her dad was better than Aryan.

"Eventually, but I kept hoping for his love but, I too stopped trying to bridge the gap between us, because by then I had come to know that not only was Aryan incapable of love, but that he was also unaware that a gap existed!! Maybe if Aryan had understood that there was a gap in our marriage and that it was growing wider, he would have tried to bridge it?" She asked hopefully.

"I do not think so, Ekta, I don't think he was capable of love, men like him rarely are, so he just did not want the marriage to work. After going through all that on your own, did you think of going back to your parents?" Sameera asked

"No, for by then I had gone out of my way to convince them that I was happily married, in fact I have not even told Aishya the full details leading to the breakup." Ekta put her head in her hands in despair.

Khusboo thought Ekta to be brave, going through all that on her own, but a part of her was disappointed, for she had always looked down on women who stayed with husbands who treated them badly She thought them weak and stupid for, regardless of the cruelty they suffered, they still made the choice of staying with them. Her mother's attitude was similar, therefore, concluded that the fault was not theirs, for Asian women had been taught from a young age that a suffering role was their destiny.

"What made you finally leave and how did Aishya find you?" Sameera asked.

"I found out he was having an affair with our neighbour, and I confronted him about it one day. His reaction to it was 'Okay I will live with her then' so he packed his suitcase and left. The only kind thing he did was to let me stay in his house; After a week of crying, I decided that at least I was lucky to have a roof over my head."

"But how did you manage?"

"I had been doing online courses for some time, so when money began to run out. I found another job, Anyway, Aishya had got my address from my parents, and when she arrived was surprised when she found out about my situation, and when she was leaving, insisted I leave my job and come back with her, Although I don't think it was the right thing to do, for now I have no job, no house and no hope of one!" Ekta cried softly. "I should not have left Dubai, for now what am I going to tell my parents?"

Sameera tightened came her arms around her and said reassuringly.

"Ekta, don't ever feel that you have no home or no family.! We will be here for you and please don't worry, you can stay here as long as you want."

"Thanks. Sameera, that means the world to me, but you have already been so kind I cannot impose on your hospitality indefinitely.

"Mum is right, you are now family, actually I think Ayesha did the right thing to bring you back with her. At least here you are amongst friends, and you are well qualified in helping women in similar situations, I don't know about Dubai, but here not only do the women face their husband's cruelty at home, but also racism if and when they leave the house!"

"Mum that is men for you, why do you think I don't want to get married." Khushboo exclaimed.

"Oh no Khushboo, you must not say that, marrying Aryan was just my bad luck, I am sure there are some nice men around"

"If there are, I have not come across them!"

However, Khushboo could not help but think of Dhruv and deep in her heart, thought of a life of companionship and laughter with him.

However, both Sameera and Ekta laughed at Khushboo's remark, and it felt good, for it was an eruption of an emotion that was not sad, even though it was short lived and was followed by a silence which was broken by Khusboo.

"Mum, I am going to bed and Ekta please don't worry, Mum is right, you are family now."

She smiled at Ekta then kissed her mum and left, glad her mother had found a friend however, as she went into the kitchen to make herself a fresh cup of tea for, she had a disturbing time ahead of her; first trying to call her father then to try and sift through his papers to find out the relevant information that the bank manager had asked for.

Chapter 55

Aadrika filled a kettle with water then pressed her hand to her forehead and closed her eyes. It had only been a day since Anil had left, but so much had happened since then. She had met Dhruv at the airport and decided he come back to stay with her.

And as she put a teabag in the mug, she thought how dependant she had become on Anil and cursed herself again at not taking her finances from him especially once she knew he was leaving for India.

Dhruv was still sleeping on the sofa in the sitting room and as Aadrika sat in the kitchen, she thought she would take the opportunity to go online to check her statement so pulled the laptop that was lying on the table towards her, but which might, she felt intuitively, set a negative series of events in motion. She went into her internet banking and scrolled down to see her statement.

She gave a cry of alarm and put her hand over her mouth for her account only showed 5 pounds! She checked her statement again to confirm that her salary had gone into her account the previous day but saw that although there had been a payment made from her office, the same amount had been taken out the day before.

She tried to recall how and when she had used her card, then saw that it had been done at the airport, and she remembered suddenly that Anil had asked if he could borrow her card as he needed some money for the journey; This he had done on the very same day that he had broken off with her; he had withdrawn all her money!

At first, she thought there must be some explanation, for she could not believe Anil to be a dishonest man. why he had even offered to look after her bills and finance. She scrolled further to see if her rent and bills had been paid, but she saw with horror that he had not paid them for the last three months. Whilst he had told her that her bills and rent were paid regularly, he had been withdrawing money to, no doubt, pay for his ticket to India!

But although everything indicated that he had taken the money, she wanted to believe that it was just a loan which he would repay on his return. but her heart sank when she recalled their last conversation, that he will not see her on his return.

She wrapped her arms around her body, trembling with the thought that some things in life just cannot be fixed easily, and this mess certainly was one of them! Reality hit her and Aadrika's mind in turn propelled a burst of white-hot fury that engulfed her body.

She closed the computer lid and put her heads on her hands, sobbing silently and cursing herself, for there was no one to blame but herself however much she tried to justify it but when Anil had offered, she had her hands full, looking after Aarush and her colleagues at work had been harassing her, all except Emma.

One of her colleagues had offered to take her out on a date followed by 'a night you will not forget! Being a single woman, many men had tried and failed. She had hated going in to work after that, fearing she might come across him, so her work had suffered, and she had to stay late on many days. And when she came from work, she was busy seeing to Aarush's needs that she. had no time to look after the bills so had gladly left the payment of bills and rent to Anil.

When she saw that the rent had not been paid for three months, she was sure that the landlord must have sent her reminders, but she then recollected that Anil carefully sifted through her letters when he came in the morning with the pretext that he was expecting an important letter. He must have kept the reminders from her so as to keep her in the dark!

A shiver that had nothing to do with cold raced down her spine as she recalled how secretive and furtive, he had been sometimes, which she had put down to family affairs. She knew that his wife was a naïve woman and wondered whether he had done the same thing to her, or had he planned to take money from her for her?

Aadrika paced the room and thought with dismay that her salary had gone into her account the day before, and Anil had withdrawn it all!

Pushing her chair back Aadrika walked towards the window pushed the net curtain aside and saw that the sky had clouded over, and it had become grey and cloudy. She leant forward to rest her forehead against the cold glass and wondered why Anil needed money, was it gambling or stock market or for his wife, but whatever the reason, all her money was gone!

She rubbed her forehead for her head had begun to ache and turned away quickly as she felt the draught of the icy air blasting through window. Tears gathered in her eyes as she thought of Anil, how he had lied to her, had she really known him or was his being a kind and decent man just a figment of her imagination?

Aadrika turned back into the kitchen, opened a drawer where she kept her medicines and took out a packet of paracetamol. She stood at the sink and downed a couple of tablets with a glass of water, not knowing if they would help, for together with her headache, was the shock and disappointment at being betrayed by a man who she had thought to be a decent guy.

She was relieved that at least Dhruv was there to help and guide her, then pulled herself together, for it was her trusting nature that had got her into this mess in the first place! She had loved and trusted Dhruv once but they had also fought, and at those times she felt Dhruv was pouring stinking water, the kind of water that was in the flowers that had wilted and died in a vase full of water.

She was so angry she took out her mobile to call Anil and when she received no answer, decided to call again the following day but for the moment she had more urgent matters to deal with.

She had stored the number of her landlords, Mr Sharma, on her mobile, and when she called them, they confirmed that her rent had not been paid for the last 3 months! Mr Sharma, a nice man, said he had sent many reminders but when he did not receive any reply was in the process of sending an eviction letter to her.

"Look, I will be grateful if we could come to arrangement, please, the man you dealt with was someone I trusted. He told me he would take care of my rent and bills, but yesterday he left for India after clearing my bank account! I am a working girl with a young son to look after" She started crying.

Chapter 56

The Sharma's were very understanding so Aadrika gave them her number, promising they would get their rent as soon as she got her salary and promising to remain in touch.

Aadrika closed her blackberry with a sigh of relief, at least that was one problem sorted out albeit temporarily, wondering, as she had their number, why she had not called them sooner.

She got up and paced the kitchen, grateful that it was Sunday, and she could have this day to think, plan and organise the next step. The first one was in deciding if she should tell Dhruv, but she was embarrassed at letting him know how things she had been scammed, all because she was so gullible.

With a white and trembling hand, she brought the mug to her lips whilst her heart hurled accusations at Anil. She had planned to go grocery shopping, but there was no money in her account and no overdraft either, was grateful that Dhruv had offered that he would get a Chinese from a restaurant the previous evening.

Aadrika finished her tea and rubbed her eyes then thought she would make breakfast for Dhruv, it would take her mind of Anil. She rose to make some fresh coffee, which she knew Dhruv liked, put some slices of bread into the toaster, then after they were done and put them on a plate, She tried to calm herself by breathing in slowly, took the tray and put the toast butter and cheese with 2 mugs of fresh coffee on it, then walked swiftly out of the kitchen to the sitting room and placed the tray on the centre table

"Hey, Dhruv, time to get up!" She pulled aside the curtains as Dhruv rubbed his eyes and sat up.

"Good morning Aadrika!" Dhruv yawned and put his hand across his mouth. "Is that fresh coffee I see?"

"It is, Dhruv, did you sleep well?" Aadrika turned and smiled.

"I did, thank you, I had a lovely dream!" He put out his hand and took the coffee," I dreamt about a girl I met at the Chinese restaurant yesterday, she had the most amazing eyes and a dimple that danced in and out of her cheek."

Although they had decided that there was going to be nothing romantic between them, both had, in their hearts, felt the chemistry between them at the airport, which Aadrika thought was not only because she had met Dhruv after a long time, but also as a rebound of Anils rejection. She, at that time wanted to feel that her life should go somewhere with someone, but now she saw that Dhruv had not changed, for everything in his life was still transitory, and she was sure he would not want the responsibility that went with practical life.

She felt disappointed, for she had hoped for his support in the tight spot she found herself in, but at least, she hoped, at the very least, he could boost her morale. She remembered the many times in the orphanage he had protected her and smiled at having doubted him, picked up a mug from the tray and sat on a chair opposite Dhruv.

"Thank you, Aadrika, you did not have to go to all this trouble. But I was tired and needed the sleep but promise from tomorrow I will be up and about before you.!" He declared. "But for now, I am going to have a toast with my coffee!"

Dhruv's hands gripped the mug tightly, then put it back on the tray, looked up and smiled as he fumbled inside his jacket and took out a cigarette pack. After lighting it, he picked up his mug again, and sat hunched over the table, drinking coffee and smoking.

"So, I see you have not cut down on smoking?" Aadrika remarked as she saw Anil puffing away on his cigarette

"Nooo." Dhruv replied sheepishly. "There was no Aad to nag me! But if you don't want me to, I won't smoke in the house. Oh, by the way, where is Aarush?"

"No, it is alright, and Aarush did not come home last night, he rang to say that as it was too late, he would be staying over at his friend's house as they were going to be practising football at his place today."

Aadrika closed her eyes, feeling Dhruv's magnetism and imagining Dhruv kissing her eyelids, barely brushing them with his lips. She thought of feeling his body next to hers, which, she thought, was the only place she belonged!

She opened her eyes with a start as she realised that Dhruv had been talking to her.

"Aadrika, are you feeling alright?" When Aadrika nodded, he continued "you should set a few ground rules for Aarush, he is away all the time!" However, when he saw Aadrika glare at him apologised." Sorry,

Aadrika you know best, anyway, I better have a quick bath and then we can decide what to do today."

Aadrika had told him that he could unpack in Aarush's room, so after picking up his toiletries from his room, went into the bathroom. As Dhruv got in the shower, he let the shampoo run into his eyes to let his sleep and tiredness wash out, after he had turned off the shower and worn his bathrobe, tying the belt around his waist, he thought of Khushboo, her almond shaped eyes in her heart shape face and the dimple on her cheek when she smiled

As he walked back to Aarush's room, he felt he could not wait to call her, but she had said she would be busy this week, so this week he would devote to Aadrika, realising that his feelings towards her had changed too since he met Khushboo.

He wore the clothes he had taken out and walked back into the sitting room where Aadrika had turned the sofa cum bed into a sofa and the room once again looked like a sitting room!

Dhruv entered the room, rosy cheeked and wearing trainers and a black tracksuit. He wiped the water that was dripping from his damp hair onto his forehead and wondered where to wipe his hands, then rubbed his track suit subtly, hoping that action would dry his hands.

He was wearing a white t shirt over the black track suit pants, and Aadrika could see his muscles ripple beneath his shirt and her heart skipped a beat, then wondered why, in all her time with Anil, her heartbeat had remained steady in his company? Maybe in her heart she had known the kind of man he really was?

Dhruv sat down on the chair and poured himself another coffee, the sunlight streaming from the window showing deep lines that had suddenly appeared around his eyes. He sat silently sipping his coffee, waiting for Aadrika to break the silence.

All the time that Dhruv was in the bath, Aadrika had been debating whether she should tell him about Anil and what he had done, and if so, how much should she tell him?

Dhruv walked over to her chair, crouching in front of her, his eyes narrowed and took her hands in his. "Aad, I know something is worrying you, talk to me and if I can, I will help." Dhruv spoke so gently that Aadrika had tears in her eyes., "Yes, oh yes Dhruv! I am and don't know what to do!"

"Tell me about it, but before that I am going to make some tea for myself, I need a change I have had too much coffee, would you like some?"

When she shook her head, he went into the kitchen, put the kettle to boil and opened the kitchen cupboard doors to find the quantity of teabags in them and Dhruv's eyes widened at the array of labelled containers of all shapes and sizes.

He knew Aadrika was fond of tea, but she had enough stock for two people! He found what he was looking for, put a teabag in a mug, then poured the boiling water from the kettle over it. As soon as he had added sugar and milk. He which had been lying on the counter, he went back into the sitting room. He knew why Aadrika was upset, for he and Anil, between them, had planned to scam her.

Both had their own motives, Aadrika had chosen Aarush over Dhruv and asked him to leave their house, and to Anil, she had just been a temporary distraction, But Anil had only taken part of the money he had taken from Aadrika at the airport, which was, he told Dhruv, 'his commission'. The rest he had given to Dhruv.

Chapter 57

But now the situation had changed, for as Dhruv earlier plan had been n to manipulate and control Aadrika, since his meeting with Khushboo, his heart priorities had changed. Now he could only envisage Khushboo in his life, however, he could not call her till the following week, when he planned to start courting her, so decided that this week he would devote to Aadrika.

He went back into the lounge, and when he saw Aadrika, felt she was so trusting she could be controlled easily, he needed another stronger woman who would be a challenge! He always had it all planned, first he would crush her ego and with no self-confidence, she would become so docile that he would become bored that he would soon start looking for a strong woman who he could squash, and the circle would start all over again!

Khusboo, on the other hand, was an exception, and suddenly he was not proud of the way he had treated women. He had only met Khushboo briefly but knew instinctively he would never hurt her and that she was the one who could break the circle and manage that side of his character.

His overnight stay with Aadrika had made one thing clear to him, he wanted to be free to run around in the sunshine and was ready to fall in love. He had learnt that marriage was all about egos and Dhruv, either they could fall in love like strangers, or they should have the courage and humility to tear off some essential and new layer of themselves, either positive or negative, and show each other how they had matured and developed over the time they had been apart.

But Dhruv had too much pride and secrets to truly strip his soul to Aadrika, especially since his chance encounter with Khushboo, He could not salve his conscience with Aadrika by going through motions that showed that everything was as it had once been and pretending, he still loved her.

He did not want to try and mend a broken relationship, he wanted to be someone's first choice, not their second. He forgot that he had been Aadrika's first choice, and she had been his, but maybe that was because fate had cast them together from an early age? He had liked Aadrika but at that time Aadrika's love had been innocent, clean and fresh. However, his meeting with had not only been surreal but at the same time mundane and highlighted the fact there was a lash of their personalities and emotions, something he had not anticipated! for he had felt attracted to her at the airport.

He thought of Khushboo's heart shaped face, pouting lips, and the dimples that danced on her cheek when she smiled, and felt he wanted her is his life forever, nor would he want to change her, could this be love, he thought, then shook his head, He had only met her briefly, but the feeling was so intense that he could not shake it off.

As Dhruv drank his tea, Aadrika told him about Anil, leaving nothing out, though, out of embarrassment, she tried to minimise their affair.

Dhruv listened in silence, and when he saw the tears in her eyes, went over to her and took her hands in his and ran his thumb across her knuckle gently.

Aadrika trembled and wiped her tears for she had forgotten the thrill, the desire and melting sensation that only Dhruv's touch could evoke in her.

"I am so sorry I was not here to protect you Aadrika." Dhruv knelt at her feet, looking deep into her eyes.

"It was my own fault, Dhruv, I trusted him to pay my bills and rent. At the very least, I should at least have checked that everything was in order. And before he left for India, I should have sat with him to go through the finances. Maybe he would have felt ashamed and left the last amount he took from the airport. I was there and still did not know, I even had coffee at a café after leaving him, and had I paid with my card would have come to know about it immediately and informed the bank!"

"Maybe, but he would have found some excuse not to discuss finances, and as for emptying your account at the airport, he was clever to take cash and from your card only, so there is no question of fraud there. Do you have a job, but anyway, what can I do to help?"

"This is very embarrassing Dhruv, yes, I do work, but my salary went into my account the day before yesterday so has been taken by Anil. Come to think of it, I am sure he planned that too, so I would not have time to check. Anyway, I was supposed to go grocery shopping, but I have no overdraft facility, so under the circumstances…"

"Oh, don't worry, I will do the shopping today, in the meantime can you arrange for a loan till I get a job for I too am..."

"Of course, thank you, Dhruv, but even though I still wear your ring, I am not your responsibility."

"Aadrika, don't say that! Despite of what happened in the past I am still very fond of you for we go back a long way! Now, I will go to the shops, and you can give me a list of the things you need and what Aarush likes? Ohhh I cannot go out dressed like this, so I will quickly change into something more suitable."

He disappeared back into Aarush's room and went over to the window, pulled the net curtains and peered outside then crossed over to chair where his jeans and T shirt were thrown.

He quickly changed into them and went back to the room he had left, wearing his black suede jacket over his jeans, and his hair tied back in the usual ponytail he favoured.

Aadrika was waiting for him with a folded piece of paper which she handed to him.

"Thank you again, Dhruv, just the basic groceries will do for now, as for Aarush's likes and dislikes, well he hardly ever eats at home, and when he does, he leaves more than half of the meal! He is a very poor eater, so it will just before the two of us."

"In that case, I enjoyed the Chinese and was thinking of having the same?"

"No thank you, Dhruv, that would not be fair, don't worry, I will make dinner."

"If you say so, Aadrika, I hope Aarush will be back by the time I come back? I have not met him as yet and think he is much too young to be out so much."

"It is okay, he is with Anika, you might remember her, she has been a good friend to me. Her son is the same age as Aarush, and she stayed with me when you left, Sometimes I think he thinks of her as his mother for she always picks hm up from school and takes him back to her house. Anyway, whilst you are gone, I will call Anil and see what he has to say!"

"Good luck with that!"

Dhruv waved, opened the door and went outdoors, glad to leave the flat for he found it to be suffocating.

There was a slight breeze, and the sun was pouring through the leaves of trees.

He walked to the store, which was nearby, but before he started shopping, went to the ATM to withdraw some money and saw that, just as Anil had told him, he had transferred only half of the money in his account he had taken from Aadrika.

Dhruv put the cash carefully in his wallet, wondering what Khushboo would think if she knew about his actions and felt ashamed.

He started walking through the aisles, one hand picking out the requested items and placing them in the trolley and the other holding the paper list that Aadrika had given him.

As he strolled through them, he passed some women wearing trousers that were low on their waists, looking at packets then putting them back, whilst others pushed crying children perched on the trolleys trying different ways to quieten them.

He had planned to renew his relationship with his wife Aadrika, and had it not been for Khushboo with her slim ankles, fine boned wrists and her beautiful almond eyes shining out from her heart shaped face, he would have kept to his original plan. and he was sure he would have succeeded, for had he not subtly manipulated her into letting him live in her flat?

In truth, he thought himself to be single and loved the advantages the life involved. Dhruv realised that it was much easier to know nothing about a woman but just enjoy an easy-going and casual relationships except when it came to Khushboo, he wanted to know everything about her.

But whenever he thought of marriage, he thought it only to a form of insanity in which love hovered permanently on the edge of frustration, and if one valued one's marriage, one built a barricade around yourself and your thoughts. And not to let one's eyes linger on, say, a pretty woman with slim ankles, almond eyes and dimples!

He was surprised at how his thoughts, since yesterday, had drifted towards Khusboo. He reached into his pocket and caressed the card with her number on it, wanting to keep it safe and secure next to his body where he hoped, one day, she would be too!

Having gone through the list and having checked out of the store, he walked home with the bags, passing a short man with thinning white hair rubbing his hands together and nervously looking around him. Dhruv looked at him curiously, and had it not been for his white hair, and twinkling eyes, Dhruv thought he looked like a man who had been up to no good!

Chapter 58

He bounded up the steps that led to Aadrika's block of flats with the bags of shopping and rang the bell. Aadrika opened the door with a smile and took them from him and went into the kitchen, where she unpacked the groceries and put them in the proper places.

"Dhruv, thank you very much, getting the groceries done has been a load of my mind, now can I make you tea or coffee?"

"Coffee would be fine Aadrika." Dhruv pulled out a chair and sat on the kitchen table taking out a packet of cigarettes from his pocket, took one out, then lighted it with flick of his gold lighter.

"Did you ring Anil.?"

"Yes, I did, and please can you push my laptop to one side?" Aadrika answered putting the kettle to boil and laying out the mugs.

She took out a plate and from the unit took out a pack of biscuits from the shelf.

"Right, what did he have to say for himself?" Dhruv asked, putting the laptop on one side and taking a puff from his cigarette.

"Once again there was no reply and went straight to voicemail." Aadrika concentrated on making the coffee.

He put his hand in his pocket and again caressed the card Khusboo had given him and wished this week would be over soon so he could call her.

Aadrika meanwhile stacked the biscuits on the plate, poured the boiling water into the mugs and brought them over to the table, and having placed them on it and sat on a chair opposite Dhruv.

She placed her elbows on the table and smiled softly, forgetting her problems, feeling warm and sleepy in Dhruv's company, as if someone had wrapped a blanket over her protectively

"I don't really need anything except coffee, Aadrika," Dhruv took the mug and held in between his hands.

"I felt guilty after you felt for you had not had a proper breakfast, just toast and coffee so thought you must be hungry. I will cook something later and till then the biscuits should tide you over."

"Aadrika don't worry, I have bought a delicious loaf of bread so a sandwich and soup will be fine." Dhruv wiped his forehead then continued to puff at his cigarette.

Aadrika got up from the table, opened the one of the units and took out an ashtray which she placed on the table.

"Dhruv you must really stop smoking I have never seen you without a cigarette in your hand!"

"That is not true, Aadrika, I remember lots of occasions where I did not smoke!" Dhruv replied indignantly.

"Yeh, right." However, Aadrika thought it best to change the subject. "Dhruv, you know that while you were out, I thought about me and Anil and came to the conclusion that I was not worthy enough to spend time with!" Aadrika wiped the tears that had welled up in her eyes with the back of her hand.

"Aadrika! You would not want a man like Anil to validate you, you should set your standards high, woman! That man stole from you and has left you without any money!"

"Yes, I know, but you know that was my fault too for trusting him!" Aadrika gave a pretty but critical shrug and to Dhruv even her gestures now seemed different, but maybe that was because he was seeing her with different eyes?

Aadrika lifted her hands helplessly, feeling a rush of emotion, then lifted her chin, humiliated at the thought that Dhruv might be under the impression that she loved Anil! She blushed and dropped her eyes, her lashes lying on her cheeks like wings.

"So, I see you had your laptop out, have you tried emailing Anil?" Dhruv asked as he crushed the butt of his cigarette into the ashtray.

"No, I don't have his email address and internet is not as easily available in India as it is here." Aadrika replied. "I was going through my account in the hope that this was all a mistake on Anil's part, and he had returned the money, but things are just as they were..."

Aadrika sighed, pulled back her chair and walked over to the window to open it and let out the stale smell of cigarettes. Didn't Dhruv understand there was such a thing as passive smoking which was just as dangerous to non-smokers? She walked back from the window, cleared the table then stood at the sink washing them after which she dried her hands on the dishcloth and returned to the table.

"Not only was I checking my account but emailed my boss if he could loan me some money"

"That is a good idea, Aadrika, they can take if off your salary so you can pay it back in instalments."

"No Dhruv it is not a good idea, for I think William, my boss, is a bigot, and I feel that this might just give him an opportunity to be indebted to him."

"Even if that is the case, would it not be worth it Aadrika? For you know our arrangement was only temporary and I have to move out at some point? I think I am becoming a burden on you whilst you are dealing with your problems,"

Aadrika flinched at the words that were uttered so casually, and it was as if somebody had grabbed her by the shoulders, spun her around and forced her to come face to face with the reality that Dhruv had not changed, He was still the irresponsible man who did not want to be tied down and who would run at the first sign of a problem.

She took a deep shaky breadth and put her hand to her forehead which was aching for she had noticed recently that she was suffering more and more from them. It seemed to her that all the niceties that made her a socially acceptable grown up had been stripped away, first by Dhruv, then by Anil and finally by Dhruv again! Now she only had Aarush to cling on to now, even though he was away most of the time!

She felt miserable when she thought that she had not really lived life, because she had only come across men who were out to exploit her, whereas all she had wanted was for them to love and treat her with respect. For that, in Aadrika's mind, would illustrate the distinction between want and need.

Dhruv had only stayed one with her, but during that time she had been wrapped in a warm and cosy bubble of domesticity in his company, but apparently it had been one sided! She thought sadly that there was nothing better than to be wanted and needed, and nothing worse to be rejected nonetheless, she decided to talk to Dhruv frankly about how she felt.

"Dhruv, I was under the impression that we could have tried again since we have both matured and the fact that you wanted to settle down now?"

"Yes, I had, and I am sorry if you got the wrong impression, I am fond of you, have been, and seeing you again after all this time brought back my feelings, for you, But the one day I spent with you also stirred up old feelings of resentment. Till now I have not met Aarush, you are still so besotted with him there is no room for anybody else, and yes, I know that he has been staying with your friend, but is he not too young to be away from his mother for such long periods of time?"

Aadrika pulled herself up and glared at him, "For your information, whilst you were away, he has been home and is sleeping in my room! He is tired and you can meet him once he is awake."

She opened the laptop angrily to check her email and noticed there was one from William, in which he had agreed that a loan could be organised for her and to come see him first thing Monday morning. Aadrika jumped up with a smile and hugged Dhruv her eyes shining, her earlier resentment about Dhruv questioning her parental skills forgotten.

"Dhruv my boss is going to organise a loan for me that would tide me over till the next paycheck!"

"I am happy for you Aadrika, you have learnt a lesson from this, don't' trust anyone! Now I need to find myself a job and a flat."

"Dhruv, you know you are welcome to stay here till you do, in fact I quite liked it, for a time it was like the good old days."

"Yes, it was and thanks for being so understanding, Aadrika, Now, I think I will go out for a walk and have at a look at the shop window, sometimes they have jobs listed there."

"I don't know what the situation for unemployment is because of the pandemic, but, but before you go, have something to eat, I'll make a sandwich."

And when Dhruv nodded his head, she deftly sliced the loaf of bread, buttered it added lettuce and cumber added some mayonnaise and pepper placed it on a plate then handed it to Dhruv after she had cut the sandwich in half.

Dhruv had watched, fascinated for she had made the sandwich quickly and deftly and when Aadrika saw Dhruv's face, smiled. "I make this for Aarush, not that he likes it, most of it goes in the bin."

"Thanks, Aadrika that does look delicious, but I will take it with me and leave you to sort your things for tomorrow is Monday."

"Alright, Dhruv, as you wish" Aadrika packed the sandwich in a bag, her mind already racing ahead to the interview with William and how she was to present her case so emailed William confirming the meeting with him on Monday morning to discuss the loan.

"Dhruv, I am going to bed now, but before you do, can you bring your things from Aarush's room and keep them in the sitting room?"

"Sure of course Aadrika, I was going to do so anyway." Dhruv said as he left the room to get his baggage from Aarush's room. "Sorry, is that why he is was sleeping in your bedroom?"

Aadrika nodded her head, put her hand to her hair twined one strand around her forefinger and twitched her mouth into an odd smile.

"Goodnight Dhruv." She said abruptly and left the room.

She went to her bedroom changed into her nightie, drew the curtains and sank into bed pulling the quilt over her head and retreated into a world where there was only her, and she thought sadly, would be only her, no Anil and no Dhruv.

She closed her eyes and pressed the back of her head into her pillow, which was so soft and yielding that it seemed to ridicule her tense and overwrought body. Aadrika's fingers dug into the quilt, twisting and turning its cover as she thought of how Anil had used her, she felt drained of energy

After some time, she took her head out of the pillows and lay quietly, her eyes wide open, an occasional tear falling and trickling down her cheek,

The room was enveloped by wind and shadows, and she looked up sharply when she heard Darpan faintly calling out to her. She trembled when she recalled how she had found his body hanging and felt she was being driven to the edge of sanity and. just a little nudge of being exploited yet again would send her flying over it. However, the thought of Aarush brought her comfort and she vowed, that unlike what occurred with Darpan, she would not let him down but take care and support him.

Since her bedroom was at the back of her flat, there was no noise or light from the street, but occasionally Aadrika would hear a car drive down the road, and when it did, its headlights would swish through the curtains on the window, and when its light swept the room, an orange glow would tinge the ceiling briefly, however she was so nervous that every little creak bump and rattle of wind against the window made her jump.

Chapter 59

Aadrika got up early the next morning feeling nervous for she was meeting William.

She wanted to make a good impression so opened her wardrobe and chose a pair of black trousers with a white shirt and black jacket, and after she was dressed, crossed the room to her dressing table.

The dressing table was very handy and practical for it had a tow of drawers in a curve with 3 mirrors, On the dressing table were her bottles of perfumes and a box that contained curlers safety pins and other odd hairgrips.

In one of drawers she kept her earrings, and she opened one to bring out her pearl studs After she had clipped them on her ears, she brushed her hair and applied lipstick then pouted at herself in the mirror, turning her head coquettishly from side to side to see that she had only covered her lips.

After giving her light make up a once over, she went to the kitchen, but before she did, opened Aarush' room to check if he was asleep, still troubled by Darpan's voice the previous night.

As she entered the kitchen, saw that as there was fresh coffee bubbling in the coffee maker, its aroma filled the air. To her surprise, Dhruv, like he had promised, had also put slices of bread in the toaster.

Dhruv was dressed and sitting on the chair, placidly texting on his iPhone, but looked up as Aadrika entered the kitchen and whistled as he saw her.

"Well, well, we are dressed to impress, aren't we?" he smiled as put his iPhone away.

"I will take that as a compliment, thanks for having breakfast ready, the coffee smells delicious. But what are you doing up so early Dhruv? You know you could sleep in."

"Thanks, Aadrika, but when I went for a walk yesterday, I saw some jobs that were listed on the window of a newsagent and one or two seemed interesting. I thought I would go see about them first thing and because I was hoping to meet Aarush before he goes to school." He tried to peer around Aadrika's shoulder.

"He is not awake, Dhruv! Anika will come and pick him up in a couple of hours!" Aadrika pushed her hair from her forehead as she poured herself a mug of coffee and switched on the toaster.

"I am sorry, you thought I was going to be home till she came, no worries I can go later."

"Don't worry about it." Aadrika replied hurriedly as she buttered the toast that had jumped out from the toaster, hot and brown. "Yummy this is nice! Anika has a key and will let herself in, in fact I am going to ring her up if she can come earlier."

She went out of the room leaving Dhruv sitting, his iPhone again in his hand, a puzzled expression on his face.

"Right, that is sorted." Aadrika said as she re-entered the kitchen. "We can leave when you are ready."

"You carry on Aadrika, I will wait for Anika. I would like to meet the woman who looks after my son."

"I would prefer you didn't Dhruv, at least not till I have spoken to her. Actually, she does not know that you are staying here?"

"I don't see why it would be any of her business!" Dhruv said angrily

"She has been a good friend to me Dhruv, and she is angry with you. When you left so abruptly, I turned to her for support. She came over the very instant with her son and stayed with me overnight. She was angry with you then and still is to this day. So please can we leave?"

Dhruv was too shocked to comment, it was if the clock had turned back to the time when Aarush was born, and he had bought Aadrika home. She used to lock herself in the room with Aarush and would not even allow him to hold Aarush. It had got so bad that she had prevented him from entering the room or holding him, then accused him of not caring! He had hoped that she had changed but apparently, she was just as possessive, and the only person allowed any contact with Aarush was Anika.

The circumstances were a pattern he was familiar with, for at the orphanage she had got attached to a sweet little boy, Darpan. Aadrika had wanted to name his son Darpan, and when he had insisted that he should be named Aarush, she had finally agreed.

Dhruv recalled her obsession with Darpan and how her whole life had revolved around him at the orphanage. She had been devastated when he had died, and it had taken Dhruv a lot of time and energy to put the smile back out on her face.

When they stepped out of the flat, they found that the rain had eased off and the sky was clear although still some black clouds still scowled in the distance ahead of them

"I forgot to get an umbrella; I hope it does not start raining?" Aadrika exclaimed in distress. "I still haven't got used to the weather and that I should carry an umbrella with me at all times!"

"It won't rain, Aadrika, I checked the weather." Dhruv assured her.

"Ah here we are." They had reached the underground station and the train from there would take Aadrika directly to her office.

Aadrika turned to him before entering the station. "Thank you for walking me to the underground, Dhruv and good luck with the job hunting! I will see you this evening, by the way I get home around 5.30 pm".

"It's alright, Aadrika, thanks I hope I find something! And good luck with your interview with your boss."

Aadrika smiled, mimed a thank you waved and disappeared among the crowd of people; those going to work were in a hurry nearly all wearing masks, the others who were not were walking slowly whilst gesticulating laughing and talking animatedly into mobile phones, their masks dangling from their ears.

A train pulled up with a screeching sound, stopped, and as the doors of the carriage opened, Aadrika stepped into one., As usual the train was crowded, but she found there was an empty seat next to a woman dressed in a black suit who had her laptop open on her lap, her fingers flying over the keyboard.

Aadrika sighed with relief and sat down quickly, aware that people were pushing and shoving to find a seat. The sliding doors of the train sputtered, closed and the train moved out. Although Aadrika did not have far to go, she spent her journey thinking about her interview with William hoping there would be no problem or hitch.

Dhruv meanwhile had walked on ahead to the shops to buy a newspaper and have an English breakfast at a café he had seen the day before.

On the way, he passed an old tramp sitting on a bench, clutching a beer can. His feet were wrapped in plastic bags and a hat was pulled over his eyes as he slouched drowsily on the bench.

Dhruv felt hurt that Aadrika did not trust him enough and made a mental note of contacting Anika but knew that Aadrika would not give him Anika's address or phone number.

He had also noticed that she had not offered him her the key to her flat so that he could let himself in anytime during the day, so feeling miserable, he brought a newspaper and located the café he had seen the day before.

Having ordered an English breakfast and latte, he saw an empty table and sat in a vacant chair. As he waited for his order, he opened the newspaper, then looked at his watch, wondering if he should ring Khushboo today or leave it for the morrow. He would have liked to call her today, for he had the whole day ahead of him with nothing and nowhere to go.

He had been lying when he told Aadrika that he would be job hunting, but at that moment the waitress arrived with his breakfast and placed the tray on the table. Dhruv had not realised how hungry he was so quickly tucked into it taking an occasional sip of coffee.

He decided he was not going to look for a job, it was just not for him., he never had had one for he had always found some vulnerable woman and lived off her.

Suddenly he thought of Khushboo and could not put her in that category, either of being vulnerable or one he would like to exploit. No, he thought, for he wanted something entirely different with her, he wanted her respect and would like to take her out on his terms, pay for their dinner, in short, he would like to spoil her and treat her with respect.

But for that he needed money, so he reluctantly opened the job listing page of the newspaper and glanced over it, but seeing nothing that interested him, folded the paper, deciding he would look again tomorrow, for getting a job had to become his priority.

In the meantime, till that happened, he thought of Aadrika. if she had been so naïve as to hand over her finances to Anil, a man she barely knew, she was still Dhruv's wife, they had history and a child together; he couldn't help but wonder how far she be willing to trust him.

But then trust was a fragile commodity and only idiots gave it blindly and only bigger fools would try to put it back together when it had been crushed and shattered once, but then Aadrika was caught in a net and would have no choice but to depend on him!

However, Dhruv had not forgotten Aadrika's earlier caginess which had been quickly replaced by a sunny expression. and found that circling around her altering emotions would be exhausting which had been partly the reason he had left her, and he did not wish to go down the roller coaster of emotions again!

Chapter 60

Aadrika reached her office, and after quickly hanging up her overcoat and retouching her make-up, looked at her watch nervously, for the thought of meeting William filled her with confusion and dread as she recalled her conversations with Anil and the kind of man, he thought he was.

She took a deep breath and knocked on William's door and soon as he said 'come in' entered the room and was surprised to see that room was quite large with a leather sofa in one corner of the room.

William was standing behind his desk holding his phone to his ear with one hand, wearing a dishevelled light grey suit, the coat of which was hanging behind his chair, a loosened tie, a white shirt, the sleeves of which were folded up to his elbows

A cigarette dangled from his lips, and with the other hand he waved to Aadrika to sit in the chair opposite him and as she did, noticed the tattoos on his strong arms. On his desk were pictures of his children and there were papers scattered all over it. From the tone of his voice and the colour of his face Aadrika thought William was dealing with a problem, then hoped that was not the case for his mood might affect his decision.

He finished the call, took one last drag on the cigarette that was between his lips before crushing it in an ashtray that was already overflowing with ash and cigarette butts.

Feeling nervous Aadrika settled back in the chair and bit her lip. And she was spot on for after he had finished his call, William stared at it as if he were going to tell her to bite it off! However, once he had cooled off, sat and had a sip of his nearly cold coffee, and although he did not have good news, thought that he did not want their relationship to become strained.

Besides which, he had noticed the fact that although Aadrika was conservatively and professionally dressed, her attire was not hiding her curves but rather, emphasising them!

He closed his eyes for a second, his mind visualising the fluid and graceful way she had entered the room and imagined what it would be like to have her in his bed, the dark waves of her black hair spread across his chest. William was a man with a need to control with an innate ability, not only to understand vulnerability but to ruthlessly exploit it; and this was an opportunity he did not want to ignore, especially when the possible victim was Aadrika.

William was like a bird of prey circling in the sky watched to swoop down on any unsuspecting victim, its talons ready to mark and tear into the target's flesh.

As he looked at her, he chewed on a pencil, and thought that the situation could pan out perfectly, at home he had Mary to bully and terrorise and, in the office, he would have Aadrika, who he had always lusted after from afar and who would, after today, feel so thankful to him that she would do anything he asked.

"Now, what can I do for you?" he asked narrowing his eyes "Your email mentioned some financial problems you are having?"

Aadrika explained the situation she was in and how she had been conned by her friend and how he had cleared her account.

"I am afraid the bank is not willing to give me any overdraft so I would be grateful if could have my salary??"

Aadrika's voice sounded so warm and lovely that William gritted his teeth, surprised at his body's reaction to it, and could not help visually what was under that professional attire. He was frustrated at his reaction too, for, she was, after all, from a different culture with a different colour skin! As such she did not deserve his care and attention, but he thought, 'she can have all my attention, but only when under me!'

As Aadrika sat biting her lip, waiting for William's answer, he looked at her and thought that she had lips that just begged for a man to explore and find out if they were as soft as they looked!

However, William knew he had to be careful as the there was a law protecting women from sexual harassment at work, as Emma, one of his employees had reminded him, but Aadrika seemed too meek and naïve to be aware of the law.

However, he had learnt his lesson first with Emma than with Anil who could have filed a case against him, which is why William had agreed to his leave. But Aadrika was a very modest girl, and to get what he wanted, he would have to tread carefully, very carefully.

"Look, Aadrika, I am sorry that you are in this position, especially since I did say in my email that I will help you." William paused, looked away then looked back at her." Since then, I have spoken to our Finance team, and they have declined this unusual request."

Aadrika looked at him in dismay with wide open eyes and put her delicate hand over her mouth. "Sir, I have a young son to take care of and…"

"I am sorry, but look I might have another solution, so what do say, we discuss it over dinner tonight? I have a meeting in a few minutes that I cannot miss. But I promise, after the meeting, I will call some friends who can loan you some money, but I can only confirm that in the evening, so we can meet for dinner, and I can update you then."

Aadrika had heard his words with a sinking heart, but when he mentioned that he had contacts who could loan her the money, her spirits rose. Also, there was something vulnerable about him as he gazed at her like a forlorn puppy. And after all, he was only trying to help her, so she agreed to meet him for dinner, and before leaving they decided on the place and time.

He walked her to the door, and when Aadrika looked up at him to thank him, felt uncomfortable for he was looking at her intently. She blushed and both her cheeks became red, and her forehead suddenly felt sweaty as she clutched her jacket tightly around her,

"So, till evening, Aadrika."

He held out his hand formally and Aadrika thought it would be rude if she did not return the gesture so put her hand in the palm of his hand and as soon as she had, he tightened his grip on her and held it for a long time.

"Excuse me sir, I have to go." Aadrika tried to free her hand confused by his attitude and the glint in his eyes.

"Okay, till this evening them."

William loosened his hold until his hand loosely circled her wrist which he brought to his lips, liking the feel of the soft skin of her delicate hand and the expression in her almond shaped eyes which had widened. He felt a stirring and thought to himself that he would surely have her one day, in fact, so strong was his desire that he felt himself not caring about the law and the consequences that his actions might have.

Aadrika quickly opened the door and fled to her office, wondering if William had other intentions than to just to lend her the money? However, she dismissed the idea, for they worked in the same organisation and would surely run into each other daily.

She went to her seat, turned back to computer screen and let her hands lay limply on the key. Aadrika had always been optimistic woman, but now wondered if she had been wating all these years for something nice that was never going to happen?

It seemed that being a wife did not complete her, neither did being a girlfriend/mistress, as a mother she was a failure for Aarush preferred to spend time with Anika than his own mother, and she felt that it was only when she had been with Darpan at the orphanage that she had felt complete!

Her colleague, Emma, was a young girl, studious looking with wide grey eyes behind narrow glasses looked at her curiously. Her long blond was braided, which she occasionally tossed over her shoulder.

"Hi Aadrika, is everything alright? How did the meeting go?"

"Thanks Emma, it was fine." However, Aadrika's face was pale for somehow meeting William had left her feeling dirty. She took off her jacket and hung it at the back of her chair.

She shook off the feeling, he had done nothing untoward but politely kiss her hand, but it was the way his lips had lingered on them and the glint in his eyes that disturbed her. Once again, she thought that maybe she had made a mistake in meeting him out of hours but what other choice did she have?

After some time, she felt restless and feeling cold she so stood up got up from her desk and walked towards the window, rubbing her arms. She stared out of her window, her eyes, looking at the fluttering red leaves of a tree, some of who, helpless against the breeze, fell to the floor.

Emma felt that Aadrika needed space, respected it and so did not talk to her, however, she something was wrong for although they were not friends, she was concerned for her for she knew that William was a womaniser and Aadrika was a naïve girl...

He had groped her once, but she had stood up to him and told him that she would sue him for sexual harassment, so, from that day on, he had kept his distance from her from since then. But she knew that he had not changed and Aadrika was too nice and meek, the kind of woman Willian could easily manipulate and exploit,

Emma was sure Aadrika was not aware about workplace harassment and bullying and wished she had made more of an effort in getting to know Aadrika so she could help her now.

Chapter 61

Aadrika made a hot mug of coffee, returned to her desk and placed the mug on her it.,

Emma tried to talk to he again, but when Aadrika replied with a polite 'I have a lot of work to catch up on' which was another way of saying that she did not want to talk. Emma did not talk to her again for the remainder of the day and at 4:45 everybody in the room started getting ready to leave for home.

Aadrika had initially planned to leave to meet William straight from work, but as the restaurant they had decided to meet near Aadrika's house, so she decided to go home change and freshen up before meeting him

She quickly wore her jacket and literally ran from the office, fumbling in her bag for her mobile to tell Dhruv about her plans for the evening and once on the train sent him a text that she would be home at 5 but would be leaving again at 7 and that Aarush would stay over at Anika's house.

Just before the train reached her station, he had texted her back saying that he too would be visiting his friend for dinner.

Aadrika was glad that at least Dhruv would have a place to live, although she had not told him to move out, but he had made it quite clear that staying with her was only a temporary arrangement.

Within a day, she had seen his restless nature unfold before her eyes and felt sad for she missed the carefree Dhruv she had known and loved, the glimpse of whom she had had during coffee at the airport. Although it was nice having him around at first, soon she found his presence to be suffocating, so much so she felt she could not breath! How dare he give her parenting skills?

She reached home and after a quick bath, decided on black jeans with a cardigan. She applied some light makeup and took out a box in which she kept her earrings, looked at them thoughtfully before deciding on a small pair of artificial diamond studs that glittered in the light. As she clipped them on, she thought of Dhruv and of his friend and hoped everything was going well.

She sighed as she looked at herself in the mirror, wore her boots, then slung her handbag over her shoulder hoped that William would have some good news for her.

She opened the front and when she saw that it was raining slightly, turned back and changed into her raincoat which she buckled tightly around her waist, opened the door and let herself out.

She was early so decided to walk to the restaurant, passing a crowd of youths on the way who were gathered in the corner of the street, smoking and passing a large bottle around, which Aadrika thought must be alcohol. If it was, she hoped they would leave soon. She did not want to stay long at the restaurant, in fact, she had thought she would meet William, see what he had to say and leave.

However, he was going out of his way to do her a favour and Aadrika did want to seem rude or ungrateful.

She grimaced when her foot sank into a pothole in the pavement, soaking her up to ankle and she was glad she had chosen to wear boots and ducked beneath the ivy hanging in front of a building and shivered as she shook the dirty water from her boots.

She reached the restaurant which was brightly lit with coloured lights, had parquet floors, small tables and bentwood chairs. She had suggested this restaurant because of its semi-formal atmosphere and friendly staff.

As soon as she entered the restaurant, a waitress walked up with a smile and when Aadrika told her she was meeting someone, was shown to a table.

She had just sat down when William entered the restaurant and when he saw her, smiled waved and walked over to her table. He had been thinking of her the entire day, of her enticing curves beneath her professional attire and her almond shaped eyes, looking up at him shyly yet so seductively. He had been thinking of a way that would entangle her firmly, yet surely in the net he was going to weave around her

"Hi Aadrika," William looked her over appreciatively for although she was dressed casually, the cardigan she had chosen did not quite hide her curves and slim waist. Her hair was coiled and rested in a thick bun on her neck with a few wisps that fell on her face and softened and framed it.

"Hello William." Aadrika smiled weakly, feeling uneasy and again confused to the reason behind it. She had thought that her earlier feeling of awkwardness in their meeting in the morning had been a result of her over-active imagination, but she was feeling uncomfortable again, so wondered again if her meeting with William in an informal environment had been a wise decision on her part?

Suddenly she thought of Emma, who she felt had wanted to warn her, for ever since her meeting with William, she had looked curiously at Aadrika. And during her tea break had brought her chair close to hers, which Emma never did for she always used that time to text her boyfriend. Aadrika had had turned away and seeing the detached look on Aadrika's face. Emma had turned back to her desk and brought out her mobile and began texting

Aadrika now felt she should have talked to her for it looked that Emma wanted to tell her something of importance.

The waitress who had seen Aadrika to the table walked over with a tablet in her hands and a smile that seemed to be permanently and artificially fixed on her face.

William turned towards Aadrika with a gleam in his eyes.

"We'll order some drinks first; would you like some wine Aadrika?"

"Coke for me please." Aadrika answered feeling flustered as William looked deep in her eyes.

"We'll order food later." He told the waitress as he ordered coke for Aadrika and beer for himself then turned his attention to Aadrika.

"So, you don't drink, not even a glass?" he asked and when Aadrika shook her head asked, "You're not driving are you?"

I do drink, but only sometimes, but I prefer a cold coke and no I don't drive, I live nearby and have walked here, the exercise will do be good,"

She smiled as the waitress arrived with their drinks and placing them on the table, stook waiting for their food order.

"Shall we order Aadrika and whilst we wait for the food, I will fill you with how I can help you."

Aadrika had intended to leave after finishing her drink but thought it would look rude so ordered a light salad for herself.

William on the other hand ordered their special and as soon as the waitress had left, picked up his glass in his strong hand and gulped it quickly, smacking his thick lips, running his tongue over them then wiped his mouth with the back of his hand.

"Aadrika, I had meant it when I said this morning that I will do what I can to help you." Aadrika had taken a sip from her glass and when she put it back on the table tapped the table with her delicate hand.

"Thank you, William, I appreciate it." Aadrika answered tremulously.

"Don't stress about it, I am sure I will need your help sometime." There was a glint in William's eyes as he put out his hand and took hold of Aadrika's delicate hand. Not wanting to let it go, he bought it to his lips and kissed her wrist with his swollen lips, his tongue lingering on her delicate arm

Aadrika quickly withdrew her hand, putting it on her lap, the expression on her face unreadable.

"Sorry, Aadrika, but you are too beautiful, anyway back to our problem, I spoke to my contacts who I thought would be able to help, unfortunately they cannot so..."

"Oh no William!" Aadrika's eyes widened, and her hand covered her mouth.

"You did not let me finish, Aadrika, although the office cannot help, I have savings which I am willing to loan you till your next salary."

"Thank you, William but I cannot accept!"

William passed an envelope across the table.

"There are 500 pounds in that envelope, take it look after yourself and your son."

Aadrika eyed the envelope debating whether she should take it, then decided she would, for it would solve all her problem and William was her boss, so, regardless of all she had heard, felt she should trust him, so with a trembling hand, took the envelope and as she did, the only thought in William's mind was 'Gotcha'

Chapter 62

As Khusboo got ready for bed, she thought about Ekta and Aryan, and how, in their conversation that evening, Ekta had revealed how Aryan, had treated her, and the knowledge only strengthened her resolve not to marry.

However, these days, whenever she thought of marriage, she thought of Dhruv with his brown twinkling eyes and her heart skipped a beat when she recalled how, when he had helped pick up the things that has fallen from her purse, their hands had touched briefly.

At that time, she had felt a spark, as if she had been electrocuted! And ever since that day, she found that Dhruv was invading her internal space and it annoyed her how deeply that brief encounter was affecting her. She put her hand on her chest, took a deep breath and called Aiysha to find out whether she would be coming back to London soon, as Chauvin's, the police officer who had killed George Floyd, sentence was due to passed soon, or if she would be sent to cover another assignment directly from Minnesota.

It was a short call because Aiysha was off to interview George Floyd's family and girlfriend for the final sentencing had been passed without any community uprising. She told her that her office was due to phone her that evening with details of her next assignment which was most probably going to be in Afghanistan.

As Khushboo finished the call and put the iPhone on the side table, she smiled slightly for it had been nice to hear Aiysha's voice, then sat on the bed with her head in her hands, for she had an urgent problem that she had to deal with.

Since the call from the bank, she had put the matter at the back of her mind, but had since received another call from them, and to her shock and dismay, was told that her father had not paid the mortgage on their house for the last three months and were in the process of repossessing the house! She was worried as to how she was going to handle the situation for her father had never discussed the home finances with her, which he should have done before going abroad!

She thought the solution would lie in her dad's study were he kept all his paper so got up from the bed and opened the door of the study and gave a gasp for there were papers scattered all over the room. As she picked up one paper and put it on the desk, thought that it would take her a long time to sift through them and have the required information for the mortgage society.

So, after some time when she had barely managed to collect the papers and stack them on the desk, decided she would get through the papers the next day, in the meanwhile, she was hoping to get through to her father who would have the answers for the bank... so yawned and went back to her room, read for a little while then went to sleep.

She woke up the next morning with the sun shining through the curtains. She looked at her clock and gave a cry for she had slept through the alarm. She quickly had a bath changed into grey comfortable trousers with a trendy top, wore her loafers tied her hair into a ponytail and ran downstairs, keeping her mobile handy for the expected call from the bank

Her mum and Ekta were ready for their visit to Reyansh, which Khushboo had forgotten.

"Khusboo, come, sit I have made your favourite Indian breakfast."

"You mean stuffed roti Mum?"

"Yes, the works, with pickle curd and I will make the tea, the Indian way with all the spices."

"Mum, how am I ever going to go back to work and miss all this?" Khushboo exclaimed "I have a good mind to resign and stay home..." She grinned as her mother placed a Chapati that was stuffed with potatoes on her plate. "Yummy." She added some butter and pickle on the chapati then put the curd in the bowl. "Mum Ekta come and sit…"

"You carry on, Khusboo have it whilst it is hot, I am making the last one and will join you as soon as I am done."

"Yes, and the tea is ready too." Ekta poured the tea from the pan into the three mugs and bought them to the table.

In between mouthfuls, Khusboo looked at Ekta. "Ekta you are looking lovely in those grey and pink trousers." She was glad to see that Ekta was back to her old self, maybe talking about her failed marriage had done her some good. She hoped so for Ekta deserved to live a normal life and she was sure any man would be lucky to marry her...

Just as she had finished her tea, her mobile buzzed and vibrated and she snatched it up quickly and when she saw it was the bank, quickly rose, pushed back her chair, excused herself and left the kitchen to take the call.

She listened for a few minutes, occasionally asking questions with a serious expression on her face, for the man from the bank was confirming the uneasy feeling she had had, and when she informed him that her father would be back in a few weeks to clear the matter, said they could not wait that long. However, once Khushboo explained the situation of having to go through his papers again, they decided to give her another 24 hours

She quickly noted down the required information and having finished the call, she did not go back to the kitchen but stood and took a deep breath. how could she tell her mother what her father had done? She had to go through her father's papers again, at least she had organised them tidily so it would not take her long.

For now, they had to see Reyansh and before she entered the kitchen, tried her father's phone again, but this time she was not even getting a connection, not knowing if it was because the Farmers protest had been denied internet access or because covid cases had spiked in India. And maybe that was why the bank was not willing to wait, for nobody was being allowed back in London, at least not unless they had quarantined.

She put the mobile in her pocket and went into the kitchen with a cheery "Shall we go mum?"

But Ekta and Sameera were busy clearing the table and putting them in the sink so did not hear her.

"Mum why don't you leave those, Olga will do them, she is late today but we will leave anyway, she has a key. I want to come back early for I have to prepare for going back to work...I used to enjoy my work, but now, I want to stay home!"

"Well thanks to corona most people are working from home, I don't see why your office is not allowing its employees to do the same." Sameera commented as she wore her coat.

"Mum, you know everything is back to normal now that everyone has been vaccinated, but you are looking nice! Ekta what have you done to her? She never used to take care about what she wore!" Khushboo exclaimed

"For starters because nobody is criticising me!" Sameera replied tersely "And Khusboo, your problem is that you, like your father do not notice, I am the same I was before, you just dd not notice!"

"Well, there is something different," Khusboo muttered as they left the house. "Oh, I know, it is the confidence that you have gained since Ekta has been staying with us. You know that makes a lot of difference to one's personality."

As they walked towards the car, they found that although it was a bright day, the daylight was bathed with the coolness of winter even though it was spring.

"What can I say, your dad never had the time to talk to me and you are always so busy."

"Are you forgetting our after-dinner talks Mum?" Khusboo said as she opened the car door.

"Sorry, they were the highlight of my day, just forget I mentioned it." Sameera said got in the front seat and tying the belt around her.

Sameera was wearing beige and brown Salwar Kameez, loose Indian pants that varied according to the latest fashion, with a matching shirt that reached her knees with a dupatta, a matching stole of the same fabric across her shoulder.

"Okay Khusboo, you are right, as usual, but you know I will miss you too for I too have got used to having you around. Time has flown so fast I think in no time at all we will be going to the airport to receive your father!"

Ekta sat quietly at the back, Sameera and Khushboo unaware that Aryan's betrayal had scarred her deeper than a convict with a chain could although Ekta did her best not to show it.

She blamed herself, thought that Aryan's cheating on her was a reflection on her, for it was she who had picked him to be her partner, a man incapable of love.

Although she had had the pride to throw him out at last, pride was a poor substitute for a human touch she craved for at night. Ekta's heart was heavy as she recalled past wounds and as they passed a park, watched the expanse of mowed grass with litter bins overflowing and women with pushchairs out for some fresh air.

Chapter 63

They were not late, and after asking for directions to Reyansh's office, walked down the corridor, passing a few people sitting on chairs, waiting to be called, some who had appointments others who had just arrived hoping they would be seen, but all who had one thing in common – they all looked anxious and distressed.

As they knocked and entered the office, Reyansh got up with a smile from behind his desk, his hand outstretched.

"Come in come in, hello Khushboo, we have spoken many times! Thanks for your help, this must be your mother and her sister?"

"Hi Reyansh, and yes this is my mother and her friend Ekta."

Reyansh was wearing jeans with a white cotton shirt whose sleeves were rolled up just below his elbow and they could feel the warmth radiating from him. He was an attractive man with thick wavy black hair that was beginning to grey at the sides, but which gave him a distinguished look. His eyes twinkled behind dark rimmed glasses that framed his eyes.

After seating them, he asked if they would like something to drink.

"It has been very hectic today, so if you don't mind, I will make myself a cup of coffee for myself and we can chat whilst I have my break! Are you sure I cannot get you anything?"

When the women refused saying they had just had a traditional Indian breakfast, enough to last them the day, Reyansh smiled and came back with a steaming mug in his hand and sat on the swivel chair.

"Hmm sounds delicious, my favourite too, unfortunately I don't have the luxury of them." He sighed.

When he noticed Ekta studying him silently, smiled at her for she looked uncomfortable, her hands on her lap.

"Khusboo, I presume you have told the ladies about our work?" Reyansh asked taking a sip from his mug and when Khusboo nodded, continued "how do you think you can help us?"

"Well, between them Reyansh I think they have a lot to offer, obviously not from the legal angle, but they are Asian women who have had similar experiences and…no Ekta you explain what you went through."

At first Ekta looked distressed but realised she must do so, so repeated what she had told Sameera and Ekta., After she had finished relating the events of her traumatic marriage and how it had affected her, she dropped her eyes, embarrassed but when her eyes flew up and met Reyansh's, they only held understanding and compassion, there was no condemnation or accusation in them, but kindness and her eyes filled with tears.

Reyansh meanwhile was wondering how her husband, no, anyone could not only leave such a kind and beautiful woman but treat her so cruelly. He had only just met her, but he admired the way she spoke about her husband, with not a hint of spite despite the way Aryan had treated her! He thought her to be a sensitive woman with a soft caring heart and a will that was even stronger.

Although Ekta looked elegant and poised, what he did not know was that she was actually a shy and modest woman, in fact she was so shy that she did not like meeting new people and when she did, had heart palpitation. Her heart was beating fast too at the moment, however, when she looked at Reyansh, was reassured by the look of kindness and feeling of warmth that radiated from him.

Reyansh, meanwhile admired her strong character, and when he looked at her closely saw that she was also an extremely beautiful woman with nicely shaped lips under a pert nose and hair that was thick and which she had plaited then knotted into a bun at the nape of her long neck. She had flawless skin under the long sweep of her lashes that fringed eyes that looked innocent and pure despite the suffering she had endured.

But when he saw the tears in Ekta's eyes, thought her wounds were still too raw and tender, for she would have to relive her ordeal each time she spoke to the women, which would only hinder her healing.

Suddenly he wanted to protect her, he wanted her to heal her so she could start her life with another man who would treat her as she deserved to be treated and his heartbeat faster when he thought he would like to be that man. So, till she was ready, he needed help with his paperwork, and she seemed to be suited to look after them till she was ready to listen to the problems of the ladies.

"And what about your mother, Khushboo?"

"Mum hasn't been through the horrible situation Ekta went through, but she had to adjust living in a new country, had no friends thereby losing her confidence and I think that by talking to other women in similar positions she and the women both would both profit by her experiences."

"I agree, but I think Ekta's wounds are still tender, and it won't help her to come to terms with them if she has to repeat her trauma to others again and again. So Ekta, how would you feel if you helped with some work in my office? I have a backlog of work so would welcome a helping hand, that is it okay with you?"

"Oh yes, absolutely, I would love to help you in any way I can! In fact, you are right for when I was talking to you about my marriage, I felt all the anger and suffering again and don't think that would be good for the women to hear."

"That is settled then, when can they start?" Reyansh asked and suddenly he was looking forward to coming to work.

"I am going to work the day after tomorrow but have some important things to take care of so would like to drop them tomorrow morning, but both would like to work in the same place, if possible, not only for morale but it would make travelling easy."

After Reyansh had explained that they would only be working in a separate department in the building they were in, he asked where they would be coming from, to give them directions. When Khusboo gave her address, he looked at her in surprise.

"But that is just round the corner from me!" he exclaimed. "I live in my parents' house, they found a smaller place for themselves, anyway, that is one problem solved; I can give you a lift sometimes, but not in the evenings I have to work late so…"

"Oh, that would be nice Reyansh, but please, they are not your responsibility."

"Thank you Reyansh, that is nice of you, but you don't have to, as for working late, you will not have to anymore for Ekta will be there to help you." Sameera smiled.

"It would be my pleasure, Sameera,"

However, although he was talking to her, he could not take his eyes off Ekta, and both Khusboo and Sameera exchanged knowing glances for they had not missed the look of affection that had briefly crossed Reyansh's face.

"And you must come for dinner one day, Reyansh!" Sameera said as they got ready to leave.

"Thank you Sameera, but that will not be necessary, Ekta, how long will you be in London for?" Reyansh asked as he ushered them out.

"Oh, permanently, so am looking for a job, but until then would love to make myself useful in any way that I can. Ekta replied softly

"That is wonderful, maybe I can help you there too for sometimes we have vacancies in our organisation."

"That would be wonderful, Reyansh, I would love that!"
As he ushered them out, Khusboo saw Reyansh's face fall as he said goodbye but then brightened when Khusboo asked what time she should drop them

"Oh, not very early, it is their first day so." He said his goodbye, his eyes lingering on Ekta before he turned and walked back into his office. As they walked towards the car, Khusboo turned to Ekta.

"So, what did you think Ekta?"

"Huh? What? Think of whom?" Ekta replied nervously then looked shyly at Khusboo.

Her nervousness confirmed that Ekta was just as attracted to Reyansh as he was to her. As soon as her mother joined her on the seat next to hers, both winked at each other, wishing, and hoping that this attraction on both sides would grow and blossom.

They made a good couple for both were kind and compassionate and after what Ekta had been through, she needed someone like Reyansh, a sincere and decent man.

Chapter 64

Khushboo wanted to deal with the bank's problem as soon as possible so drove home robotically trying to keep her mind empty, and when she stopped at a red light, looked at the time on dashboard clock and as soon as the lights changed, put her foot on the accelerator.

As soon as they reached home and Khusboo had parked the car she followed her mother and Ekta into the house. As they entered the landing Khushboo gave a cry for on table in the landing was a vase with red roses that had darkened and wilted.

"Mum, wasn't Olga supposed to get rid of the flowers?"

"Yes, she was, the vase was in the dining room, she must have bought it here on her way to throw the flowers, she must have forgotten, poor thing she has a lot to be worried about!"

"Yes, she does, no worries I will do this, I love flowers, especially roses, but not when they are all droopy and shrivelled!"

Khushboo carried the vase into the kitchen, leaving a trail of red petals across the floor behind her, which Sameera picked up as she followed her,

But only after Khushboo had thrown the flowers in the bin and cleaned the vase did she notice that there was blood on her finger for she had gripped the stems so tightly that she had not felt the thorn pierce the delicate skin of her finger!

Sameera saw the blood on her finger and gave a cry.

"Khushboo, you need to have that seen too! Here sit, I will get the first aid box out," She rummaged in the drawer, but Khushboo stopped her.

"Mum, it is only a slight prick, I have some work to do upstairs but will run the finger first in cold water."

"As long as you do it, Khusboo, do not leave it."

"Mum you worry too much." Khushboo kissed her affectionately on the cheek before disappearing upstairs.

She mounted the stairs and opened the door to her bedroom and having quickly run her finger in cold water and splashing her face, went to her father's study again.

She had to sift through her father's papers and when she thought what he had done, not only hurt   but made her angry! But Khushboo shoved both feelings at the back of her mind, aware that neither emotion, however justified, was not only unhealthy but would distract her from focusing on the problem at hand,

She had considered telling her mother for she was very wise and always knew what to do, however, when she recalled how happy she was and eager to begin her placement with Ekta, she dismissed the idea.

"Khusboo, would you like some tea, we are making some." Sameera came out into the landing and frowned when she saw her daughter's face and she became more concerned when she declined to join the for a 'chin wag'

"Yes, I would love a cup, Mother, but I will have it upstairs for I have to finish some work, just give me a shout when it is ready, and I will come down to get it."

"Okay, I'll call you when it is ready…." Sameera shouted over her shoulder as she re-entered the kitchen where Ekta had begun to clean all the dishes they had left in the morning.

"You don't have to do that Ekta," Sameera scolded her gently. "I am surprised at the mess, for Olga was supposed to be working today, maybe she did not have time to do the kitchen because I left a note for her to concentrate on changing sheets and cleaning the rest of the house."

"Don't worry about it, Sameera, I like to make myself useful, and since she was concentrating on the rest of the house, she must have forgotten t to empty the vase! But you can finish making the tea, Sameera, I have put the water on to boil in a saucepan, for spicy Indian tea!" She smiled as she continued to wash the plates. "How is Olga anyway, Sameera, we have not seen her for some time. I hope she is okay."

"Yes, she is, that is as far as I know, Khusboo is in touch with her, and once we start working with Reyansh, I think 'Raksha' will be the safest place for her, very aptly named, they give a place to stay for women who are trapped in bad marriages. Olga, hopefully, can go there directly without involving us in any way, I know that sounds selfish but..."

"Not at all, Sameera, you have to look after yourself and your family, and yes, I think so too, the sooner she leaves that man the better!"

"I agree, and thanks Ekta, for putting the water to boil, it will save time, Khusboo wants to have hers upstairs so we will go to the sitting room to have ours and then decide what to do about dinner. In the meantime, shall I fry some samosas?"

"Not for me Sameera, a hot cup of tea is all I need." Ekta wiped her hands on the kitchen towel, opened the cupboard unit and took three mugs from it.

After the tea was made, Ekta took the two cups to the lounge, whilst Sameera went to the landing and called out to Khushboo who hurried down the staircase, took the mug from her hand and went back to her father's study.

She had been through the papers, however, there was only one place left for her to look, which was in her father's desk drawer, but Khushboo hesitated when it came to forcing it open.

Her throat was dry, and she was glad of the tea her mother had made. She took a sip before continuing, for she thought that the action of breaking into her father's desk to be underhand   But when she recalled the bank manager's conversation, justified it was her father who had started the ball rolling by betraying them and all she was doing was doing was discovering to what extent he had gone to, and all she was doing now was only exchanging dishonesty for deceit if that..

Once she had the drawer opened, she found that everything was stacked in front of her neatly, not like the untidy papers that were strewed on his desk. In it were bills, payslips, chequebooks, bank statements and piles of important looking letters.

She took a deep breath, pulled up a chair, sat and rifled through the papers, and her heart sank with each document she read, but found the most damning of all from the bank confirming re-mortgage of their house It was dated three months ago ,followed by two letters requesting payment of the mortgage, the last three months payment had been overlooked,, and a third saying that if a payment was not paid immediately, the bank would start proceeding to repossess their house.

Amongst the papers, she discovered letters confirming that Anil had surrendered his insurance policy, and they had paid a substantial amount that had been converted to Rupees, paid into his account in India.

As Khusboo went through the papers once again, she took long breadths and a wave of nausea swept over her. She had been hoping to find something that would have explained her father's actions, but all she had found was evidence to support the bank manager's allegation!

After a while, she got up went up to the window and opened it, breathing in the fresh air feeling hot and cold then went back to her chair and picked up where she had left off. Khusboo read the papers a third time, hoping that what she read to be false and closed her eyes but when she opened them, was forced to face reality – that was the betrayal of her father.

Suddenly she pulled herself together, wondering why she was stressing, for her father would return and sort everything out himself, in the meantime, she was sure the bank manager and herself could arrive at an amicable agreement.

With a slight smile, glad she had not involved her mother for she only had a couple of papers to through before she was done. She took one letter and as she read it gave a gasp for it was from the travel agent confirming her father's one way ticket to India!

He had told them that he would be back with his brother within 4 weeks! With trembling hands, Khushboo read another letter from his bank, confirming that they were closing his account and transferring it to an account in India, as per his request!

Chapter 65

She couldn't believe it! Her father had re-mortgaged the house, taken all the money along with the insurance money and left them with nothing!

Khushboo sat weeping on the floor, her arms wrapped around her knees, after some time she reached for a tissue then blew her nose furiously. She was not only crying for what he had done to her, but to her mother for this would surely break her heart; she was so naïve and trusted her father implicitly.

She tried to concentrate, forcing herself to exhale slowly, to stop gulping for another breadth of air before she emptied her lungs of the one before.

And as she did, tried to calm herself, thinking of something positive, she had a decent job, had spoken to the bank manager so they would not repossess the house, no, it was not the financial but the emotional betrayal that she felt intensely.

Her father had always been a stranger to her, but that he would stoop so low? He had lied all along, that he was working so hard for her wedding, all lies! Suddenly, she thought of something else and felt sick, was there another woman? Maybe he was married to her and had a family in India, .and why they could not get through to his parents, for they must be privy to their sons plans.

Khusboo sat back in the chair angrily, but the anger turned to hurt and then back to anger and she wiped the tears that had gathered in her eyes. She rubbed them and decided to check on his clothes so went to her parents' bedroom and opened her father's wardrobe, where before his clothes had been hanging neatly, it was now nearly empty. She remembered her father was travelling light from home, but his trolley was heavy when they went to drop him to the airport so, how?

He knew Sameera was not allowed to open his cupboard, in fact there were many a times when she had heard them argue about it till eventually Sameera had given in and ignored that side of the room. That meant he was having an affair here and gradually taken his clothes to her place?

Khusboo shook her head, for that was the least of her problems, the more immediate one being to talk to her bank then tell her mother.

As she went downstairs, she thought how ironic it was only that day they had met Reyansh who provided shelter to abandoned women. Well, her mother was not going to be one of them, she thought angrily as she joined her mother and Ekta busy making plans for the morrow.

Khusboo smiled as she heard them talking about the novelty of travelling on trains and buses, for en-route they could go window shopping! Seeing the happiness on her face, Khusboo decided she would not dampen her mother's spirits curled on the sofa, glad of the respite.

"Mum, Ekta, I am going to drop you in the mornings and most evening, and let me tell you, it is only nice if you travel once or twice on the train or bus and shop on the way! Mum, you know what the weather is like here, it is terrible waiting out in the cold or rain!"

"Of course, we are grateful, it is just that we would love to go shopping and thought we could include it on the way. But thank you, Khushboo we appreciate it."

"Bye the way Khushboo, what is the situation with Olga? I thought she was supposed to come daily and then you'd drop her home with some food for them?"

"Oh, I forgot to tell you mum, Alexei and his friend Dimitri decided to go on holiday leaving Olga alone at the flat. She sounded relaxed when I spoke to her, so I told her to take it easy and not come in."

"Don't you think you should have told me? Anyway, I hope her husband and friend have gone back to Russia?" Sameera asked hopefully.

"Is he one of the friends who raped her?"

"Yes, he is and that is why it is a good thing he is not staying with them., But Alexei is very possessive, he rings her about 3 times a day to find out where she is, and when he asked why she was home every time he phone, she told them that she has been fired."

"Why did she do that, we love having here and it makes her financially independent." Sameera asked with a frown.

"Actually, I had told her to tell him; since she is preparing to leave him and when she does, there will be no connection leading to us…"

"So how are you going to get in touch with her to let her know the plan?"

"Oh, I will think of something, ring to ask her that I am confused about where she has kept my clothes or something." Khushboo waved her hand in the air.

"Is she serious about leaving him, Khushboo? You know suppressed women often change their minds for they don't have the courage to do so, on top of which they are frightened of the outside world..." Ekta commented." I know I did, many times. Men like Alexei and Aryan have a certain hold on us women that makes us afraid to leave them, and they know it too.!"

"Oh yes, she does, the only reason she is waiting it is because she doesn't want to involve us in any way. I think she is afraid of him, afraid to what lengths he would stoop to! I mean what kind of man would allow his friends to rape his wife?" Khushboo shuddered. "Maybe he was not loved in childhood, maybe he only saw violence in his life. Who knows? Whatever the reason, Olga should not have to bear the brunt of his inadequacies!"

Chapter 66

The following morning, as it was a Saturday, Aadrika washed and dried her hair then after tying it in a loose bun, put on her favourite black jeans with a casual pink zip jumper which complimented her skin and hair and walked into the kitchen. She was surprised that Dhruv was again cooking breakfast humming as he opened the cupboard doors to find what he was looking for.

"Hey, Good morning Dhruv, you did not have to make breakfast every day!" Aadrika exclaimed.

"I like to, anyway, where is Aarush? I thought I might see him as today is Saturday."

"I think he might have left early or stayed over again at Anika's. house. Whatever the case, he is supposed to let me know!" Aadrika said angrily.

"Hey, calm down, maybe he left early for football practice.! Now don't worry, sit down and I will get you your breakfast, I remember how you like your eggs."

He winked as he placed a plate with a fried egg on plate in front of her, brought his hand up and touched a strand of hair that had slipped out of the loose bun, then turned to take out the slices of toasts from the toaster.

"Do you still like coffee in the morning or have you changed to tea?" he asked as the kettle boiled wishing it were Khushboo he was making breakfast for.

"No coffee would be fine," Aadrika replied.

She buttered one slice of toast for herself than instinctively buttered one for Dhruv, like she used to. She marvelled at how easily she had fallen into a familiar domesticity with him, yesterday she had felt so alone and having had to face the harsh reality that he had swindled her of all her money,

But this morning, seeing Dhruv, she felt relief, mixed with something else that was hard to define. Could it be happiness or delight but whatever was it was mixed with part anxiety part certainty, then remembered he would only be staying with her temporally,

Neither talked about Anil and what he had done, and although Aadrika wanted to tell Dhruv about her interview with William, decided to wait for Dhruv to bring up the subject, if he chose to do so, after all, she was not his problem.

She ate her breakfast in silence till it was broken by Dhruv who saw Aadrika, looking sad and broken,

"Aadrika, I know I had mentioned that I would be moving out soon, I don't want to add to your troubles, but when I had dinner with my friend yesterday, he said he could not put me up immediately and if I could stay here a little while longer?"

"Oh of course, you can stay as long as you like!" Aadrika exclaimed. "In fact, I have to sort out this problem so will only be too glad for your companionship."

"Thank you, Aadrika, it is sweet of you. So, what do you want to do today? The sun is shining, and it is a bright day. It seems like a lovely day so far, but there is prediction of rain later on." Dhruv came to the table with two mugs of tea.

"I don't mind staying in Dhruv, I am not in the mood to go out anyway."

She looked down at her hands that were encircling the mug of tea and noticed she was still wearing Dhruv's wedding ring. She looked up and saw that Dhruv had noticed it too, so he tenderly reached forward and rubbed her hands and despite the confusion Aadrika felt, she felt safe with him for he was kind and thoughtful. Andi in her present dilemma, it was nice to have Dhruv stay with her, but was she happy with the way her life was turning out? But then it had never turned out well for her.

Her time at the orphanage came to mind and she had often wondered why they were moved around so much, but when she had asked about it once, was told that the homes were overcrowded! But it was mainly Aadrika and Dhruv who were moved, and she now wondered if it had something to do with racism.?

She voiced her reservation about that time.

"Dhruv, why were we moved around so much in the care home? Most of the other children were sent to foster homes or adopted, did they discriminate because we were Asian?"

"How come you are thinking of this now?" Dhruv looked up and his striking eyes twinkled with mischief "Maybe, but thankfully we are out of that place now!"

"Yes, we are, but it had an effect on me, so much so that I had to go into therapy after you left. In the home, the children were always making comments about my race and background, even though they knew I knew nothing about, it! and when I went into therapy, I was told by the counsellor that actually that was bullying and a kind of racism that I had I faced and that it my symptoms were actually the result of what I had been through, result of the trauma I faced at that time..."

Dhruv looked at her with confusion. "Ad, I knew that the children taunted us, but I did not know you had taken it so seriously for I always told them off and thought that I had scared them away! And what made you think you needed to see a counsellor?"

"Our GP referred me to one because after you left it all became a bit too much, and I was having symptoms from chest tightness, panic attacks to insomnia. I was reluctant to go at first but when the symptoms continued, I thought it best that I should see a GP. Anyway, the counsellor told me that it was not only the bullying but my grief at the death of Darpan. She showed me how angry I was and how I hated him for leaving me. I did not realise that I had also been feeling guilty that I should have protected him. Anyway, that is as far as we got, because I have not been back since. I mean that was such a long time ago and I have moved on and I have Aarush to look after now."

Aadrika was shaking inside as she recalled her sessions with the counsellor, and the issues just the one session had uncovered, so spoke automatically, repeating details as if she were living out the consequences as told by her counsellor.

"And that is why you are so protective about Aarush!" Dhruv smiled slightly and there was compassion in his eyes. "I am sorry for my part in all this, Ad, but you should have continued seeing the counsellor. How are you feeling now?"

"Dhruv, leave it, I don't want to talk about it anymore!" Aadrika said abruptly and her voice snapped like a violin string.

Chapter 67

It was the first time she had spoken to anyone about her visit to the counsellor, but with Dhruv the words had come easily, but whilst talking, she had felt a terrifying sensation, as if she was running desperately to catch something of vital importance, but which was eluding her.

When she had spoken to the counsellor, Aadrika had felt a pure primal pain of grief and anger, then a frantic desire to claw hit or kill something or someone. That wave of intense emotion had shaken her to the core, so she had stopped keeping her appointments.,

She planned to deal with the pain on her own and felt she had effectively suppressed her negative emotions and moved on. At the most, nowadays, she only felt a mild dull sensation settling softly and suffocatingly in her being, and it was at these times she felt she could not breathe! Sometimes she felt there was a heavy fog around her heart, felt very sad and tired, when recently she had heard Darpan calling out to her.

She did not want to tell Dhruv that she felt so tired that she thought her only link to normality was to continue to perform mindless daily functions like going to work washing looking after Aarush; and that Anil had only been a distraction from her daily routine

"I am sorry, Aadrika, I won't mention it again." However, Dhruv was startled at the sudden change in Aadrika's tone of voice and the bright look in her eyes.

"Sorry Dhruv, I did not mean to sound rude, but I don't know how the stay at the home has not affected you! I still have nightmares at night, and I get up feeling I am still in that place.!" Aadrika shuddered. "Anyway, I am going to the lounge and will clear up later.

She got up to go into the sitting room and was followed by Dhruv who was surprised that she had seen a counsellor but come to think of it was no surprise, for he knew how Darpan's death had affected her.

He began to feel sorry for her and wondered if he had gone too far in his payback, for it was Dhruv who had orchestrated the whole scenario; of her being stalked and it was his friends were the hooligans that had been hassling her, finally timing it such so that Anil would come to her rescue.

Anil was a friend of a friend who had told him about the kind of person Anil was, that he was only interested in making money, so Dhruv had asked him to introduce him to Anil, and together they had come up with a plan; that Anil would start an affair with Aadrika, and then scam her of her money.

Anil had phoned to tell Dhruv that he was leaving for India and that Aadrika would be at the airport, to see him off. If he wanted to see his son, that would be the right time as Anil would be breaking off with her so she would be feeling vulnerable. Dhruv had gladly agreed however, he had not foreseen his electric meeting with Khushboo, an encounter that was so intense that he forgot his original plans.

Dhruv reached for a cigarette, then leaned forward and looked at Aadrika. "Forget about those days, Ad, I have."

"I had, maybe seeing you again brought back the horrible situations we had to go through. I have got over it."

"So that is the affect I have on you, not of the times I saved you from those boys, not of the happy times when we first got married in a small registrar's office?" Dhruv asked, his eyes twinkling. "Sorry I could not afford a proper honeymoon which you deserved and have always felt guilty because of it. I went on a cruise once, working as a waiter of course, and thought how nice it would have been if we were on our honeymoon on the cruise!" he smiled as he raised the coffee cup to his lips.

"So, you did miss me?" Aadrika asked then changed the subject. Anyway, I think everything came back to me because there is so talk about racism and discrimination being discussed everywhere and people protesting all over the world. I think these issues were always there, but people are becoming more aware of it since the video of George Flloyd went viral."

"You mean because of the video of a policeman's knee on his neck? I didn't know that you had been following the case, Ad? But you are too sensitive, most people who saw that video cried, Aadrika, I am not surprised it has affected you too, look I am going to make myself another cup of coffee would you like some?"

Dhruv smiled with such an engaging boyishness, and in his blue turtleneck sweater and eyes that were fringed with long lashes, lashes that a woman would envy, Aadrika nearly found herself falling in love with him again, then thought of his temper. However, she could not help wondering, as she had before, if it was it possible to hold 2 opposing points of view, love and hate, at the same time?

Aadrika looked so pale that he and hoped she was not taking events of the video to heart, for that would not be good for her mental health, which, he had discovered, was fragile., he recalled the times he had had to hold and comfort her because she could not breathe, but after he left, she would be alone.

"No thanks Dhruv, no tea for me." Aadrika replied, then as she heard Dhruv moving about in the kitchen

For one weak moment wished she could feel his arms around her, that she could lay her head on his wide shoulders; but wishes were just wishes and reality was that he was only a good friend who would be leaving her again.

Although she was sure he did not love her, he, at least listened to her, whereas most women, when they were spoken to by their men, would find that their problems would run off them like oil on water.! Most men, Anil included, would let the women do the talking, so as they did not pay attention to them, did not reply or respond, but Dhruv was different, he always listened thoughtfully and responded accordingly and for that Aadrika was grateful.

Suddenly Aadrika thought she heard her mobile ring and when she put it against her ear, heard the babble of children's voices. Dhruv re-entered the room and saw her close her mobile and put it away., but she seemed distracted by something in the distance and was strangely, almost bizarrely silent.

"That was Aarush, he said he is going to be home for lunch, so I better go and make something for him to eat for he is usually very hungry after play" Aadrika finally spoke.

Dhruv followed her "I did not hear your phone ring Aadrika anyway, do you need any help? I can go shopping again if you want?"

"No thanks Dhruv, just milk for now please? Oh, and Dhruv don't forget your mask, it is not necessary but better to be careful"

"Thanks for reminding me, Aadrika I had actually forgotten."

As soon as he had left, Aadrika decided that before she started cooking, she would make herself another cup of tea before making lunch for Aarush

Chapter 68

Aadrika was still sitting in the kitchen when the bell rang, when she opened the door. Dhruv was standing outside with a bag of groceries in his hand.

"Dhruv, only milk was enough for now, you did not have buy anything else, but thank you."

"No. problem Aadrika," He replied, handing her the bag, hung his coat in the landing and followed her into the kitchen.

However, as soon as he entered the kitchen, his eyes widened in surprise when he saw that the sink was still piled with dishes and their teacups were lying on the kitchen table counter.

Aadrika put the bag on the counter, took the bottle of milk from it and put it in the fridge.

"So, it seems you have not decided about what to make for lunch Aadrika? That is a good, for on the way I passed a fish and chip shop. and when I got o whiff of them, I just had to get some! I hope Aarush likes them?"

"Thank you Dhruv, that was sweet of you, but Aarush will not come for lunch and does not like Fish and Chips anyway, but I do!"

"Yes, I remembered so shall we have them whilst they are still hot?"

He opened the unit cupboard door to take out some plates and seeing Aadrika's puzzled face explained "whilst you were washing your hair in the morning, I took the liberty of familiarising myself with where all the cutlery, spoons plates were kept. I hope you don't mind?"

"Of course, not Dhruv! "Aadrika watched fascinated as Dhruv deftly placed the fish and chips on two plates and bought them over to the table

"So, what did you do while I was out?" Dhruv asked as he pulled up a chair and sat on it.

"Nothing much, I had to make some urgent phone calls, Oh yummy! This looks delicious!"

Aadrika poured some ketchup over the chips before she positioned her knife and fork over the fish that was soft, hot and not overly fried., and just as she liked it. She sliced the fish onto her fork than added a few chips on it and popped it into her mouth.

"You know, Dhruv, this is the first that I have had fish and chips since you left."

"Oh, and why is that Aadrika?" Dhruv had got some beer for himself and took a swig from the bottle, eying Aadrika through half closed eyes.

"Well don't read too much into this, but it would not have tasted the same, we used to have fish and chips in the house too, remember?"

Aadrika poured coke that Dhruv had thoughtfully brought for her into a glass that Dhruv had already placed on the table.

"And it would have just bought back times that I would rather have forgotten."

"Mine included?" Dhruv smiled as he took the fork to his mouth and took a bite of the fish on it…" You are right, this is delicious!"

Aadrika had finished her fish and chips quickly then run her finger across the empty plate then licking it.

"I see you enjoyed that Aadrika, we shall have it often I promise!" Dhruv took her empty plate, placed it on his than put them in the sink. He came back and took her delicate hand in his, lacing his fingers though hers.

"Now tell me what is worrying you Aadrika! I know you well because you always chew on your bottom lip when something is bothering you! Are you thinking about Anil? Did you try and call him again?"

"Yes, I am thinking about him, and I did call him, Dhruv, but as always, it goes straight to voicemail. I should know by now that he won't return the money either! What can he say or do now?"

Dhruv had been surprised that he had not found Aadrika crying but that she had taken matters into her hands, had rung up her landlord so would not be evicted and had even had an interview with her boss to arrange for an advance on her salary.

Was it possible that she had grown into a strong and independent woman? No, she had been broken when she learnt of Anil's deception, but she had managed to pick herself up quickly. And unwittingly, she had given him a piece of information about herself that he thought would be useful; the knowledge that she had being seeing a counsellor.

That piece of information would be like a secret weapon to Dhruv till he could figure out how and when to use it. Till then, he would keep it buried and only reveal it on occasions and even then, he had to do it subtly.

He would enjoy holding the knowledge in the palm of his hand, caressing its contours and considering its power over her, but as soon as the idea came to him, he thought of Khushboo and what she would think of him.

Aadrika had been crying and was standing looking thoughtfully out of the window. Till the time she came crawling to him, he had to go out of his way to make himself indispensable and charming, but the thought was now half hearted, for he wanted Khushboo to come to him, and not crawling!

"Aadrika is something troubling you, I mean apart from Anil?" Dhruv asked again softly "And don't say nothing because I know you. But if you do not want to talk about it, that is fine too, I just wanted to let you know that I am here for you. If you are worried about telling Aarush about me, we can put it off, but that will only make matters more difficult I think."

"No, no thank you, Dhruv, we should tell him, but he is not coming for lunch as I thought, I don't know how he will take it, but I hope he likes you..."

Dhruv's voice cracked then he spoke in a deep voice," I am sure he is a well brought up boy, Aadrika," He cleared his throat and then coughed slightly.

"Yes, he is." Aadrika replied proudly. "He is so sensitive and gentle, so much like Darpan" Dhruv looked at her in surprise. "Aadrika, you still remember Darpan? I mean it was a long time ago, and you told me you had moved on."

"Of course, I remember him Dhruv! He was like my little brother, a family I did not have, I still do not understand why he committed suicide, he had his whole life ahead of him!" Aadrika shook her head in confusion, then when Dhruv sneezed, remarked. "Oh, you better be careful; it looks you might be coming down with something!"

"I am fine, Aadrika." Dhruv replied with a smile remembering why it was that he had fallen in love with her; it was her goodness, and she was so beautiful it was as if she purified him. And it was this very goodness, naivety and trusting nature that enabled him to manipulate her, and it was those very qualities which had led to her fragile mental state of mind.

There were only two times she had rebelled against him, once when it had something to do with Darpan and the other when Aarush was born.

She had only once allowed him to see Aarush, and that was when they had come back from the hospital. Dhruv had thought him to be so tiny so had picked him gently, but he was wrapped in so many blankets, he could not see barely see him, but after that day, Aadrika had stood between him, and Aarush and she had not allowed him near Aarush,

Chapter 69

The sun poured through the window in the morning through the net curtains, waking Khushboo who drowsily rubbed her eyes, when she suddenly became conscious of the fact that after seven relaxing days with her mother, she would have to re-join her office today.

She turned to the side table and looked at the clock and saw that as it was still early, so could take her time so looked around her room. Her bedroom was done in her favourite colours, beige and turquoise, with a dressing table that had 3 mirrors, a stool of peacock and a picture of a peacock in its full splendour showing its colours hanging above it.

But she sat up abruptly as she recalled the events of previous days, how her father had gone to India, withdrawing all the money from his account, re-mortgaging their house, leaving her to sort out the finances quickly lest their house would be re- possessed!

She lay back on her pillow and recalled the various conversations she had with her friends when discussing their parents, and they had had all one thing in common, they had fathers that had flaws and failings, mostly significant and noticeable ones, which they had put down to generation gap. But she had always thought her father to be different, he had a certain formality and coldness about him, a trait which not only detached itself from his family, but showed itself in black moods,

However, those failings all seemed minor and common now, and her father's good qualities, if he had any, seemed fraudulent and a cover for his true character proving that each man was for himself and there was no room in his life for duty obligation or even love; she thought her father's life was like a diamond, it reflected a different colour, depending on the angle of the light that was shone on it e.g. it could look warm and glowing; on the other hand, the same stone could look no more than a piece of glass!

Her emotions, which for her mother's sake, she was trying to control, alternated between disappointment, fury and hurt.

Finally, she got up slowly filled with unusual sense of capability and purpose for she had a long day ahead of her. After dropping her mother and Ekta at Reyansh's office, she was resuming work after a week of fun and relaxation.

During the week, she had been in touch with Stella, her paralegal, who had told her that there was a lot of work pending for although Isabella, was very efficient, Khushboo's clients had insisted they only wanted to deal with her.

Khushboo wore her trouser and jacket, tied her hair in a bun, applied some make up and pearl studs in her ears, took a deep breath and ran downstairs. She stood for a while at the end of the steps, one hand still on the banister rail, listening to the sounds emanating from the kitchen.

Her mother and Ekta were laughing in the kitchen, and there was the familiar noise of cutlery and aroma of fresh coffee, a change from the usual Indian tea they all enjoyed

Khushboo could not believe what the events of the previous day had unravelled, and they had affected her so deeply that she could not think so was worried that her mother was very perspective and might sense something was wrong,

So, before she entered kitchen, she took a deep breath, stood straight with her shoulders held back and smiled as she entered, amazed at how, since the departure of her father, the heavy atmosphere in the house had been lifted and her mother now laughed and smiled frequently. Being married to Anil had curbed Sameera's spontaneity, and in his presence, she had become so meek and docile, so eager that she did not disobey him, that she behaved as if she was treading on eggshells.

Anil had been brought up in a society that dictated that their culture and tradition make man the boss of the house; customs that showed that women and their bodies only existed for the use of men, for not only their pleasure, but as an outlet for their rage and use them as punching bags too.

Ekta's company had given her mother's confidence a boost, and she did not want to shatter the happy bubble she was in by telling her the truth about her father. So, she decided that she would shoulder the responsibility of the finances of the house and protect her mother from the truth for as long as possible

She couldn't help wondering if her father's suggestion for volunteer work doing was a push, subtly, in Reyansh's direction, for part of his work was to guide unfortunate women and provide them shelter. Her mother did everything for her father's comfort and this is how he repaid her! She tried to brush away the contempt she felt for him, but the feeling stuck to her like a cobweb dusted from a wall.

"Hello mum, Ekta, are you ready? I will drop you to Reyansh's office before I go to work."

She walked towards them with keys held conspicuously in her hand so that they would see she was in a rush

"Yes, we are, ready, but before we leave, have your breakfast; now sit," Sameera ordered, but with a smile on her face as she placed a mug of tea on the table. "I have made the Indian breakfast you love."

"No mum, I am in a hurry, and you know this Indian breakfast, which I love by the way, is only for weekends and holidays! Although I would love to, If I have it, I will feel sleepy the entire day and I have a lot of work to catch up on."

"I know Khushboo, I thought you might say that so have made toast for you."

Sameera took out 2 slices of toasts from the toaster and placed them on the plate. "There is butter and sugar on the table, and Ekta, we can have the stuffed chapatti, they would be filling, after all it would be our first day and we don't know whether we will have time for lunch!"

"Yes, that would be fine by me, my, you do look nice in your professional suit Khushboo! I had got used to seeing you in casual dress!" Ekta remarked.

"Thank you Ekta and Mum! Of course, you will, have time for lunch, Reyansh is not a slave driver! Oh, all right, I will have some toast with tea." Khushboo remarked after she had checked the time on her watch. "Oh, my Mum you never wear trousers!" Khushboo commented as she noticed that her mother was wearing casual grey trousers with a pink jumper.

"And Ekta, you look lovely, and what have you done to my mother?" She said as she smeared butter cheese on her toast.

"Just thought she might be comfortable in trousers…" Ekta smiled gently.

Chapter 70

"Hmm I don't know what you said to convince her, I have been trying but to no avail!" Khushboo finished her coffee, then picked up the car keys she had dropped on the table.

"That is only because your father did not like me to wear trousers, in fact he was quite adamant about it." Sameera informed her

"Of course, I should have guessed he would want to control you on how you dress too." Khushboo said sarcastically

"I think it is the Indian men, Khushboo, Aryan was like that too" Ekta said as she looked sadly out of the window.

"Ekta, you look nice too, but then you always do!" Khushboo said as she looked at her approvingly.

Ekta was wearing casual black trousers and jacket with blue blouse with and had done her hair in an elegant bun which showed off her long neck. She had not slept at night for her mind had kept wandering back to Reyansh.

She had thought she would never have any kind of relationship with a man, but Reyansh had awakened something in her, and the thought of not ever seeing him again scared her. She was not expecting a big wave of emotion that would engulf and drown her, or to be swept of her feet, no, all she wanted was a clean and beautiful emotion with a decent man, one that would not end in pain.

Ekta had been thinking of Reyansh whilst applying her make up too, making sure that her lipstick was of a perfect soft neutral colour that would complement her skin, for she did not like anything bright or garish and had a feeling that neither did Reyansh.

Suddenly she felt nervous, for if there was ever an opportunity to get to know Reyansh, she would not know what to do or say, she was not the romantic type, so it was not in her nature to be seductive, and what little allure she had had, had been trampled upon by Aryan.

However, even after she began work and could have made friends back in Dubai, she found she was shirking from human contact. So over time, she had cut herself off from people by hiding behind what she found to be a convenient wall of diffidence so that now when she needed the social skills, she had none.

"Oh, er thank you, Khushboo!" she smiled softly. "Sameera, I think we are making Khushboo late."

"You are right, Ekta, we will take the Chappatis with us." She quickly wrapped the stuffed Chapatis in foil paper than put them in a plastic container. "I will take some for Reyansh too, he is such a nice boy, and works throughout his breaks."

"Mum hurry up we will be late; Olga will be coming today so she will do the rest, even though she has told Alexei we have fired her, she insisted that she would come for at least a couple or hours each week"

"I know, but there are other things she needs to take care of. Don't forget she only comes for a few hours. Just give me a few minutes…"

Sameera quickly cleared the breakfast dishes and put them in the sink, opened the tap water so the water would run over them whilst she opened the fridge door and put the bottle of milk in it, wiped down the kitchen work surface, swept crumbs into the palm of her hand and dusted them off in the sink.

When she saw Khushboo looking at her in frustration, she quickly put down the wet sponge, dried her hands on tea towel that hung in the middle of oven and hurried out of the kitchen with the container of chapatis.

"Khusboo, can you hold this whilst I wear my coat?" she asked Khusboo as she handed her the plastic container.

"Just a minute, Mum it is very thoughtful of you to think of Reyansh, but he might be too busy to spend too much time with you. Ekta, Mum has never worked so does not know how an office works." Khusboo said as she wore her trench coat and tied the belt tightly at the waist before taking the plastic container.

"Ekta, will you be warm in that?" Sameera asked as she watched Ekta throw her grey cape over her shoulders.

"Yes, don't worry, I am fine, "Ekta replied in her soft voice and Khusboo wondered if she ever got angry?

"Mum will you ring and tell me how you will come home? I am going to be very busy, so if you cannot get through, can you please ask Reyansh for directions? He will guide you as to what underground station would be nearest etc or help you get an Uber."

She opened her wallet and handed her mother some cash. "And if he is too busy, leave a message for I will regularly check them and will call you as soon as I can."

"Khushboo, do not worry! We are not children!" Sameera said indignantly as she got in the front and tied the seatbelt across her waist.

Ekta sat at the back of the car and rested her head against the headrest, closed her eyes listening to the soothing stream of banter between mother and daughter,

Khushboo, with a deft flick of her wrist turned the keys in the ignition, turned her head to see that her mother had tied her seat belt then looked in the rear window, and when she saw it was clear, steered the car onto the road. She drove capably and briskly around the road that was quiet and deserted at this time of the morning

The sun hung low in the sky shining weakly through clouds and was casting long shadows on the gardens of the houses they passed. Khushboo drove mechanically, her mind on the problem her father expected her to deal; he had abandoned her to carry the burden alone; but it was an impossibly heavy burden for her to hold and she needed him to lift it from her shoulders!

She turned to her mother, "Mum have you heard from Dad?"

"No, I have not, I tried yesterday and again today but it goes straight to voicemail. I tried his parents too but again no answer. I hope everything is alright there." Sameera replied with a frown.

Chapter 71

'Come on Dad, be a man and make all this go away, make it go away! You need to clear up the situation or put it to right!' Khushboo thought as she drove silently.

All through breakfast in the morning, amidst her mother's and Ekta's cheerful banter, she had felt as if she had been walking around with a jar of acid in her hands, a jar that was full to the brim with no lid, a small mover on her part and it would just spill out!

And this was only for a few hours, how was she going to keep it from her for another three weeks? She looked at her mobile which was pinging every few seconds with messages and emails confirming that she had a busy day ahead,

Her mother looked so relaxed and happy that she couldn't help but think that if her father had been present, her mother would not have been the loving and affectionate person she was today. He would have made sure of that - by undermining her on every occasion, so maybe they were better off without him?

Just before they reached Reyansh's office, she gave her mother the house keys than called him on her mobile saying that she was dropping Sameera and Ekta.

As soon as she reached the office building, found that he was standing outside for them, looking smart in jeans, with the collar of a white shirt visible beneath the black cashmere sweater.

"How nice of him to come and receive us," Sameera said then whispered and winking muttered "I think we know why!"

Sameera undid her safety belt and opened the door, just as Reyansh opened the door for Ekta with a smile

Reyansh too had been awake the whole night too, thinking about Ekta. Most of the women he came across were either too dominant or victims, very few women who had been through what Ekta had and survived the emotional trauma and come out the other end with their head held high and with dignity.

But Ekta, he thought was mysterious and self-assured, a woman who he was sure would not need to fill silent gaps with needless conversation, something that most women did and something he detested. And considering what she had been through, there had been something brave about her as she sat with a straight-backed posture, yet at the same time, he had observed the modesty in her eyes as she had looked at him shyly.

When Reyansh opened the car door. his heart skipped a beat as he saw how her long neck was accentuated with the elegant bun. Her dreamy eyes with their long lashes and looked up at him shyly as she stepped out of the car in black pumps that encompassed her small feet. She looked her usual calm and cool self, but underneath her poise, her heart was beating so hard and there was an unfamiliar sensation at the centre of her heart.

Reyansh held out his hand with a big smile, and she had turned her head away coyly. Although she did not intend it to be affectation, Aryan had criticized her many times about it...

"Reyansh, I might not be able to make it on time. I will try, but it is my first day back and it is bound to be hectic. I know you are busy too, but can you just explain the best route to our house to Mum, or better still get them an Uber?" Khusboo wound down her window.

"Oh, don't worry Khusboo, I will look after them and don't worry, I live nearby so will personally take responsibility of that!"

He turned and ushered the ladies back and as soon as Reyansh reached the building of his office, he turned and waved to Khushboo before following her mother and Ekta into his office admiring Ekta's figure for she did not have a single extra ripple of flesh on her graceful body and moved with a fluid grace which he admired.

Khushboo smiled, waved and began a U turn, but when she looked in the rear window saw a truck that she had not seen honking angrily. She waved at him to calm him and completed her u turn.

She drove straight to her office, wondering what the situation there was going to be, for she recalled James friendliness with Isabelle, and hoped that her job was not in trouble, for now, more than ever, she needed a steady job…

She listed the calls mentally that she had to make, sometime in the morning, the first one being the one to the bank manager.

Maybe she should take Reyansh into her confidence for she was too involved to find a legal way round this dilemma. But that would have to be a last option, for he was a friend of her father then wondered how her father, a swindler and conman, could have a decent man like Reyansh as a friend, then remembered her father mentioning that they were only acquaintances who were interested in a common cause.

She hated the fact that she would have to economise at home, and do so without arousing her mother' suspicion, and was glad she had fired Olga, for although she did come sometimes, did not take any pay or money from her, she would talk to Reyansh about her, soon, and she was sure he would accommodate her in one of his organisations.

There was a traffic jam on one of the roads, and as she sat tapping her hands impatiently on the wheel, Khushboo thought how difficult it had been to keep the knowledge of what her father had done to herself and not blurt it out, even unintentionally!

There had been no equality in her parents' marriage for her father had set so many limitations that her mother had finally succumbed and become putty in his hands. Khushboo hated the culture that forced and declared man to be superior and wondered for a split second whether Dhruv had a similar approach to women?

She hoped not, for more than ever, she needed a friend to talk to as she could not offload to Aishya. She was grateful to Ekta for she had restored her mother's confidence enough to work in an office and she could also depend on her to support her mother when she was told the truth.

She decided she would take Ekta into her confidence as soon as possible for not only was she wise, but she could also not carry this burden alone.

As soon as she reached the office building, she parked her car and went in past the reception towards the elevator. She was expecting the security guard to stop her, as was his custom, but was surprised that he just smiled and waved at her.

Chapter 72

As she waited for the lift, she looked around her at the steady stream of people wearing business suits and carrying leather attaché cases some under their arms others holding it in their hand. They were pushing through the revolving door, some with coffee in hand, some already on calls or reading emails on phones, all having started their busy day even before reaching their office.

Khushboo heard sound of the lift as it arrived on the ground floor and as its doors slid open, she, with a few others, entered and pressed the button of the floor they were going to. As soon as the lift reached her floor, she got out and walked to her office. Stella was not at her desk, so she quickly went through to find Isabella at her desk and looking over her shoulder at James.

She was surprised to see Isabella at her desk, for she knew that she was due back today, and fought a sinking feeling that Isabella was an ambitious woman who wanted to take over her job? But Khushboo had kept in touch with Stella who had assured her that Isabella was a nice woman and that all was well.

"Good morning, James, Isabela," Khushboo greeted them as she hung her coat on the coat hanger in the corner of the room. Startled James looked up.

"Khushboo, Good morning, I thought as this was your first day, you would come in later. Anyway, how are you, it is good to have you back." He quickly crossed the room to shake hands. "Is everything okay?"

"Yes, thank you James."

Khushboo thought that when he saw her, his friendliness with Isabella had quickly turned into professionalism.

"Yes, it is, James, it is good to be back, in fact I was going to ask you the same for you rarely leave your office!"

She looked at Isabella in admiration for she had forgotten how beautiful she was with her blonde hair, slim yet curvaceous figure and wide eyes that held a glint of invitation in a piquant face. Not only was she beautiful, but she also seemed to be the kind of woman who could fascinate and entertain James with talk of fascinating anecdotes for Khushboo was sure Isabella was well travelled.

Her mind ran through a series of emotions, surprise that was giving way to wariness.

"Now that you are back, Khushboo, I will leave you two to get on with it." He said heartily as he left the room. "Isabella, now that Khushboo is back, you can update her on the new cases you have dealt with."

"Yes of course James." Isabella got up from the chair to make room for Khushboo who had seen the stack of messages and files on her desk and the red light that was flashing on her phone.

"Thank you." Khushboo said as she sat on her swivel chair, she took the call, read the messages then turned to Isabella with a frown. "Are these new cases Isabella? I have more than I can handle as it is!" she exclaimed as she looked down at the stacks of files and papers…as if her life wasn't under enough pressure!!'

Not waiting for her answer, Khushboo caught up with the voicemail messages on her phone and checked her texts and emails, she had only been away for a week but was going to be buried under a blizzard of paperwork for another week!

After some time, she took a deep breath and put her head in her hands. "Whew, this is too much, and I have barely started! How come you took on new clients?"

"That is what me and Stella thought too, however, James came in one day when we were discussing how to best let the clients know that we could not take on anyone new, though women needed representation, anyway, it was James' idea not to turn them away. Sorry, look it is your first day back, let me get you coffee and we will talk."

She walked over to the side table where there was fresh coffee in the coffee maker, mugs sugar and milk on the tray.

"Sorry I was late so could not get any doughnuts; I am sure Stella told you about our morning ritual?"

"Yes, she did, coffee, doughnuts and gossip to start the day! I noticed it gets busy later."

"Yes, we find that it is a good start to the day, and we will go back to it from tomorrow, thanks Isabella, I need that cup of coffee, I had a hectic morning before I came to office." Khushboo took the coffee whilst Isabella perched herself on the side of the desk.

"You know, I spoke to Stella whilst I was away, and she did not mention taking on new clients. That was not fair of James to pile you with more work whilst you are getting used to the pending work, but I see you are very efficient." She smiled "Maybe that is why James thought you could handle the extra work."

"Actually, he suggested a few changes, I don't know whether I should wait for him to tell you, no I think I will, then we can go ahead and start the day."

"Isabella, is everything okay?" Khushboo asked, alarm bells going off in her head, for everything was going wrong with this day! Was Isabella going to confirm what she had been thinking all along? That she was going to replace her, or were they closing ranks around themselves to keep her out?

"Yes of course, it is, just that whilst you were away and seeing your heavy workload, James created a new post and not only because of the workload, because you are very efficient, but because I love the job, specially being in a position to help the women!, Anyway, now I will be working beside you, and you will not have to shoulder all the work on your own."

Khushboo was shocked and surprised that Stella had not mentioned it and wondered if this was proof and confirmation that she was going to be phased out?

Chapter 73

"Oh, does Stella know that she will be working for both of us!" Khushboo asked.

"No, she has not been told…! Isabella replied. "I thought I would wait for you to do so."

At that moment, there was a knock on the door and Stella entered with a smile. "Welcome back Khushboo, sorry I missed you earlier, I was on a call"

"No worries, how are you, Stella?" Khushboo smiled and hoped she would be able to take on the increased workload as she was a single mum with a young child and usually liked to leave on time.

"I am fine, Khushboo, oh, Isabella, I just thought I would let you know there are some removal men outside. They have got some furniture that they said you ordered?"

"Oh yes, that will.be the." She left the room whilst Khushboo and Stella looked at each other with raised eyebrows

"Stella, before you go, there will be a few changes here, Isabella is joining me, so you will be working for both of us. Promise we won't work you too hard!"

"Oh, I don't mind, Khushboo, as long as we still have our coffee and doughnuts in the morning! You don't know how much I missed those. Anyway, I have to get back but if you have any questions, you know I will be outside."

But as soon as she turned to leave the room, it was blocked with the removal men bringing in first a desk then a swivel chair. Whilst Stella waited for the removal men to finish their job to Isabella's satisfaction,

Khushboo waved to Stella to come closer and as soon as she was whispered,

"Stella, I need to make some very important personal calls as soon as possible and I don't think I will get any privacy here."

"I think the men are nearly done." Stella said as she saw the removal men rubbing their sweaty brows and leaving." you can make the calls outside whilst I help Isabella here."

"Thanks Stella, I think I'll do that!"

Khushboo left the room with the two women deciding which was the best place for the desk and chair, Khushboo turned and smiled at them "My desk and chair must stay in the same place, Stella!"

"Of course, Khushboo", Isabella replied hurriedly, brushing back the strand of hair that had fallen on her forehead.

Khushboo left the room and sat at Stella's desk, dreading her conversation with the bank manager, for she had not known the extent of her father's l deception, financial and emotional.

Her body trembled and shook with nerves, followed by a sense of urgency as she thought of the consequences of her father's actions and how they could lead to their being homeless. A tremor ran down her shaky arms, as if they were fluttering like leaves in a breeze.

She had just opened her handbag to take out her mobile when it rang before she could. She quickly fumbled for it, anxious to talk to whoever it was before it went to voicemail. Whether it was her father or the bank manager, it was essential she talk to either of them.

She heard the bank manager's voice at the other end as she answered quickly explained the situation to him, that she had gone through her father's paperwork and accounts and then hesitantly telling him that he had cleared his accounts and transferred them to India.

When the manager asked if it would be resolved once he was back, she had to tell him that, unbeknown to them, he had got a one-way ticket so had no intention of coming back. He was very understanding when she explained that she held a good job in a reputable firm and would take over the debt payments, in instalments.

They ended the call on amicable terms, but before he did, assured her that he would be sending her the paperwork confirming their arrangement and that no further legal action would be taken from his end.

As soon as the conversation ended, Khushboo sat back with a sigh of relief, and with shaking legs, stood up, and went to the bathroom to wash her hands and face. After she had dried them, she went back to Stella's desk to see that the red light on her blackberry was flashing. As soon as she answered, heard Reyansh's cheerful voice.

"Reyansh, is everything all right? Mum Ekta how are they doing?" Khushboo said with a lump in her throat.

"Very well, Khushboo and that is what I wanted to talk to you about. I think we spoke about this yesterday, that they would be useful in different departments. I thought it best that Ekta work with me whilst your mother has gone over to the women's branch where, with her experience, she will be talking to other women to give them advice."

"I thought Ekta was more suited to that since she has been through all the trauma of being abused manipulated and then abandoned, Reyansh?"

"No Khushboo, again, I think I mentioned this yesterday, I feel her wounds are still raw so she will be working with me in my office where I will see to it that she is well looked after. Another reason for that being that she is looking for a job, and we do need paid workers so if she gains experience from our organisation that might help her"

"Reyansh, you know best, but I do need to talk to you about something personal, actually I don't even think I should, but I might need your advice in the future."

Reyansh was immediately sympathetic. "Anytime Khusboo, you are a lawyer and know all the legalities, but if you ever need a listening ear, I am here for you. Oh, by the way, I know you are busy today so you do not have to worry about picking up Ekta and Sameera, or for them to travel by public transport I will personally drop them."

"Thank you, Reyansh, that is very kind of you, and it is a load of my mind for I am very busy."

As she put her mobile back in her handbag, she smiled for as he seemed smitten with Ekta, his underlying motive in keeping her close to him had not escaped her. Well, well, she thought, love does strike out of the blue then thought of Dhruv and wondered if it had struck her too? She wished them well in her heart and hoped something would come of it for Ekta deserved to be happy.

She was so nice and gentle and had suffered so much and Reyansh too, she had heard, was divorced and had had an unhappy marriage.

She picked up her handbag and walked back to her room to find that between Isabella and Stella, the room had been transformed.

Isabella's desk was placed in the corner of the room, and Stella had even managed to find a pot of plants to put at the corner of Sophie's desk. Behind the desk was hanging a painting of flowers that had petals with beads of dew clinging on them and a few droplets on the floor next to the vase.

"Very nice, Isabella! I thought the room would be too cluttered with the extra desk and chair, but it still looks spacious, and the painting and plant give it a nice finishing touch!"

Chapter 74

"That was Stella's doing! Thanks for your help." Isabella smiled. "But now, I think, Khushboo we should get down to work, I need to update you on what I have done whist you were away, although most of the women wanted to deal with you. One thing I came to realise was that it was important to establish trust a connection with them. Anyway, Stella said you had some important personal calls to make and if you are done, we can start! I hope everything is, okay?"

"Yes, thank you and you are right, we have not really done anything this morning." Stella tuned to leave the room with a 'Call me if you need me' when Khushboo stopped her.

"Thanks Stella, please can you hold all calls this afternoon? We do not want to be disturbed."

"No problem Khushboo, I will take messages so you can call them back."

"Thanks Stella, much appreciated." Khushboo eased herself into the leather swivel chair behind her desk "But before we start, Isabella, I think we need another cup of coffee to stay alert, I don't know about you, but I do!"

"Ahead of you Khushboo," Isabella said as she put in a new filter in the coffee machine and heaped in the coffee grounds. She poured it in two mugs and brought it over to Khushboo.

The rest of the afternoon was spent in silence broken only by Stella who bought them sandwiches for lunch, and seeing them hard at work, placed one on Khushboo's table and the other on Isabella's desk before she left the room.

Although she was immersed in work, Khushboo found herself waiting for something to happen; maybe the ring of the phone, a knock on the door? But the afternoon continued to be cloaked in a soft safe silence.

After some time Khushboo got up, stretched and walked over to the window through which the sun was spiralling its light into the room. She took a deep breath and looked out into garden where the leaves of creeper on the back wall was exposing the bare brickwork underneath. Peonies and roses that were planted years ago stood in rows, blooming soft pink and cream,

She turned back into the room and made herself a cup of coffee "Isabella would you like one? As you can see, I am addicted to it!"

Isabella smiled and leant back in her chair. "Yes, thank you and so am I!"

"Isabella, I had planned to leave early to pick up my mother, but as my friend will take them home, I will stay late, but you can leave, and thank you for all your help. In fact, I am glad to have you as a partner!" Khushboo took over a mug to her then went back to her desk.

"I am glad too Khushboo! Thank you!" Isabella replied taking the mug. "I will leave in another hour."

Both were bent over their desks an hour later when James knocked and entered, He was wearing a dark suit, white shirt and tie under a heavy cashmere coat. In his hand he held a brown briefcase and looked looking very business-like

"Ready Isabelle?" he asked, then whistled in appreciation as he looked around the room. "Very nice!"

However, Khushboo had not missed the look that had passed between them and wondered if their body language, could be construed as flirting?

"Thank you, sir, bye Khushboo I will see you to tomorrow, and don't work too hard!"

Isabella took her coat from the stand and after putting it one, took the gloves from its pocket and slipped them on her hand after which she followed James, who waved and mimed goodbye to Khusboo with his lips.

As they left, thought about their body language, then wondered why it was bothering her so. She liked Isabella and her personal life was none of her business.

Maybe it was bothering her because of an incident, that had happened so long ago, he had almost forgotten about it. It had happened when she just joined the organisation. James had asked her out once and she had politely refused, and the matter had not been discussed since.

Could it be that James had felt slighted, remembered it and was showing her, in no uncertain terms, the consequence of that refusal? No, that was not possible for she had since discovered the importance of networking and harmless meetings of colleagues for a drink after work.

She sighed and at that time, Stella knocked and entered.

"I will be leaving soon but, Khushboo there were a few calls from your clients who insisted they speak only to you. I have noted their numbers so that you can give them a call back." She started to rattle of a few numbers,

"Hey, hold on Stella, not so fast, I suggest you write them on a note pad and put them on my desk."

"Okay will do and also a Mr Sharma called a few times demanding to see you and no one else so I pencilled him in for tomorrow 11.a, m. which you can see on your computer calendar Before I go is there anything that needs to be done?"

"Is he a new client? I wonder what he wants, anyway I will find out tomorrow. And no thank you Stella, have a good evening, I will be leaving soon too."

She was on the verge of asking her about Isabella and James for she knew that office grapevine was dependable, then dismissed the idea for she was not one to gossip. She had bigger problems to deal with, for although she had them under control, she still had to tell her mother.

As soon as Stella left, Khusboo cleared her desk, wore her trench coat over her suit and tied the belt tightly around her waist. when the phone rang. Khushboo quickly picked it up, her heart thumping/

"Hello, Khushboo?" Dhruv sounded relaxed and friendly "how are you and how about dinner today? I know it is a bit last minute but..."

"Hi Dhruv." Khushboo's heart was beating fast. "Hey, I never agreed to dinner only a coffee" she exclaimed.

To Dhruv, her voice not only sounded soft and smoky but also sexy and utterly enchanting. Just hearing one syllable of his name fall from Khushboo's lips, and it seemed to him that his life stood still, and the letter seemed to hover between them, pulsing with a life of its own.

"Yes, you did!" He teased, turning on his charm that nearly melted her cool reserve.

"No, I did not." Khushboo said firmly, however she pressed the phone to her ear as if to wrap his voice around her. "Anyway, I cannot make it today."

"I am sure you can Khushboo, everyone needs to eat, and I was looking forward to meeting you, properly this time and promise, no bumping into each other." Khushboo heard humour and disappointment in his voice.

Part of her wanted to keep him on the line, not only because it was good to hear his voice, but also because she wanted him to say something warm so she could place him in a category of relationship that suited her, then asked herself which category would she want him in; was it fun or a fling where no one got hurt or a more permanent one?

Finally, she agreed, for not only was Reyansh dropping her mother and Ekta home later, but she needed to relax and unwind after the hard day she had had. Plus, she wanted to meet him and get over her infatuation, for that is what it must be, she thought.

They agreed to meet at an Indian restaurant that was close to her house for she wanted to go home and freshen up before she met him, the thought of meeting Dhruv filled her with unbearable confusion, would she cry, fall in his arms and blurt out her problem or slap him for the effect he was having on her? Whatever it was, she needed her wits around her.

As she waited for the elevator she thought about James and wondered if, as an employer, he knew about the main cultural differences when employing workers who were not British nationals, then felt silly for doubting him for being CEO and a lawyer of a big organisation he surely would.

Apart from that one incident, Khushboo respected him and was sure he was aware of the employment law which covered sexual harassment at the workplace. However, she could not but help wonder that it should have helped him to understand habits and behaviour of people from different cultures and what constituted acceptable and unacceptable behaviours. Therefore, he would not have asked her out, unless like with Isabella, it had only been innocent and made in an effort to know her better out of the office?

She shook her head and tried to dismiss it from her mind, suddenly looking forward to the evening for she hadn't been out on a date in fact, it was her practice not to do so, but somehow with Dhruv, it seemed she was breaking all her rules! Khushboo smiled slightly as she left the building.

It was late evening, and the light was changing, making everything look indistinct and shadowy after the disappearing sun, much like her meeting with Dhruv!

Chapter 75

As she drove home, Khushboo reviewed the situation, pleased that the bank manager had been so understanding, though her father should not have put her in that position in the first place!

She took her hand off the wheel for a moment, tucked a strand of hair from behind her ear, rubbed her forehead with shaking fingers and waited for her anger to subside as she put her hand back on the steering wheel.

As she drove into the driveway of their house; she saw that the curtains were drawn across some of the windows, as a message to burglars that someone was home. However, Khushboo felt that maybe the house was trying to tell her something, maybe it wanted her to close her eyes against reality or was it cautioning her to keep reality buried. from her mother?

As she entered the house and opened the front door, a heavy silence rushed out to envelop her and she frowned, then remembered that Reyansh had told her that he might be late in dropping her mother and Ekta.

She peeked into the lounge before going upstairs and saw the comfy sofas and bookshelves that were crammed with her books.

But as soon as her glance rested on some family photographs on the mantlepiece, she was filled with anger at her father's smiling face looking up at her! She felt so incensed that she wanted to throw it out of the house, or at the very least, cut out it out, as he had cut them off from his life!

Khushboo mounted the stairs, switched on the landing light before crossing over and opening her bedroom door. She took a quick bath and changed into a simple beige dress with cap sleeves and a boat neck that emphasised her ivory white shoulders. She tied the black patent leather belt that had gold studs and a double buckle. around her small waist,

She crossed across to her dressing able and applied makeup, making sure it was subtle, finishing by applying the bronze gloss lipstick on her lips. Her soft brown hair fell in natural curls around her heart shaped face and her warm brown almond eyes, that were fringed with long lashes looked bright with anticipation of the evening ahead.

She took a final look in the mirror, and although satisfied overall, found that there something to be missing, so finished her attire with tiny gold studs in her ears that not only glittered in the light, but also matched the studs on her belt. She looked at her watch and gave a cry, for she was late, so she hurriedly zipped up her brown boots, grabbed her soft brown leather handbag and after transferring her wallet mobile and keys into it ran downstairs, after having hurriedly put on her light brown coat and sliding on matching brown gloves over her hands, she opened the front door

Outside, Although it was dusk and the sun had disappeared over the horizon, the sky was still streaked with faint colours of pink red and lavender that were fading fast.

As she walked towards the restaurant, she called Dhruv to let him know that she would be late and was relieved to hear that he too was running late was but was on his way there.

They reached the restaurant at the same time, and as Khushboo looked at him thought he looked sexy and stylish in a black cashmere sweater, leather pants and leather jacket.

She saw Dhruv's muscles ripple under the tight cashmere sweater and his legs looked powerful and strong in the tight leather pants.

He smiled as he greeted her and held out his hand that were broad with strong fingers with a sprinkling of dark hair covering them. Khushboo hesitated for a second then put her delicate gloved hand in his and flinched when it was tightly gripped. Dhruv saw her wince and immediately let go apologising profusely.

"Don't worry about it Dhruv, I am fine." Khushboo smiled

They entered the restaurant, and as they waited for a waiter to show them to their table, they stood awkwardly, and anybody who saw them thought they made a lovely couple. Dhruv looked handsome in his ponytail and semi casual attire and Khushboo looked striking and exotic in her beige dress, brown boots and thick brown hair and big brown almond shaped eyes.

Finally, a waiter in a red jacket came up, welcomed them, then escorted them to a table. As they followed him, Dhruv lightly brushed his fingers across Khushboo's lower back and as his fingertips ran slowly and softly all the way down it, she shivered.

The tables in the restaurant were all covered with red tablecloths and had gleaming silver cutlery on them which shone in the dim light, and the wallpaper of the restaurant was covered with the traditional Indian paisley design of red and gold with classical Indian guitar playing softly in the background,

The waiter escorted them to an empty table and withdrew discreetly.

"This is nice," Dhruv sat on the chair and looked around appreciatively, and with his dazzling smile, asked. "Would you like some wine?

"Er yes, I have had a difficult day at the office so could do with a glass!" Khushboo smiled as she handed her coat to the waiter who had been standing beside her, and as she smiled, a dimple danced on her cheek.

The weight and timbre of Dhruv's voice was deeper in person than on the phone and also a bit throaty which Khushboo found attractive. Although she tried to ignore Dhruv's broad shoulders, she couldn't help noticing how toned his body looked under his sweater and jacket.

Dhruv ordered wine for both of them, and his heart, which was beating too fast, had started to quieten down, but leapt again as she smiled, and for a moment all he could hear was the blood pounding in his ears.

Khushboo sat in her chair, her hands gripping its arms, her heart beating fast too...She was surprised that nobody noticed anything extraordinary about their silence or heard the pounding of their hearts! But that was of no consequence, for they were in their own little bubble, separated from humanity, Finally, it was Dhruv who broke the silence.

"So how come a beautiful woman like you is single?" Dhruv asked with an endearing smile

"How do you know that I am?" Khushboo looked at him in surprise.

"I did not feel a ring on your finger when we shook hands earlier."
"Oh, Oh, of course" Khushboo replied softly.

She had been certain that she would not be affected by Dhruv's magnetism again however, every time she looked at him, she felt a sudden lack of oxygen and felt that she had to quickly breathe so that would kick her brain into gear!

She still felt strongly attracted to him and at the same time resented him because he had overpowered the emotional defence that she had set up around her and that shook and infuriated her at the same time.

But notwithstanding her varying emotions, Khushboo found him to be good company, one who, she was sure, would be comfortable in any setting or in any company.

As they chatted over their wine, which was strong, heavy and dark, its colour a deep red, it seemed to Khushboo that it was absorbing not only the light but the atmosphere and its overtones too!

She felt relaxed in the pleasant atmosphere and Dhruv's stimulating company when the waiter came for their order, and when he had taken it down on his tablet, withdrew.

Dhruv was such an easy person to talk to that Khushboo wanted to confide her dilemma to him, but both were feeling so calm and relaxed that she did not want to spoil the mood. After all, it was her burden to carry and after all, what did she really know about him? So, much as she wanted to, she tried to check the flow of any personal conversation, but during it, Dhruv's eyes never left hers.

Chapter 76

Smoothly and expertly, Dhruv embroidered fiction over facts and told her that he was without a job at present, and how he had been in a care home all his life and had not known his parents.

Khushboo felt sorry for him, for not having known the warmth of a family life, and found she was making plans for her future, a future with him, a future of companionship and laughter and even children one day?

Abruptly she shook herself for it would not be wise to go down that route with Dhruv. For not only was it too soon to think about a meaningful relationship, but it would be difficult to come back from it! She was amazed and alarmed at the same time at not only how she was thinking about shaping her future with a man she had only just recently met, but because she had always been resistant to the idea of marriage and to the ordinariness and humdrum of everyday life that would entail.

The waiter arrived with the food and placed it on the table, and after inquiring if they needed anything else, withdrew discreetly.

"This does look delicious, excellent choice of restaurant, Khushboo."

"Thank you, not only did I hear good reviews about it from my colleagues, but it is near home so will be easier and quicker for me to get back." Khushboo answered.

"Don't worry about that, Khushboo." Dhruv said as he helped himself to some rice and mutton curry. "I will drop you home..."

"Thank you, but you don't have to, I can walk down, oh wow I did not realise I was hungry!" Khushboo said as she first placed the rice and chapatis on her place then put some lentils and mutton curry in the small bowls provided.

"I insist, Khushboo, on the way here I saw some unsavoury youths lounging about on the streets,"

For some time, they ate in silence, Khushboo nibbling at her food whilst Dhruv looked at Khushboo from under his lashes. Her head was bent over her plate, her hair forming a dark wavy dark curtain that fell over her ivory shoulders, hiding her face whilst the small earrings twinkled in the soft light.

Khushboo looked up and as she swept her hair from her cheeks, saw the flicker in Dhruv's eyes that had flashed momentarily. His gaze was so intense that when it caught hers, she blushed. She cleared her throat as her shoulders rose and fell as she drew in deep breadths.

"I enjoyed that, now what shall we have for dessert? You have been nibbling at your food!" Dhruv asked wiping his lips with his napkin. "I am sorry, I think I monopolised the evening by talking about myself."

"I didn't mind at all though I do feel sorry that you had such a rotten childhood. And no dessert for me thanks you go ahead, though I wouldn't mind a coffee."

Khushboo felt that Dhruv had had a hard life, which might account for the fact that he did not have job. It must have been difficult growing up in a home with no parental involvement, and no work ethic which explained glimpses of his devil may care attitude that she had seen, and, she felt, it was this very devil-may-care attitude that was his charm!

"How about some liqueur to go with it?" Dhruv asked.

"Not for me, Dhruv but don't let that stop you., and after that I really must leave." Khushboo said as rose and picked up her purse." But, for now, I would like to powder my nose."

Dhruv got up to hold her chair and saw her disappear and as he sat back in his chair, thought how very different she was to Aadrika whose name he had omitted to include as his friend in the home, nor had he told her that he was married to her for he had been careful to take of his wedding ring. He had liked Khushboo initially, and withholding that information was not intentional, He wanted to ensure that they would meet again, when he would tell her everything. Somehow, she brought out the best in him, something he was not used to,

After he had given the order for 2 coffees and one glass of liqueur, he looked around the restaurant, his eyes resting on a man who had been looking at him intently.

As soon as he saw that Dhruv was alone, he walked over to his table. He was distinguished looking with slight grey at the temples and was wearing a dark suit with white shirt and tie. His eyes were intelligent looking and kind, and he smiled slightly as he neared the table.

"I see you have not recognised me; my name is Doctor Wilson and I helped bring your son into this world. How is your wife Aadrika now?" He asked anxiously

. "They are both fine thank you." Dhruv replied as the Doctor looked at him in surprise and raised his eyebrows, however when he saw Khusboo returning fumbled in his pocket and took out a card.

"Sorry to bother you, but I think we need to talk, call me as soon as you can..." He put his card on the table and returned to his seat, still frowning.

"I noticed that man looking at you during dinner, an old friend?" Khushboo asked as she took a seat then bit her lip, for she did not want to seem nosy. "Sorry it is none of my business."

"It is alright, you don't have to apologise, but yes, a blast from the past." Puzzled Dhruv put the card in his pocket, wondering if the good doctor had mistaken him for someone else, but he had remembered Aadrika. All the same, he was amused by the worried expression on Khushboo's face.

However, when the waiter placed two coffees and a glass of liqueur on their table, he forgot about the doctor.

"Are you sure you would not like a glass of liqueur, it is Bailey's I think, very light with a flavour of coffee."

"Thank you but I have enjoyed the food and the cup of cappuccino looks perfect." Khushboo said as she took a sip of the frothy coffee, surprised at how easy going, relaxed, polite and considerate Dhruv was.

The evening had taken longer than expected and time had just flown by. Dhruv's company had been like a breadth of fresh air, for Khushboo had forgotten about the betrayal of her father and the financial debt he had left them in.

She figured that it was a strange twist of fate that their paths had crossed at a time when she needed the reassurance that there were still kind men in the world.

Little did she know that Dhruv was a man of many faces, that everything in his life was transitory and didn't want the responsibility that went with a solid life. For Dhruv, truth was something that could be shaped in whatever way he wanted., so, he could get what he wanted. However, he was finding it strange that all his different faces where being fused into one!

They half-heartedly decided to leave the restaurant after spending 3 hours of easy conversation and laughter. Once they had collected their coats and left the building, Dhruv insisted he walk her home.

"Khushboo, the street seems deserted, and the street lighting is not very good either."

"Okay, Dhruv, thanks again for a pleasant evening and walking me home, although you did not have to, my house is not far from here." Khushboo said.

She shoved her arms in her coat whilst walking, then buttoned it with jerky movements. They were walking leisurely, neither of them in a hurry to end the evening.

Dhruv took out a pack of cigarette and a gold lighter from his pocket. After igniting the lighter, he held the flame to his cigarette and having lit it, he puffed at it then inhaled deeply before putting the packet and lighter back in his pocket.

"Whew! I Needed a smoke!" Dhruv said as he puffed on the cigarette and blew out the smoke.

"Thank you for agreeing to have dinner with me, Khushboo, I enjoyed the evening."

"I did too," Khushboo said as they reached her house.

"So, what do you say we do this again one evening? And this time, I will choose the restaurant!" Dhruv's eyes twinkled as he looked at her.

"I think I will like that Dhruv, and thank you for walking me home, you were right, I would not have felt safe walking home."

Khushboo waved to him then turned and ran up to her house and Dhruv decided to wait till she was safely in the house. She was fumbling in her handbag for her keys when the door opened, and a man stepped out and began talking to Khushboo.

Dhruv clenched his fists at his sides, surprised at how possessive he felt. As he recalled her throaty chuckle, a shudder went down his spine, so he threw his cigarette butt across street. turned and walked to Aadrika's flat, which was also nearby.

He thought of the Dr who had accosted him, angry and frustrated for he had ruined his evening. He looked at the card again and found that he was a neurologist. Dhruv was puzzled for had he not told him that he had helped deliver Aarush?

Khushboo meanwhile was just about to open the door when Reyansh stepped out.

"Reyansh! How nice to see you, is everything all right?" Khushboo exclaimed.

"Yes, it is, I am sorry I got late in dropping them, did you have a good evening?"

"Surprisingly yes! "Khushboo answered. "Thank you for dropping them, I hope it was not out of the way."

"No, I live nearby, so it was no trouble at all. In fact, if it is okay with you, we can make this a daily routine? Your mother is very nice and reminds me of my mother who I miss very much.,"

Khushboo agreed, readily, for that meant that not only would she be free to go out again with Dhruv, but she could put in extra time at the office.

In addition to which she had a feeling that her mother would need Reyansh when she broke the news about her father, which she now decided she should do as soon possible.

Chapter 77

"I am just going to park my car, Khushboo, we got late so I picked up some takeaway and your mother was kind enough to ask me to join you."

"Oh wonderful, Reyansh, I am sorry, we can talk later."

Reyansh turned quickly to look for a parking spot, hopefully nearby, whilst Khushboo went into the house. She closed the door behind her, dumped her coat on the banister and went to wash her hands.

"Khushboo, is that you?" Her mother called from the sitting room.

"Yes, Mum I will change and join you in a minute."

She went to her bedroom and after she had changed into slacks and a black sweater, thought she would try calling her father, dreading, yet sure that it would go to voicemail and an automated voice would announce that the person was not available! It was the same thing every time, and each time it infuriated her. She heard the same automated voice, and on hearing it she felt a surge of fury so strong that she felt dizzy and had to sit down till the pounding in her heart began to subside.

After a while she stood up and paced the bedroom, her hands shaking and itching to do destroy something till she remembered her mother was waiting for her so should try and control her feelings.

As she went downstairs, she heard her mother's voice and the soft tinkling laugh of Ekta, which both Sameera and Khushboo had come to love, and she smiled to herself thinking that another name was going to be added to the list!

"Hi Mum Ekta," Khushboo threw off her shoes and collapsed on the settee. Although she had been seated and had been inactive the whole evening, her legs ached, and her head was ringing from being the focus of the conversation during the evening. She was felt heady when she thought of Dhruv, how when he had looked at her, she felt a sensation that was akin to a glass of champagne!

"Ah Khushboo, I see you had a good evening!" Sameera smiled as she saw her daughter's flushed faced.

"Yes, indeed I did, Mum!"

"I am glad, Khushboo, Reyansh dropped us home and insisted he get some take-away, so I won't have to cook! He lives alone, and as both felt he should not be dining alone, we invited him back, so he will be joining us for dinner. You look fresh and comfortable, Khushboo, Ekta, why don't you too go and change into something comfortable?"

"Yes, you will definitely feel better, and Mum, I met Reyansh on my way in."

Ekta's face had brightened at the mention of Reyansh, and she smiled "Yes you are right, it has been a long day, Sameera, I will do that but will be down in a jiffy." As she ran upstairs, Khushboo and Sameera looked at each other, the same idea crossing their mind.

"Well, I do hope this goes somewhere, Khushboo, they make a lovely couple, anyway I too will change into something more comfortable; I don't know how you girls can wear trousers for a whole day! Anyway, I see Reyansh has found a parking space." She said as saw Reyansh walk up the driveway through the window.

As soon as she had gone, the doorbell rang and Khushboo opened the door to Reyansh.

"Hello again, Reyansh, I want to thank you once more for bringing mum and Ekta, it meant a lot to me, and however keen they were to travel by public transport, I think they would have found it difficult." She led the way to the lounge "Reyansh would you like a cup of tea before dinner, and thank you for that too,"

"No thanks Khushboo, but listen we are alone, do you want to talk, I know something is troubling you."

Instead of telling him about her father, Khushboo told him about James and how her replacement had managed to get a permanent job working with her.

"But that does not worry me because Isabella is a sweet girl, but she and James are quite cosy and I cannot but help fearing insecure, and I just cannot afford to lose my job! Not now."

"You know he cannot legally fire you, Khushboo. "Reyansh replied, his eyes on the door, and just as Khusboo thought his mind was elsewhere, he turned to her and asked, "What do you mean 'not now'? Is there something else bothering you?"

"There is but that can wait for another day, but Reyansh you can help me in another matter. I need to talk to Mum alone tomorrow, so is it possible that you take Ekta to your house after dropping mum here so that I can talk to her?"

"Of course, no problem, I will invite all of you for dinner tomorrow and we can arrange the details later."

"Thank you, Reyansh, I will call you from office tomorrow, anyway, enough of shop, how were Ekta and mother?"

"I think you should not worry about them for they were fine."

Reyansh's eyes brightened for at that moment Ekta had entered. the room quietly. She had changed into a light cotton maroon of the shoulder embroidered top with black jeans and her damp hair inched down her back to reach her waist The only make up she had on was some light lipstick of the same shade as her top and a line of koel in her big eyes.

"Khushboo, can you help me in the kitchen please!" Sameera called.

"Coming Mum, excuse me Reyansh, you must be starving!"

Khushboo heard the clatter of her mother laying plates and spoons on table and left the room leaving an awkward silence behind.

Reyansh had never felt so tongue tied as he felt now, He was usually never short of words as and when the occasion demanded, be they charming funny or encouraging. But he now felt that he could not speak and if he did, the words would be reduced to functional words only, even a mere yes or no would also stick in his throat! Reyansh ran his tongue along the roof of his mouth and cheeks as if looking to see as if they might have got stuck there!

The glow of the lamp shone on Ekta's ivory shoulders and although she looked calm, her heart was beating fast. Her skin felt like every square inch of it that had been asleep was now waking up, and she was surprised, for she had expected them to remain asleep forever!

At that moment Khushboo called out that dinner was ready, so Reyansh got up and put out his hand to help Ekta.

She put her delicate slim hand in his and as she rose lightly, he touched his fingers lightly on her waist and as he did his heart pounded as did Ekta's.

However, Ekta had not wanted to feel drawn to Reyansh, and had resisted at first, but had finally given up and admitted that she did crave human contact!

Both of them were blushing slightly as they entered the kitchen where Sameera and Khushboo had laid out the takeaway food on the table and when all were seated Sameera said

"Reyansh, it was very nice of you not only to drop us but get the takeaway, saving us making dinner! It all looks so delicious"

Chapter 78

"It all looks so delicious; it is a pity I have had dinner." But Khushboo realised she was still hungry, for during dinner, she had enjoyed listening to Dhruv and only nibbling at her food..

"It does, and I am ravenous, I barely had time for a sandwich at work. "Reyansh helped himself to some rice. "Oh, Sameera, it is settled with Khushboo that I will drop you home in the evenings."

"Thank you, Reyansh, that would be nice, but you said you often have to work late, so we don't want to keep you from your work." Sameera remarked.

"Not at all, it will be my pleasure! In just one day, Ekta has been cleared such a lot of backlogs that had piled up, I don't think I will have to stay late anymore! And thank you for inviting me to stay for dinner, I am used to dining alone and at work we are so busy that I barely have time to have lunch or any kind of break. But now that Ekta and Sameera have joined us, it makes it so much easier, that is if you will continue to come, I have not asked you how you found working there?" Reyansh added helping himself to some curry.

"Oh, I liked it, but to be honest, it was difficult at first for I have not been out of the house but thanks to Ekta, I am now confident enough to be of some help! Anyway, Ekta, how did you like working with Reyansh? He is such a kind man I am sure he must have gone out of his way to make you feel at ease."

Confusion flickered across Ekta's face as she thought that Sameera was implying that there was an involvement with Reyansh.

She looked at her for a moment, her brow furrowed then shook her head. Reyansh had seen her confusion, knew that being a sensitive and modest girl, would have misunderstood and cleared his throat.

"Apart from working with people, there is a lot of Admin work which I thought she could take care of as she has experience in that line. And because I was led to believe that she is looking for a paid job, this experience would look good on her CV."

Reyansh wiped his mouth with a tissue whilst both Sameera and Khushboo felt that the 'man doth protest too much.'!!

"You really have given it a lot of thought and you are right, that kind of work would be useful. Ekta, you are very quiet, we are talking about you, you know?"

Ekta smiled as she sat at the table toying with her food, moving her head slowly side to side as she listened to the conversation. thereby stretching her elegant neck. She twisted a strand of hair around her finger and cocked her heard before answering.

"Of course, I liked it Reyansh, though I had forgotten a lot and you were very patient with me.!"

"Don't worry about it, it was your first day." He rose from the table. "Sameera, Khushboo thank you for a lovely dinner, I will see you tomorrow. Oh, how are you planning to come, do you need directions?"

"No thank you Reyansh, for the first week I will drop them in the morning," Khushboo replied.

"And I insist you have dinner with us from now on," Sameera said as Reyansh wore his coat and gloves.

"Thank you, but you don't have too, but I would love to, so from now on, it will be my responsibility to drop them in the evening." Reyansh smiled but although he spoke to all of them, his eyes were on Ekta. "Oh, and Sameera, a small suggestion, if you could wear Indian attire from to tomorrow, the women would find it easier to relate to you. Goodnight, all" he wrapped his scarf around his throat, waved and vanished into the night

. "Before we turn in for the night, can we talk in the lounge, and I will make tea to round up a lovely dinner?" Khushboo asked" not omitting the company of course?" she smiled impishly

"That would be nice," Ekta replied shyly for she had not missed the hidden implication. "How about you Sameera?"

"Oh yes, I would love some tea before I go to bed, I am tired. You know, it was a different experience, work I mean, Khusboo I wish I had thought of this before, though I think your father would not have allowed it and who knows once he is back…Come Ekta, let us go into the lounge. Oh, and Khushboo, you are not off the hook, I noticed how flushed you looked after your evening, so we need an update on that too?" She winked slyly at Ekta as she steered her into the lounge.

Khushboo felt a surge of anger and frustration at the mention of her father and pushing the strand of hair that had fallen across her face, she went to the kitchen and switched the kettle on to boil. She opened the unit door and took down the special Indian Spice chai and put a tea bag in the three mugs. Waiting for the water to boil, she opened the fridge door and took out a carton of milk and after the water had boiled, she put the mugs on a tray and carried them to the lounge,

She hid her anger behind a mask of watchfulness, for when it came to her father, she was not sure how long she would be able to control her feelings. However, she smiled when she saw her mother and Ekta comfortably exchanging the day's events.

"Thank you, Khushboo, that looks nice and hot!" Ekta said as she took the mug from the tray.

After Khushboo had given a mug to her mother, she took her mug and seated herself on the sofa.

"Now, tell me, Ekta, Mum how was your day?" she asked as she placed her tea on the table and plumped up a cushion than placed it behind her back before she reached for her mug. "I know you said it was okay but...I mean Reyansh is not here. Oh, and Mum that was very nice of you to invite him over, it was nice of him to drop you home, that is the least we can do. But you did have a good day, yes?"

"Oh no, that is what we were talking about, it was a nice day, and we are both looking forward to it tomorrow."

"I was thinking about what I should wear Sameera? I mean he suggested you wear Indian dress; I wonder I should do the same instead of trouser suit?" Ekta stared at her mug and swirled it around.

"Don't worry about it, you look nice in whatever you wear." Sameera reassured her.

"I don't think that is what she meant, Mum, you will be talking to women whereas Ekta is updating her office and computer skills so might find trouser suit to be more professional and comfortable."

Khushboo wanted to confide in Ekta, but when she saw her lovestruck face, concluded that as was on cloud nine, would not be able to give her any objective advice anyway...

"Right now, how was your evening and who is this Dhruv you had dinner with? Is he the guy we saw at the Chinese restaurant? I can see from you face that he has had quite an effect on you, so, when do I get to meet him? You have never gone out for a date, I told you that when the right man comes along, you forget your way of thinking!" when she saw Khushboo's red face exclaimed "Hah! I knew I was right."

"Mum I have only met him once, I don't know much about him except that he is unemployed at the moment, has no family and was brought up in a home."

"Oh, poor fellow, but maybe you should suggest volunteering at Reyansh?" Sameera made a noise that was something between laughter and a scorn.

"Mum, will you be serious please? There are other more serious matters at stake here, I have not heard from Dad, neither have you, do you have Adarsh's number, maybe he contacted him?

"There is no reason for him to do so, Khushboo, Aadarsh is my cousin, and you know how your father is, he does not want anything to do with my family. I mean, he had to in the beginning because Aadarsh helped him with a job, but not now. Anyway, why are you worried, he will be back in another three weeks."

"And till he does, I spoke to Aishya, and she will be coming back soon, for the policeman who killed George Floyd has been sentenced, but she will be going to straight to Afghanistan. But, if by the time she returns, I have not got a job and moved out, can we stay here?"

"Of course, it is, Ekta, but she has only been gone a week, it is difficult to get a job in so short a time, and being Asian, it will take longer. But I am sure that the experience you gain with Reyansh will be invaluable, and he will give you a glowing reference. I am sure you will get a job in no time. In fact, you never know, Reyansh might have a vacancy in his office!

Khushboo smiled as she traced her fingertip around the rim of her mug which brought dimples to her cheeks. She pushed the hair that had fallen on her forehead back.

"Mum you must be tired, I think we should go to bed for it is going to be another tiring day for us, we will leave at the same time. That reminds me, Mum have you heard from Olga, has she been coming?"

"No, she has not, at least not regularly, but I was not worried because actually you said she is not supposed to come here.at all! Khushboo, you told me that she was fine as Alexie had gone for a few days with his friend. Although I did not like that, and also that he still managed to control her from wherever he had gone. I hope she is okay."

"I hope so too, it is a bit late, but I will give her a call now." Khushboo took out her mobile and began dialling. It seemed half her life these days was spent on the mobile, most of which went to voicemail and were a waste of her time.

This time there was no reply, and as Khushboo put away her phone, she was slightly worried, for it was not like Olga not to take her call, however, late.

"Mum she is not picking up, maybe I should go to her flat to see if she is okay?" Khushboo asked with a frown on her forehead.

"I don't think that would be a good idea, for if Alexei is there and she is fine, your presence just might provoke his anger and make things worse for he!"

"You are right mum, I did not think of that, I only hope she is okay."

They went upstairs to their bedrooms, each engulfed in their own thoughts, Sameera worried about Olga, Ekta thinking about Reyansh and Khushboo still feeling heady after her evening with Dhruv; which had been so relaxing that it served as a distraction from her problem.

Khushboo lay awake n bed, marvelling at the effect he had on her, for although they had only spoken to each other and had had no physical contact, nevertheless, their bodies transmitting subtle promising implications, and both felt their magnetism. Whether it was chemical, romantic or just a delusion for Khushboo, the truth was that he was penetrating the braking wall of force that she had set around her.

Meanwhile, Ekta too could not sleep, amazed at the powerful attraction she felt for Reyansh, his twinkling and kind eyes that seemed to look straight through hers and the warmth of his hand as he had helped her up from the sofa.

Chapter 79

Whilst Dhruv walked to Aadrika's flat after leaving Khushboo, he thought about what he should do next, whatever it was, he had to tread carefully with Khushboo for she was a beautiful woman with a mind of her own. He felt that she was not the kind of girl who dated much or who would only date him for a few weeks and move on. No, it would be all or nothing with her, and wondered what destiny had in store for them? Were they destined to be star-crossed lovers clinging to each other and escape from the world, or would Dhruv take her to Paris, just for a weekend or could he do the right thing?

However, all he knew for certain was that Aadrika seemed to be the boring dull woman in his life, for her personality paled to that of Khushboo's.

At that moment his mobile phone buzzed and vibrated so he quickly took it out of his pocket, hoping it was Khushboo, but saw with disappointment that it was Anil

"Hi Anil, how are you?"

"I am fine, Dhruv, how are things with you and Aadrika? Has she discovered that she has no money and that I took it?"

"Yes, she did, Anil, but she seems to be much stronger than we thought, she did mention what you had done, but that was after she had contacted her landlords and her boss for a loan."

"She asked from a loan from William. That is a surprise! Anyway, he will want something in return don't worry, she will not be able to cope, what with her office, looking after Aarush…By the way how have you got along with him? That was the main purpose of getting back, right?"

"Yes of course, but Anil, maybe we are taking this too far? As for Aarush, she has not changed in that respect for, you are not going to believe this, but I have not even met him as yet! He is either at his friend's house where he stays overnight or is playing football."

"I have not met him either, which is strange considering I was always at Aadrika's flat early in the morning., after which for we left together after breakfast." Anil replied, surprised.

"I do find that strange, Anil, neither of us have either met or seen him!"

Suddenly Dhruv remembered Dr. Wilson who he had met earlier that evening and how surprised he had been when Dhruv told him that both Aadrika and Aarush were fine.

So as soon as Anil had rung off, Dhruv looked in his pocket for the Doctor's card, and when he found it, although it was late and not expecting an answer, he called him,

He was surprised when the doctor picked up the phone. "I was expecting your call, can you come by my office tomorrow, I will text you the address. I think you realise that we need to talk."

The doctor had sounded serious, however, he was happy with the way the evening had turned out, so whistling, he knocked on Aadrika's flat.

She opened the door then turned her back and went back into the lounge, but Dhruv could see from her attitude that she was sulking.

"Is everything okay Aadrika?" Dhruv felt a little annoyed for he was still feeling euphoric.

"Yes of course it is, I had to out for some milk and passed the Indian restaurant near the corner."

"Oh yes I had heard they serve very good food there so we should try it sometimes."

"Maybe, that is if your friend won't mind"

"Aadrika, what are you talking about? Anyway, where is Aarush, should he not be home by this time?"

"He is home," Aadrika replied indignantly. "He was tired so is upstairs asleep."

"I will peep in his room to have a look at him, I have not seen him as yet and am dying to see what he looks like…Does he look like you or me? I hope he looks like you Aadrika you are beautiful."

"No, I think you better not do that, Dhruv, Aarush is a light sleeper and any sound, even if is light will wake him and he needs his sleep."

Aadrika was dressed in black, and her dark hair was tied back in a ponytail. Her mouth was set in a hard flat line and her eyes shifted from left to right.

Her manner seemed evasive and shifty compared to her usual calm demeanour. She was talking fast and irrationally, and her body language too was all wrong, it was as if she had tucked into herself, head down, hands clasped tightly together.

Her eyes narrowed, and taking into account her swinging moods, Dhruv felt that the knowledge of Anil's departure and his deception might have affected her mental fragile state. Although initially his motive had been revenge, as he had pointed out to Anil, he did not want to jolt her already fragile state of mind. She trusted him, had always trusted him and he felt a twinge of guilt.

"Aadrika, don't worry, I won't disturb him, now come sit down and tell me what is worrying you. No, first cup of tea?"

Aadrika shook her head and sat down and waited for Dhruv who came back a little later with a mug of tea. Dhruv always used a particularly masculine authoritative tone when he wanted things done in a certain way, especially when it was time to get things under his control, except this time he used it to get information.

"Aadrika, let me what is the matter? Is it Aarush, I have told you before that you do not take the stress alone, we can both sort the problem?"

"No, there is no problem with Aarush, it was seeing you with that woman at the restaurant, both of you looked so happy that I felt miserable, for it suddenly occurred to me that I have been left, first by you then by Anil and again by you."

"But I thought we had decided that would be nothing between us. Just living together for 2 days has showed us that."

Dhruv took a sip of tea from the mug, wondering if he should tell her about Dr Wilson, then decided against it, for he had got the feeling that the doctor wanted to talk to him alone. However, he was a bit disturbed for Aadrika was behaving oddly, and wondered if it was because she was jealous, or because it was the after effect of the lockdown, Anil's deception or maybe it was everything combined? Maybe contacting William had not been a good idea, for Anil had told him that he could matters worse for her.

"Hey, Ad, you are not jealous, are you?" Dhruv but although his tone was light, he was concerned for he felt he was sitting in a room full of secrets.

At the very least, it was something underhand going on, something he needed to know, and intuitively felt it had something to do with Aarush. The sooner he spoke to the Doctor the better, for it seemed that he alone could shed a light on the mysterious circumstances, for Aadrika was behaving so strangely, he doubted she would tell him.

It seemed that the relationship that he had had with Aadrika had been based on fiction and built and fuelled by old fashioned suspicion and jealousy on his side. He had first been jealous of her bond with Darpan, then resented the love and attention that Aadrika had paid Aarush and now he was even beginning to doubt her conduct and behaviour!

Aadrika sat on the sofa feeling restless, then narrowed her eyes as she remembered Dhruv laughing with the lovely girl in the restaurant. Although they had decided to go their separate ways, Aadrika experienced a pang of regret that he had moved on.

Chapter 80

Aadrika was racked irrationally with a spasm of hatred at everybody, she was even angry at the girl at the restaurant, till finally it spread throughout her body like poison.

The feeling was so intense that she wanted to kick, punch or kill, however, she took a deep breath aware that she would have to learn and live with these waves of animosity that she felt towards each and everyone.

Dhruv saw the various flitting expressions on Aadrika's face and felt that she needed to be handled with kid gloves, Anil's betrayal had devastated her, had made her insecure and she now believed she could not cope with the world. At one time, he had thought she had matured into a strong independent woman, was he wrong?

"Aadrika, I don't mean to pry, but how did your meeting with your boss go? Is he going to pay you advance salary so that at least you can sort out your finances?"

"Ah I meant to tell you, yes he has, but not from my salary, I think there is a rule against it, since we are a small company. But he was very nice, and offered me to lend some money himself, from his savings and…"

"Did you accept, Ad and if you did was that wise?"

"I have no choice Dhruv, and that is a load of my mind, but whilst you were away, Mr Sharma, my landlord called. They seemed so understanding when I spoke to them earlier, but now have told me that I have to evict the property!" Aadrika cried, her voice loud and shrill.

"Oh, that is awful Aadrika!" He came over to Aadrika and took her hands in his." Has he at least given you some time to find somewhere else?"

"That is not going to be possible for every landlord wants a deposit of at least a 1000 pounds, unless I take a room only. Even that I cannot afford, after I paid all my bills and three months, I owe Mr Sharma. However, he did say he would try and help me find someplace."

Aadrika's voice was so low that Dhruv had to strain his ears to hear her, and it seemed as if the roller coaster of emotion that she been through had finally exhausted her! '

No wonder Aadrika appeared so uptight, Dhruv thought, she seems so fragile it as is as if she is made of fine China that would shatter at the slightest touch!

Aadrika sat with her hands clasped on her lap, and she suddenly shivered, as if someone had crept up behind her. Dhruv thought of Khushboo and wondered if he should ask her to help Aadrika, for, she had mentioned during the evening that her work involved helping women in her situation?

"Aadrika, you know the woman you saw me with, well, I actually was having a meeting with her regarding you and…"

Aadrika sat up angrily, "How dare you talk about me behind my back, what have you told her?"

"Nothing, nothing," Dhruv tried to calm her. "She works in a law firm and helps women in similar situations like yours, but rest assured, I did not talk to her about you, anyway, I did not know you were being evicted, I was going to ask you first, Aadrika, she is a very nice woman and…"

"And a very beautiful one too!" Aadrika replied suspiciously with narrowed eyes. "Will you be meeting her again? We are still married, you know, bet you did not tell her!"

"Aadrika, why are you behaving this way? Yes, we had planned to meet again, and I was going to tell her then."

He was puzzled, so in between taking sips from his mug, Dhruv had been taking a puff on his cigarette.

"I see, it did not take you long to move on!" Aadrika's eyes were wary and when she saw Dhruv look at her in confusion, added, her voice calm and well-modulated. "Yes, yes I know that is something we had agreed on."

She turned her face to one side and laced her fingers tightly together, the expression on her face unreadable. Her heart was black with bitterness, cold and grief. Aadrika felt she was shedding people like an old bark from a maple tree in autumn! First Darpan, then Dhruv, then Anil and now Dhruv again, though she was beginning to feel she never had them in the first place?!

"Aadrika, I think you better go to sleep; you look knackered! And don't worry, we will sort the problem of your house together."

Dhruv had at last got his revenge, but the victory seemed empty. He wondered at the cause, was it the effect of Khushboo that had mellowed him or was it seeing the fragile state of mind that all this had on Aadrika.? Whatever the reason, now he genuinely wanted to help her. He had wanted to talk to her about formalising the divorce but thought he would leave it for another time, now he was sure she could handle it.

"Yes, I think I will, goodnight, Dhruv and thank you for your moral support, it is very nice of you, I am not really your problem..." Aadrika rose, smiled weakly as she rose.

"Goodnight, Aadrika, I hope I will see Aarush tomorrow."

Dhruv looked at Aadrika's face closely, hoping that the expression on her face would provide him with an answer or at least a clue to the mystery, but Aadrika simply turned and walked out of the room.

As she snuggled into the pillow after fluffing it, she drifted off to sleep, thinking she was alone, once again. An unexpected wave of longing ripped her heart. Even when she had been with Anil, he rarely spent the night with her, but she still missed having someone, anyone and the faint hope that it might be Dhruv had finally vanished into thin air.

Chapter 81

Khushboo had not been able to sleep as she recalled the pleasurable evening spent with Dhruv. She had tossed and turned and watched the ink black of the night fade into the silver of a pre-dawn sky and from there to a slate grey sky.

It was still early so she went downstairs to the kitchen, still in her pyjamas, to make a cup of tea, then having put the kettle to boil and having put a twining teabag in her favourite mug, she went to the fridge to get some milk.

When she opened its door, she smiled slightly for Olga had arranged everything neatly, with a separate shelf for vegetable, another for storage boxes and had also set aside a compartment place for milk and bottles.

Sameera had heard her moving around so entered the kitchen with a frown.

"Is everything alright, Khushboo? It is not like you to get up so early, something or someone keeping you up?" she smiled meaningfully.

"Mum! Everything is fine, I could not sleep so decided to have a cup of tea before getting ready for work. Can I make you one or would you like to go back to sleep? It is still early."

"Oh, I could not be able to go back to sleep anyway, Khushboo, so will join you..."

She sat on the table and put her elbows as Khushboo took down another mug, added teabag and milk in it and came over with the 2 mugs and placed them on the table.

"Now, Khushboo, can you tell your mother why you could not sleep? It wouldn't have anything to do with a certain young man you had dinner with, could it?"

There was a twinkle in Sameera's eyes as she held the mug in both her hands, blew on it then took a sip of the tea.

"Mum!" However, Khushboo blushed then changed the subject. "Mum, I need to talk to you alone, so I spoke to Reyansh, and he agreed that he will drop you here and then take Ekta to his house where we will have dinner. This will also give the two of them some lone time." Khushboo winked, looked at her wrist, gave a cry and got up quickly.

"Very clever, Khushboo that is a very good idea., but why do you want to talk to me?"

"I'll explain later."

Sameera got up with, a a puzzled look on her face, and they walked out of the kitchen together. When they neared the door, Khushboo suddenly stopped and turned to her mother, and in a low voice whispered.

"Mum, please don't tell Ekta about our plan, Reyansh will handle it. And I do need to talk to you, hopefully I will be able to leave a little early, I will meet you here at 5.pm"

They went upstairs to their respective rooms and after some time came down, Khushboo wearing her professional outfit, crisp white shirt, black pencil skirt with a black jacket. She was wearing delicate pearl studs, her ensemble completed by subtle makeup and high heels.

Sameera was already in the kitchen, wearing, as Reyansh had suggested, an Indian outfit of cream a **Salwar kameez**, which comprised of pants with to-the-knees shirt and stole of pale pink.

"Hi, Khushboo you look nice!"

"As do you Mum, can we leave soon please for then I can leave office early."

"Yes of course, Khushboo,"

She quickly switched on the coffee maker, put some slices of bread in the toaster, then opened the unit door and took down a mug for Ekta.

"We are just having toast and coffee and as soon as Ekta comes down, ah here she is looking lovely as ever!"

Ekta was looking tall and willowy, for she was wearing a cream roll neck cardigan with grey trousers that accentuated her long legs. Instead of her usual bun, she had let her dark hair fell to her shoulders. Her make-up too was subtly made up, but today it was to disguise the black circles under her eyes.

They quickly finished their light breakfast and as they walked across to where her car was parked, unlocked it and climbed into their usual seats, Sameera in the front whilst Ekta sat at the back. Khushboo, having got in the front seat and after tying the belt around her waist, slammed her door, and in her hurry to be on her way, almost collided with an oncoming van.

The day that had started cloudy and cloudy and dull but changed its mind and decided to twirl about and show of its summer colours.

"Hey Khushboo, steady on! You are going to get us killed! What is the hurry?" Sameera asked in alarm as she clutched the handle of the door. "Ekta, are you okay?"

"I am fine thanks Sameera."

"Sorry ladies, I was thinking of something else!"

"Yes, I know who you were thinking of, just do your thinking safely at home please..." Sameera said tersely.

The roads from thereon were deserted so in no time at all they were at Reyansh's office. Before Sameera undid her seatbelt, Khushboo turned to her and kissed her on the cheek.

"Ah, that is nice, Khushboo, you never do this!"

"Have a nice day, Mum and I will see you in the evening."

She waited in the car till both had entered the building, then turned her car towards her office, and resuming her daily routine, she stopped at the bakery for fresh doughnuts, but this time she included an extra one for Isabella.

Having parked the car, she walked over to the bakery and passed a bearded homeless man who was sitting barefoot on a wall, puffing hungrily on a cigarette that was nearly burned out. Around him were black plastic bags that looked to be full of his belongings

As Khushboo carried the box of doughnuts back to her car, she felt sorry for the man and almost felt guilty that she was having doughnuts whilst the homeless man was trying to appease his hunger by smoking a burnt down cigarette.

She placed the box of doughnuts on the seat beside her, but as soon as she had put the keys in the ignition, somehow, she could not start the car, thought it was a sign that she should be thinking of others less fortunate than herself, So, she quickly took out her wallet, opened the car door and walked back over to the homeless man

She opened her wallet and held out a note of five pounds. him a few pounds. He held out his hand which was in mittens quickly, and after taking the note, gave her a toothless smile. He put the note in the pocket of his old, frayed coat, and it seemed as if he was drifting barefoot through life with his sweet gentle smile that showed his weakness?

Khushboo drove off, thinking she had a lot to be grateful for and braked suddenly, for a bus in front of her had stopped at a bus stop, dropped some passengers then moved off.

Khushboo took her foot of the brake and followed slowly, till she could safely overtake it. She went past a few shops one of them being a hair salon. In the salon, there were ladies siting, some swaddled to foiled around their heads, others sipping coffee while others were waiting for their turn, reading magazines.

She arrived at her office and having parked the car and taken the box of doughnuts, she caught a lift that took her up soundlessly to her floor.

Chapter 82

Although she was early, Stella was at her desk, one hand holding a receiver to her ear and with the other, writing something on a post-it-note. She paused to smile to wave to Khushboo, who waved back and pointed first to the doughnuts then to her office. She found that Isabella was already at her desk, the office filled with the aroma of fresh coffee as it bubbled away in the coffee maker.

Khushboo hung her coat on the stand and took her seat behind her desk when Isabella looked up and smiled.

"Hi there, I did not hear you come in!"

"Well, you seemed so busy in your work I did not want to disturb you!" Khushboo smiled. "Anyway, I think I told you about our morning ritual. Before we start our day, we have fresh doughnuts and coffee. I bring the doughnuts because I pass this bakery which makes doughnuts that are out of this world! Stella usually keeps the coffee ready, which I think it is, so as soon as Stella comes, we will have five minutes free time to ourselves. The day then becomes so hectic that we rarely get time to talk or sometimes even have coffee!"

"That sounds like a wonderful way to start the day, Khushboo," Isabella went to the table where the coffee was bubbling, poured 3 mugs and bought it over to Khushboo's desk who had opened the box

. "Those do look yummy, I did not have time to have breakfast, so am starving and they do look delicious."

At that moment Stella walked in and joined them and as soon as they had finished the doughnuts Stella took her coffee back to her desk, but as soon as she reached the door, turned to Khushboo.

"Khushboo, remember you have an appointment at 11 a.m. with a Mr. Sharma but he did not say what it was about. Shall I show him to the conference room?"

"Yes, that will be fine, I hope by that time I have sifted through the messages, there are so many I don't think I will get a chance to check them all.

"Do you want me to see him Khushboo?" Isabelle had only been in the office for a brief time, so wasn't sure with whom it was safe to talk to safely, sarcastically and whom to talk to with respect! But it was her nature to treat everyone with respect so thought that attitude would, at least, would keep her within the boundaries of conduct and she liked Khushboo and Stella.

"No thank you Isabella. I will take care of it."

Both were working quietly when an hour later, Stella knocked and staggered into the office with red roses in a big vase. She went straight to Khushboo's desk and placed the vase on it.

"It seems you have an admirer Khushboo," She winked turned and left the room. "There is a card there."

Khushboo quickly read the card, which read simply 'thank you for a lovely evening',

Khushboo blushed slightly and put the card in her drawer recalling that he had shaken hands with her twice, first when they had met, then whilst saying goodbye. Both times Khushboo had squeezed his hand slightly, but now hoped that he had not mistaken that as a sign of suppressed passion?

All during the morning, he had been sending her texts, jokes that he wanted to share with her, and they had made her smile.

She rubbed her forehead and walked over and made herself another cup of coffee for it was nearing 11.am and she did not know how long the meeting with Mr Sharma would take. She took the mug and went to the conference room to wait for him and hoped he would turn up and not cancel the meeting at the last minute, as many did.

She sat tapping her fingers on the table when she heard a ping from her mobile. It was another text sent by Dhruv and she thought that considering his upbringing, he was surprisingly pleasant, knowledgeable, and intelligent man with a sense of humour.

Out of the blue, she thought that if ever they were to have a relationship, which she doubted, for seemed a care-free man, but hoped, it would be a unique one, and maybe it was because of that very reason she was attracted to him and found him to be exciting? She was sure that if he were to ever change in any way in the future, it would have a negative impact on their relationship.

Whilst waiting for Mr. Sharma, she took out her mobile and rang Reyansh to confirm that he would drop her mother at her house by 5p.m. and that they would later join him and Ekta for dinner.

At that moment there was a knock on the door and Stella walked in followed by a man who she introduced her to Mr Sharma and left the room.

Mr. Sharma was a tall and stockily built with a large bony head, curled up ears and kind compassionate black eyes under thick eyebrows with few wisps of air in them.

Khushboo got up from her chair and held out his hand and smiled." How can I help you Mr Sharma?"

"I am very sorry to bother you but there is something I need your advice on." His voice was muffled and Khushboo could see that he looked worried.

"Of course, Mr Sharma, I am here to help, would you take a seat please?"

"Thank you". Mr Sharma sat down but then bent his head and rubbed his hands on his bony head.

"Now, Mr Sharma, what can I help you with? Has it something to do with your wife?

"Oh no! In fact, I have come here without telling her, anyway, let me start at the beginning. I am a landlord and one of my flats was rented by a single woman with a son. Now I did not meet them, and she used to pay the rent regularly, that is till about 3 months ago. She phoned me a few days ago surprised, that it had not been paid although I had sent reminders. She told me that her friend had offered to take care of her bills, and she had trusted him, making sure that she did not see our reminders, but, instead, he scammed her of all her money! She called crying, and at my wife's insistence, we came to an agreement in which she could stay on and pay the backlog of rent in instalments."

As he spoke, Khushboo's heart went out to the lady, for she reminded her of her mother, both so trusting and naive, both been conned by people they trusted.

"I am afraid I cannot help you in this case Mr Sharma, unless the woman wants to take the man to court."

"No, she is much too naïve for that, and would take a long time. But since we last spoke, I need her to vacate the house and have told her to do so, within legal time limit of course, but she has no money, and I was wondering if you could help her?"

"I will be happy too; in fact, my mother is volunteering at an Asian woman's shelter who deal with these kinds of issues. If you leave me your number, I will see what I can do then ring you with their details."

"Oh, thank you so much! She is such a kind sweet girl I hate to put her and her son out on the street."

He handed her his card then wrote something at the back.

"That is my property's address where she lives..." He smiled, handed her the card and left the room, looking relieved.

As she took the card, it pleased her to think that there were good men for Mr Sharma did not have to look out for his tenant, yet he had taken time out to see her.

She went back to her office and told Stella and Isabella that she would be leaving at 4:45 p.m.

Chapter 83

She left the office at 4:45 p.m. and as it had started drizzling slightly, her coat was somewhat wet when she got in the car and drove home, her thoughts with the poor woman who had been swindled, all alone with a son to take care of.

Her knuckled gripped the steering wheel till they turned white, and her lips formed a thin hard line. If it had not been for the fact that she had seen the letter confirming her dad's one way ticket to Indi with her very eyes, she would have continued to believe that her father would return and sort out the problem.

She stopped on the way to do some shopping and got mango Walls ice cream, her mother's favourite flavour, hoping that it would help soften the shock.

As soon as she entered, she took the shopping in the kitchen, unloaded it on table and stacked the ice-cream in the freezer then went to her room for a quick bath.

After her bath, she decided to call her father and waited for an answer whilst she dried her damp hair with the towel, and then with the corner, wiped away the trickle of water that was dripping from her hair down her neck

When there was no answer from him, she rang Olga who also did not pick up, so Khushboo placed the mobile on the side table whilst she finished dressing a frown on her face. She hurriedly wore her jeans with a jumper, then stretched her arms above her head feeling her neck and shoulders tense, when she heard a noise downstairs, and presumed it to be her mother.

She ran down to the kitchen and saw that her mother had put the kettle on. "Khushboo, is everything alright? Reyansh said you wanted to talk to me alone and we will go their house for dinner later which Ekta is going to prepare!"

"Well, that is good news for that means she is comfortable in Reyansh's house, Now, shall we have our tea in the sitting room to talk or here if you prefer."

"No Mum the lounge is fine, the chairs are much more comfortable."

As soon as Sameera had made the tea, she carried the mugs to the room and sat down, a puzzled look on her face.

Khushboo had collapsed back on the cushion with her feet tucked under her a mug of tea in her hand but her shoulders felt tight, as if she still was wound too tight and thought about how she was going to tell her mother about her father who had flown off into a country with different days and different season and a different lifestyle, wondering how in the world it had come to this, then decided the best way was to be truthful and honest.

"Mum I wanted to talk to you about Dad, he has left us and is not coming back."

"That is not true, Khushboo, he will be back." Sameera replied angrily." How dare you say something like that?".

"No Mum, he is not." She then told her mother everything, from the time that the bank manager had rung her, to her finding the papers. How he had re-mortgaged their house, claimed in insurance money into an account in India and closing all his accounts here, and ending with the letter from the travel agent which confirmed the one-way ticket to India.

"That is why we have not been able to get through to him, Mum he does not want anything to do with us."

Sameera listened to Khushboo in disbelief, with lines between her eyebrows, not grasping what Khushboo was saying, for she had become used to living in her husband's shadow and always thought he would be there. Although his constant disappearing acts had hurt her, she had silently borne them in the knowledge that he would come back to her, and he always had.

Khushboo's words were like spikes of ice that stabbed at her between her ribs, each one sharper than the last and she felt she was riding a roller coaster of emotions. Sameera's anger turned to sadness, then she felt a sense of loss as she thought that even if he returned, too much had been lost between them that might never be repaired. Re-mortgaging their house for such a large amount, then vanishing without paying his previous mortgages? Sameera was an honourable and decent woman and for Anil to have left them with nothing was something she could not understand for she had always thought him to be an honourable and decent man.

Her lips clamped together, tears running down her cheeks, which she wiped quickly with the back of her hand, taking then tool a tissue which Khushboo held out to her, her eyes glistening. But now that Sameera thought about it, it all made sense; the meetings that went on till late at night, calls at home that were quickly ended, switching off the computer screens when she got close.

She blew her nose delicately, dabbed at her reddened eyes, sank back into the soft couch then dug her fingernails into the couch for she had been spurned and rejected by her husband in the worst possible way!

There was an eerie silence in the room, as each of them was caught up in the personal pain of betrayal, Sameera as a wife and Khushboo as a daughter. Sameera was a kind forgiving woman but was hurting so much that she could not think of her husband or what he had done.

Her anger was mixed with betrayal and humiliation but wanted to conceal the hurt. She did not want sympathy, neither her daughter's nor of her relatives, if they ever came to hear of it, which they undoubtedly would. No, she preferred to wrap her grief around her like a layer of cling film.

Although she was hurting, her instinct was to ease her daughter pain, for it was she who would have to deal with the financial debts her father had left them in.

She stood up abruptly, and left the room, and with shaking hands unlocked the garden door, flung it open, and without a word, went out into the garden. She felt maybe by staying clear of the shadow of house, might make the truth go away, so she tipped her head back and sucked in lungsful of air.

Khushboo sat quietly, knowing how much her mother was hurting and that she needed time to process the information, but that. although her mother was naïve and gullible, she was also a very strong and resilient woman, Khushboo had been angry before, but when she saw her mother crying, she wanted to claw and scratch her father's face!

Khushboo crossed over to the window and saw her mother pacing around the garden, then stop and pluck a rose from the rose after which she resumed her calmly walking around the garden.

"Mum shall I make you another cup of tea?" Khushboo went out and asked with a frown. She was worried for it was essential her mother show anger but apart from a few tears she seemed to be in perfect control.

Before closing the window and returning to her seat, Khushboo smiled as she saw a fat pigeon trying to balance itself precariously on a fence and when could not succeed, wobbled, shifted its weight then fly off,

She went into the kitchen to make some tea and returned just as Sameera came back and sat down, still looking puzzled,

As she handed one mug to Sameera, she kissed her on the cheek. "Mum I want you to know that I have got everything under control. I have spoken to the bank manager who was very understanding and with my salary, we can get back on our feet. I am sorry Mum that is no comfort to you, but at least we won't be out on the street."

"Oh Khushboo, I am so sorry, you are so young, you should not have to carry the financial burden! Can you explain again what he did?" Sameera asked with tears in her eyes and Khushboo repeated what she had told her earlier.

"You know the strange thing Mum, all this time I thought we were fighting outside negative forces like racism discrimination and bigotry. I never thought something sinister was taking shape in my own home!"

"Me too, Khushboo, I thought your father to be a decent man and always took his side against yours. I am sorry." She whispered

"Don't worry about it now Mum, anyway I promised Reyansh that we will join them for dinner."

When her mother shook her head, added "Mum you must eat, and change would do you good and at this time it is nice to be surrounded by friends."

At that time there was a knock on the floor and Khushboo ran to answer it...As soon as she opened it, was surprised to see a policeman and wondered who had told them about their father.

"Mam do you know a person by the name of Olga?"

"Yes, she used to work for us, is everything okay?" Khushboo asked in alarm.

"Mam her husband is threatening to kill her and would only speak to you, please can you come immediately her husband is in a temper and we are afraid for her!"

"Oh my god of course, give me a minute to change." Khushboo ran up to her room, quickly changed, rang Reyansh to explain the situation and if he could pick up her mother and take her to his house.

"Reyansh, I have had to give some very bad news, so please look after her."

She ran downstairs before realising that she had not tied the shoelaces of her loafers wondering how she had not tripped over them, so sat at the bottom of stairs to tie them, then, put the key to the door in her pocket, but before letting herself out of the house, went to the sitting room

"Mum, a policeman is here, I have to go with him for Olga is in some kind of danger from Alexei who only will only speak to me. I have spoken to Reyansh, and he will pick you up."

"Oh Khushboo, I can't take any more of bad news, I hope she is okay."

Chapter 84

Reyansh's office was fairly large, warm and tastefully furnished with one wall entirely covered by bookcases and a desk which he had chosen to have by the window. There was a computer on his desk, a small fridge in the room a small leather sofa in the corner and cabinets full of files, and a printer was at the corner of a room on a small table, and on his desk were stacks of silver memory sticks.

Ekta had been surprised when sometime during the day Reyansh had told her that he wanted Ekta, Sameera and Khushboo to have dinner at his place. He would be dropping Sameera at her place where she and Khushboo would join them later, whilst he would take Ekta to his house.

"If it is okay with you, Ekta, I'll drop Sameera first then pick you up and take you to my place. I will have to come back to office though so will get some takeaway food on the way back."

"Not at all, but Reyansh, you do not have to get food, I will cook something whilst I am waiting, I am not a bad cook you know!"

"Is there anything you cannot do? But Ekta you do not have to; you will be tired too."

"Don't worry about it, it will be my pleasure."

"But I don't know if I will have all the things, you need and..."
"Reyansh don't worry about it."

"Thank you, we will leave at 5 then."

Ekta went about the day with a smile on her face, for she was looking forward to seeing where and how Reyansh lived. She would love to cook for him, for she always had arguments with Aryan, who had resented her ability to organise his life for him. In the beginning, she had cooked different dishes for him for she wanted to improve Aryan's taste buds, but he only wanted junk food. She had, many times, cooked a special dish for him after queuing and slaving over the cooker for a long time after work, only to see Aryan gulp it without any appreciation or thanks, till she had finally given up.

Reyansh, all during the day be he on a call or working on a file, would watch Ekta through half closed eyes as she moved gracefully around the office, arranging his paperwork and files.

He thought that Ekta brought all the seasons with her, the delight of a summer sun, crisp freshness of autumn and spring followed by the sparkling magic of winter! At 5 p.m. Reyansh looked up from his desk. "Ekta are you ready? Shall I get your coat for you?"

"Yes, I am," she replied. "But thank you, I do not have a coat, it was not cold in the morning."

"But it is now, here you can wear mine." He put his coat around her shoulder, and as he slid his hand along her back, he left a trial of warmth everywhere he touched and suddenly he tipped her chin up studying her face which was soft and pink

She smiled at him, her eyes sending messages of promises, a thank you with her eyes and smile, her face like a gift of the kiss of surrender for paying attention to her. Ekta had always felt hurt that no one noticed her or acknowledge her as a person; so, had put up her inhibitions as a shield that would protect her from others.

Ekta dropped her eyes embarrassed that she might show her feelings, but Reyansh only smiled slightly as his hand tightened on her upper arm and guided her to his car.

As, soon as they were seated Reyansh turned towards Ekta. "Ekta about the cooking, you don't have too, you know!"

"I know but I want to!" She gently touched his cheek for in the brief time she had known him, she had come to love the contours of his face, and in his eyes, she could clearly see sparkle of sincerity.

When Ekta had touched his cheek gently his heart had begun to beat faster, and he wanted the same again, wanted them to be together forever, and for the rest of the journey home, he clung to that wish...

Ekta looked around her as they passed familiar looking roads and she remembered that Reyansh had said that he lived nearby, and as soon as they arrived at a house with red brick wall and ivy running down its walls, he stopped

"Is that your house, Reyansh? It is beautiful!" Ekta put her hand on her mouth as she gazed in awe.

"Well, my parents actually, they have moved to smaller place out of London and as I am their only son, wanted me to move in, especially as I was living in small flat..."

They were walking up the driveway and when they reached the door, Reyansh took out a keyring and opened the door

"Now make yourself comfortable, Ekta, I won't be able to show you around, but that is the kitchen, where I hope you will find everything you need. If not, please do not hesitate to ring me and I will get takeaway! Oh, and this is the lounge where you can make yourself comfortable till the ladies show up."

He turned and left, closing the door behind him and Ekta went to explore the house, admiring the spacious lounge that was dominated by big plasma TV on the wall. The room was decorated with cream velvet chairs with gilt fringed cream and gold cushions, and on the side, table was a cream and gold lamp. The windows were framed by ivory velvet curtains and there was a fireplace in the room,

Ekta admired his mother's taste and went over to the windows to draw the ivory-coloured curtains and to switch on the yellow lamp on the side table which, when switched on, gave the room a warm glow.

She peeped into the dining room that had bay windows that looked out into the garden before going into the kitchen to make herself a cup of tea and see what she could cook for dinner. As she located the tea bags and mug and put the kettle on to boil, she thought that most women have secret plans and hopes, and although she had put her hopes and desires on hold, most women, she thought would love to have a house like this. She discovered that although she had put her hopes and desires on hold, she now felt unbound by them and freely acknowledged that she too would love to live in the house, but only with Reyansh beside her.

She looked at the time, gave a cry and hurriedly got up for she was going to need more time to work in a strange kitchen. She went quickly to the fridge, found some lamb, thought she would make mutton curry, then looked through the cupboards and collected all the ingredients she would need for it...

She then found a chopping board and proceeded to first chop meat and put it on a plate, then chopped the onions and put them onto fry and once they were brown put in the chopped meat. She then stirred in tomatoes, 2 teaspoonful of curry powder then ginger garlic and paprika., and as she cooked, was surprised that all the ingredients were available in a bachelor's house, for she doubted he cooked for himself,

However, she recalled him saying that his parents had lived here and most probably would be visiting him often. She put the pot with the meat to simmer till it was tender, and in the meantime found the rice and put the water to boil for it. However, she could not find any Chapatis or Nan so thought she would phone Khushboo to pick them on the way.

The curry that was simmering on a gentle heat was giving of a rich aroma, and satisfied with the result, Ekta thought she should make some desert, and as she had seen some fresh fruit, and a tin of mangoes, thought fresh fruit salad would be fine.

She went into the dining room and having found silver cutlery, located placemats and napkins in a drawer of the mahogany sideboard which she lay on the table. After she had laid them out on the table went back into the kitchen to see if the meat curry was done, and when she found it to be tender, switched it off and turned her attention to the rice, The water had boiled, and after putting in the rice and curry leaves, she put it on low, dried her hands and went to the sitting room to ring Khushboo.

She looked at her watch and found that it was only just after 6 pm and dinner was ready. She went back into the kitchen, saw that the rice was done, switched it off made herself another cup of tea and went back into the lounge, wishing that she had made more than one dish.

Before making herself comfortable, she went over to the mantel piece and saw a few photographs in silver frames. One was of an elderly couple, smiling, who were definitely Reyansh's parents, for he had the smile as his father and another of Reyansh. She stared at it for some time overcome by the powerful attraction she felt for Reyansh, who was smiling into the camera, and it was as if she could feel his twinkling eyes looking straight into hers!

She had heard stories about single women falling in love with any man available and wondered if it applied to her? Were the stories true or untrue and was this feeling she felt for Reyansh love or just infatuation? She shook her head in bewilderment and went to sit and wait for Reyansh, then remembered she had to call Khushboo.

Usually, Khushboo did not take long to answer, but just as Ekta was going to end the call for she did not want to disturb her, when Khushboo answered, breathless.

"Khushboo, are you alright? You sound terrible!"

"Oh, Ekta it is all my fault, I should have acted sooner, it is all my fault."

"Khushboo what are you talking about you are not making any sense! Where are you?"

"Oh Ekta, I am at Olga flat, Alexie has killed her and it all my fault!" she sobbed.

Chapter 85

"Oh my God! Khushboo, what do you mean, what has happened?"

"I will tell you the details later, for now, Alexei her husband and his friend are in custody and out Olga is no more."

"I am at Reyansh's house Khushboo, I will leave immediately and come to your house. Does Sameera know?"

"No, you stay where you are, I have told Reyansh he will pick Mum up and bring her to his house. She knows that Olga was in danger for the police came to collect me from my house, but she does not know the details. Oh, it is awful, I will come to Reyansh's house later and tell you everything." She ended the call with a sob leaving Ekta stunned.

Just as she had finished the call, Reyansh opened the door with his key and entered followed by Sameera. Ekta ran and hugged her, took her by the hand and took her into the sitting room.

"Ekta, Reyansh got a call from Khushboo in which she told him about Olga, it is all our fault, we were concerned for her but enough! We did nothing and let her go back to her husband knowing the danger she was in."

"That is true, Sameera, but we only went by what Olga wanted." Seeing Reyansh's puzzled face, she explained the situation from start to end and how they were going to give the address of one of Reyansh's shelter so she could escape there

"So why didn't you, Sameera, you know we are all about helping women to escape from their partners."

"I think it was Olga's idea, for her husband had threatened to kill anyone who helped her, so if he found out that Khushboo had helped her, anyway, it was Khushboo's idea she stops working for us and as; her husband had gone for a holiday with his friend, we thought she was safe,"

"You call raping her, having his friends rape her not violent?" Reyansh roared

"I know and we feel so guilty, thinking of ourselves…"

At that moment they heard a car drive up, and when Reyansh looked out of the curtain, saw that a police car had come to drop Khushboo. He quickly went to open the door to find that Khushboo was just standing outside, trembling, and when she saw Reyansh quickly went into his arms and started sobbing.

"Oh Reyansh, poor Olga, it was all my fault."

"No, it was not." Reyansh gently took her elbow and took her into the lounge, where all three ladies hugged and cried.

"I think we all need tea, which I will make." He disappeared into the kitchen and came back with a tray with three mugs of tea and a bowl of sugar. "I suggest that even if you don't take sugar, do so now for you have had quite a shock."

After some time, Sameera asked in a small voice, "So what happened, do you know? Alexie was supposed to be away."

"Yes, he was but he came home unexpectedly and found her with a friend, another Russian girl and went ballistic. Then he found my card in her coat, and when he saw that I was a lawyer, thought she was going to leave him! And when she said no, she was not, demanded to see me/ The friend had in the meantime called the police".

"Didn't he know that she worked for you so would have your card?"

"He was so blind with rage; he was not thinking rationally. Anyway, I went, hoping to defuse the situation, but froze when I opened the door, for there stood Alexei, a man who was more than six foot tall, all muscle and boiling rage, holding our tiny Olga by her throat with his forearm and crushing it!"

"Oh my god! Couldn't the police do anything?"

"He held a gun to her head and threatened to shoot Olga if anyone came near. Poor thing, Olga; s eyes were popping out of their sockets, wide with terror! Her small hands clawed at his arms, looking at me in terror, her eyes pleading for help. She was gasping for air, her delicate legs thrashing against his strong thighs, but Alexei stood like a man made of rock, holding his wife by the throat, a girl who was so tiny and fragile that she was no threat to him!"

"Oh, that is awful!" Ekta put her hand over her mouth in horror

"That is not all Ekta, looked at me and said nobody leaves him and when I tried to tell him that she was not going to, he just looked at me with wyes that were wild and said, "so why does she have your card if not to leave me?" He had tightened his hold on her jerking her off the ground and snarled "nobody leaves me!"

"What were the police doing, could they not free her or something?" Sameera kept repeating. "They are supposed to help that is what they are trained to do in these kinds of situations.".

"No, the closer they got, the tighter became his hold on her." Khushboo was sobbing as she relived the horrible situation. "In fact, he held her so tightly that when she stopped struggling, he just tossed her on the floor like a bag of flour than stepped over her, saying that she was not pure Russian anyway and that is where she belonged!" Khushboo put her hands over her eyes. "She died protecting us and I let her down, she whispered." I ran over to her, but it was too late, he had strangled her, right in front of my eyes, and neither me, nor the police could do anything to help her!!

"Ekta went over to her and took her hands in hers.

"Khushboo, if the police could not do anything, nor could you so please don't blame yourself, now I have made some rice and mutton curry, have something to eat, you will feel better."

"Nothing for me, Ekta, but look after Mum, she has had too many shocks today, see that she eats something."

"No Khushboo, I don't think I can eat either."

When she saw the confused expression on Ekta's face, she added "Mum will explain, I just need to be on my own."

"Maybe it is best we leave her alone, we are all feeling so bad, can you imagine having to witnessing the murder of one of your friends?" Ekta shuddered then led them to the dining room.

"Wow this looks nice, Ekta, you have been busy." Reyansh remarked as Ekta took out a bowl and rice dish that she had found amongst the cutlery in the mahogany table and served the riced and mutton curry in them.

They ate in silence, Sameera occasionally wiping her eyes with the napkin when Khushboo walked in and saw her crying.

"Oh, Mum have you told Ekta and Reyansh about Dad and what he has done?"

"No, I have not Khushboo, that is not something I want to have broadcasted and is trivial to what happened to dear Olga."

"No Mum I did not mean that, it is just I think Reyansh might be able to help, and you need Ekta by your side!" Khushboo sat on an empty chair. "We have learned one lesson today; that it is no good waiting, never know what the morrow will bring."

"Right, Khushboo, I noticed for some time that there was something on your mind, not everything to do with Olga. Now how can I help?"

"Thank you, Ekta, but I think it might be too late for that." Khushboo had put some rice on her plate and was drawing patterns on it with her fork and repeated what she had told Sameera earlier.

"What a scumbag! Sameera what a day it has been for you two!" Reyansh exclaimed.

"It most certainly has, but I feel sorry for Khushboo, carrying the burden of her father's deception alone so as to not hurt me. Olga too died protecting me and I am not worth it!"

Yes, you are, Mum, I only told you because I felt you needed to know, we were both calling him when it is clear he wants nothing to do with us. Anyway, the financial aspect is all sorted out"

"Look ladies, I suggest you sleep here tonight, it will not only be nice to process this together, I also don't trust Alexei's friends, Khushboo they will be blaming you for Alexei's arrest."

Khushboo thought it to be a good idea, for they could not bear to go into the house that Olga had so lovingly looked after for them.

Considering the delay to be on her side to find somewhere safe for her, resulted in Olga's tragic end, she thought the first thing she would do was to look up the tenant of Mr. Sharma.

Chapter 86

Dhruv had got up the following day with a smile, for he had dreamt about Khushboo, hoping she had liked the flowers he had sent. As he rubbed his back, he hoped he could lodge with his friend soon, for although Aadrika meant well, the sofa cum bed was not comfortable; in addition, he was finding it difficult to cope with her fluctuating moods.

It was still early, but he could hear movement in the kitchen, and when he entered, hoping to meet Aarush, found that Aadrika was sitting on the table, her eyes shadowed in dark circles from lack of sleep.

"Hi Aadrika, you look like you have not had a good night's sleep! Is everything alright?" Dhruv poured some coffee into his mug and brought it over to the table.

"What do you think Dhruv I am being evicted from my house, have no money have to look after a son...do you want me to go on?" Aadrika answered tersely then put her head in her hands, then got up from her chair, wiping her cheeks and opened a drawer and took out a knife.

"Hey Aadrika, what are you doing! Put that down!" Dhruv looked alarmed.

"I took it from a drawer that has spoons tin openers meat skewers knives and cleavers! I like this knife because it is sharp!" Aadrika took the knife to the sink, ran water over it then reached for teacloth and wiped the blade, taking care not to touch edge then turning it over.

"Aadrika give the knife to me!"

"Why? You have your fancy woman to go to, Aarush has his friends, no one needs me!"

Aadrika ran the knife down her forearm, then dropped the bloody knife on the floor as the blood from arm dripped in deep red drops onto the kitchen floor.

"Oh, don't look so worried, Dhruv, it is just a small cut, you don't really care, anyway, I better get dressed to go to office?"

She turned from the doorway looking calm "Did I tell you that my boss has been continuingly phoning me, demanding sex if I cannot make repayment of money, he loaned me just a while ago, or else he will fire me!!" Aadrika wiped the tears from her eyes and ran to her room.

Dhruv was stunned, he knew that Aadrika's mental state had always been fragile, but the episode with the knife had really scared him. But that did not surprise him for he was swamped in problem and was glad he had made an appointment today to see Dr Wilson.

So as soon as Aadrika left for office, Dhruv quicky dressed and took a tube to his hospital.

As he sat in a seat in the train, he looked around and saw the people on the train all had faraway expression that one usually sees on faces of regular travellers.

He got down at the underground station near the hospital and since he was early walked slowly. Having arrived near he saw a lot of people outside the hospital talking amongst themselves, there were paramedics, doctors and nurses Everyone was rushing around looking tired, their eyes flitting and sliding about.

After he had got directions to Dr. Wilson's office from reception, Dhruv walked through a corridor, passing people standing outside glass panelled rooms, hoping to catch a glimpse of their relatives or friends, some of whom were lying on beds attached to bleeping equipment's, others who were heavily sedated with intravenous drips that had been inserted in their arm.

Dhruv stopped outside a door with the name Dr. Wilson, Psychiatrist on it and knocked, and as soon as he heard 'come in' opened the door and entered.

Dr. Wilson stood up with a smile, shook his hand, and gestured towards a chair. "I am glad you have come to see me. I was afraid you might not think it to be urgent." Dr. Wilson sat on his swivel chair, leant back and chewed a pencil.

"Look Doctor, I am confused, at the restaurant you told me that you had helped bring my son into this world, but I find that you are actually a psychiatrist so that in itself is not true to start with!"

"I am sorry about misleading you, but after the birth of your son, I was called to access your wife."

"But why? And why did you now feel that it was necessary to talk to me urgently?"

"You mentioned that your son and wife were fine, so why have you come to see me?"

"Well, Aadrika has been acting very strangely recently, but that may be because she was conned recently and was told to evict her flat…I mean, where is she going to go with a son to look after?"

Tell me, have you seen your son since your return?"

"No, Doctor, I have not, but he is always busy. He spends time at his friend's house, so he comes late and is picked up by Aadrika's friend whilst Aadrika goes to work. But look Doctor, why are you asking me these questions?"

"Because your son died at birth, Dhruv, and I was called in when there were complications as to her mental health. Your wife was distraught with grief, convinced it to be her fault when she found out that the child was still born. And she kept repeating that as she could not protect someone named Darpan, so she was responsible for her son's death. We thought that when she had been discharged from hospital, she would come to terms with it, but it seems that she has been carrying on the illusion of her son being alive, looking after him sending him to school etc?"

"Yes, but..." Dhruv said in a shocked voice.

"Has anyone seen the boy?"

Dhruv remembered his conversation with Anil. "No, no one. I am his father, yet she always has an excuse for his absence. And now that you mention it, even after we came home from hospital after his birth, she would not let me near him, in fact that was the reason we broke up, for she was spending all her time with Aarush in his room and ignoring me. Oh my God! But what I cannot understand is, why didn't the doctor tell me? I am her husband, and he was my son!" Dhruv had tears in his eyes.

"I wanted to, but the hospital only consulted me once, but reading her file, I was concerned, for she had not got over the death of Darpan, and suddenly having to face another loss was too much for her. Had I stayed on the case, I would have suggested that you be told of this,"

"If not you, at least the nurses should have told me, how does one pretend to take an invisible baby out of the hospital?"

"I agree but women like Aadrika are very clever at deception, and no doubt she told the nurses she was fine and would tell you in her own way. At that time, I had thought her to be at border line of mental illness. But if you are telling me that she thinks Aarush is still alive, and acts that he is, then, that is worrying, and it looks like she may be suffering from delusional disorder. Delusional disorder is a type of serious mental illness and people who suffer from it can't tell what is real from what is imagined.

I don't know who Darpan was to her, but it seems she was very attached to him, and blames herself for his death., In her mind, she is validating her guilt by keeping Darpan alive in Aarush..."

"That sounds serious, and now I remember, when we got home from the hospital, she wanted to name the baby Darpan, I should have sensed something was wrong for I was the one who helped her get over the death of Darpan., he was a boy she was very fond and protective of, someone she considered to be like her brother. Even I was taken in, in more ways than one! But why was I not told of this by the hospital, and that being the case, why were no outpatients follow-up appointments made for her?"

"I am afraid I cannot answer that, like I said, I only saw her once, voiced my concern to the doctor, who since, I believe has left the hospital which could be the reason of no follow-up appointments being arranged. But she must have a GP who would have seen that something was wrong."

"Yes, she does, and told me that he had recommended her to a counsellor, and she did go once, but that as it was too painful, so thought that she could manage herself. And here I was thinking she was independent and strong, working, looking after the house and bills on top of having to look after a young boy!" Dhruv ran his hands through his hair

"I suggest you contact your GP at once." "

"But Doctor I think it is much more than her just being delusional," Dhruv explained the incident that morning with the knife and her jealous and altering moods that he had witnessed in the last few days.

As soon as Dhruv finished, the doctor immediately picked up his phone, spoke into it for a while, then after he had finished, explained that he would be contacting her GP who would be in touch immediately.

He rose and when he saw Dhruv's downcast face, held out his hand. "Look, I know you don't think but we have caught this in time and don't worry, we will look after her. In the meantime, continue as before, that you believe Aarush is alive and well."

"Poor thing, I have been pushing to meet him, that must have contributed to all the other problems."

Chapter 87

Dhruv walked back slowly, his mind in a daze. He had not met Aarush, but he had always liked the thought of having a son. He had never in his wildest dreams thought that he was a figment of Aadrika's imagination. He had heard of children having invisible friends, people who created multiple personalities internally to escape some kind of trauma, but Aadrika? He shook his head in bewilderment, she seemed and behaved so normally, at the most, he had thought of Aadrika as being an overprotective mother and recently, of fragile mental state.

As he walked back down the corridor, he passed the people who had been waiting for a long time for news of their loved ones, their face tired and tense with an occasional cry of either compassion or pity.

Before going home, he walked around for a while wondering how people were going around normally, shopping taking late lunch's meeting friends whilst he felt his world was crashing around him! Hoping that the fresh air would clear his mind,.

By the time he took the underground to Aadrika's flat, it was evening, and he waited on the platform, looking at the evening exodus of bowler hatted civil servants that were also waiting for a train. Finally, a train arrived, and he managed to get a seat next to a young boy wearing a baseball cap that was perched on the top of his head and wearing a black hooded top with jeans that hung halfway way down his backside.

How could Aadrika have carried on the charade of Aarush being alive and well for so long? She had convinced everyone that she had a son He had not met Anika, who, Aadrika told him, looked after Aarush. But when he had asked her about Anika, was told that she had moved in with her mother and did not have a phone. Most probably, after staying with Aadrika for only a day, found out there was nobody named Aarush,

The train halted at his stop, so he quickly stepped out of the carriage and walked out of the station, walking slowly, wondering how he was going to handle the situation. He wondered if racism was part of the reason of her breakdown, for she had slipped through the system, both at the care home and at the hospital.

Aadrika had told him that after he left, women had belittled her for being a single mother. She had naively thought that the women only wanted to meet Aarush to criticize his upbringing, but he was sure they suspected there was no child. That stigma, and the discrimination she had faced all her life, the sexual harassment she faced, and the stress of the lockdown, must have contributed towards worsening her mental health problems?

They had trapped Aadrika in a cycle of mental illness. which in turn had delayed or stopped her getting help. Added to which was the social isolation she had faced due to lockdown. Dhruv felt a twinge of guilt because he too had abandoned her, not only that, but he had also contributed in a big way to her feeling insecure.

He was so busy in his thoughts that he was oblivious to the people walking past, the cars passing on the street, people walking on the pavement, however, strangely, he could not ignore the smell of diesel dirt and grease mingled with greasy takeaway food.

He took out his mobile to ring Aadrika if he should get a takeaway, but before he could do so, the phone rang and was surprised to hear the soft and husky voice of Khushboo

Khushboo cleared her throat and said softly. "Hello, Dhruv." "Hi Khushboo," Dhruv smiled slightly, his heart beating fast, thinking that this was the best thing that had happened to him today.

"Dhruv, I am near the vicinity of the restaurant we went to last time, and I have had such terrible news that I need a relaxing evening, so thought of you."

"Of course, you know I would love that, I just have to take care of something, and I will meet you at the Chinese restaurant next to the Indian restaurant, we went to last time, how is that? In another hour?"

"Perfect, but first I have to see a client of mine and, oh thank you for the flowers!"

"I am glad you liked them, Khushboo, I will see you there."

Khushboo was glad she had phoned Dhruv and arranged to meet him in the evening for the last couple of days her thoughts had been veering between her father's deception and poor Olga who had trusted her and, in the process, got killed by her husband.

As she drove to Mr Sharma's property she recalled the previous day's events, then slowed as she neared the property.

She looked in the rear window before parking, then placed her left hand back on the wheel and used her right hand to turn off the ignition before cautiously lifting her foot from the brake pedal

But before getting out she brushed her hair, applied some lipstick and picking up her briefcase got out of the car. She was professionally dressed in tailored conservative black trousers with a black jacket over a frilly white blouse and tan coat draped over arm was a tan coat, her makeup, as usual was subtle and she had a scarf tied loosely around her neck.

She ran up the few steps and rang the bell that chimed in an old-fashioned tone, and after a few minutes, the door was opened by a woman who stood in the doorway, her eyes wide with groggy terror as she saw Khushboo.

"Why have you come to my house, do you want to kill me so Dhruv will be with you?"

Khushboo looked at her, confused and shocked, not only at the woman's appearance, but that she had mentioned Dhruv. Who was she and how did she know him?

"Look, I don't know what you are talking about! I have come only because Mr. Sharma, your landlord, came to me to see if I could help you find a home."

Aadrika looked at her closely, then calmed down when she saw that the woman standing opposite her was Anil's daughter or someone who looked like her.

"Oh, Oh I am sorry, I don't know what came over me, come in." Aadrika said calmy, her manner changing.

"Thank you." Khushboo replied.

She followed her, perplexed at the strange behaviour of the woman in front of her. No wonder her landlord had seemed concerned, though she now thought it to be more a case for Social Services.

"Mr. Sharma asked you to help me?" Aadrika asked. She stepped back and slumped against the door as her eyebrows gathered in a frown.

"Yes, he did, but if I may ask, you looked terrified when you opened the door. Is someone harassing you?"

"Yes, my boss, he lent me some money and now he sends thugs around who knock the door and then disappear. And every day at work, he just stands and stares at me!"

Suddenly her manner changed, and she looked slyly at her. "I thought you looked like the daughter of a friend of mine, Anil, he has left to go to India and taken all my money with him…!"

Khushboo looked at her, shocked, who was this lady, first Dhruv now her father? But Mr. Sharma had told her that his tenant had been duped by her friend, had her father done the same thing to this lady and what was her relationship to him?

"How did you know this man, Anil? Your landlord said your rent had not been paid for the last three months because your friend had not done so? You trusted him?"

"Oh yes, I thought he was a decent man. We worked in the same office so he would come to my house first thing in the morning, we would have breakfast then go to work together. I was too busy looking after my young son, so he offered to pay all the bills and rent, and it was only after he left that I found out that he had not only not paid the bills and rent but had taken the salary that had come into my account."

"How did he do that? Surely the account and card were in your name?"

"Yes, you are right, they are, and that was my fault, I had gone to see him off at the airport, and it was there that he asked if he could borrow my card to take out a few pounds that he might need on the journey, how could I refuse, how was I to know that he would empty my account?"

Chapter 88

Khushboo was stunned and angry, then gradually she began to feel sorry for her, but she felt responsible for her too. It was one thing deceiving them for he knew Khushboo was independent and had a job, but to do that to a single woman with a son to look after was despicable! No wonder the woman seemed unstable, and on top of everything, she was having to cope with sexual harassment at work! She was glad that she had decided to visit her as soon as possible.

Khushboo sat silently fuming, trying to turn her emotion of cold fury into anger, thinking that it to be a safer emotion than fear which she had felt when she first saw Aadrika and had heard the cruel edge to her voice.

But although she thought Aadrika had calmed down, she saw her looking at her slyly, an odd look in her eyes., and the look sent a shiver down her spine,

Aadrika had explained about her relationship with her father and thought Khushboo was a woman who looked like his daughter. If that had such an effect on her, what would she do to her if she found out that she really was? She also wanted to know about her relationship with Dhruv, but that she could ask him Dhruv later.

Abruptly, Aadrika came and sat beside her looking at her so intensely that it made Khushboo uncomfortable.

"I have to meet a friend so think I better leave." Khushboo stood up and Aadrika stood up too.

"You are the woman who was in the restaurant with Dhruv!" She exclaimed suddenly. "

"Yes, we did go out once, I did not know you knew him?"

Aadrika's manner changed, and she snarled "He is my husband."

She paused and her voice dropped to a whisper but suddenly, with surprising speed Aadrika grabbed Khushboo's wrist and jerked her off balance leaving Khushboo wide eyed with shock and from then on everything became a blur.

Aadrika seized Khushboo's scarf around her neck from behind, and Khushboo, shocked by the force of attack by a woman she had come to help, flung up her arm defensively and twisted her head for breadth, stunned into silence. Whilst on her tongue she felt the bitter acid tang of fear, was one single thought piercing through fog of confusion in her mind Why me?'

Khushboo's neck was clamped in the crook of Aadrika's arm, and she gasped for air, but as the hold was too strong, could not push her arm away so turned her face aside. Khushboo fell between the table and sofa and turned to escape, but Aadrika grabbed her by the ankle and gave it a vivacious twist as Khushboo fell on her hands and knees. Her head hit backward and with a thud, struck the radiator behind her.

Aadrika first grabbed Khushboo's head then forced her down to the floor. She grabbed her hair whilst pressing down on her tugging and viciously at her hair, whilst Khushboo tried to manoeuvre herself into a sitting position by bringing her knees up, trying to avoid being pinned down on the floor.

"Let me go, why are you attacking me, I only came to help you!" Khushboo cried as she looked into Aadrika's wildcat eyes. She tried to turn her neck, but it was trapped and, she looked at Aadrika in terror, her eyes wide, her vision had become so blurred that she had to blink hard.

Finally, somehow Khushboo managed to push Aadrika away and dragged herself free She got off her knees and stepped clear of Aadrika who had fallen in the fight and stepped over her arms, rushed out of the room and was running towards the door when Dhruv entered, for he had decided to come to Aadrika's flat to change before his date with Khushboo,

"Hey, Khushboo, what are you doing here, oh my God, what happened?"

Dhruv, seeing her dishevelled appearances and the scratches on her face, opened the door wide and as he tried to usher Khusboo out of the kitchen, Aadrika came out brandishing a knife.

"I knew it! She wants to kill me and wants you to herself!"

Dhruv was shaken, not only at the sight of Aadrika, but that she had attacked Khushboo. He put a comforting arm around Khushboo,

"Don't worry, I am here now, you are safe, go outside." He whispered as Khushboo sobbed uncontrollably

"No Dhruv, she wants to kill me, I don't know why but she wants to kill me." She took a deep breath then tremulously asked, "but she said she was your wife?"

"I will explain later, did you say she tried to kill you?"

"Yes! You saw the knife she held in her hand! She looked at me with such frenzy that I got afraid and wanted to leave, but she would not let me, repeating over and over that I had come to kill her and take you away from her!" She recalled Aadrika, her cheeks red, and her eyes shining with rage and fury.

"She is right, but I will explain everything, here take my keys and sit in my car but for now I need to ring a doctor."

Aadrika meanwhile alternated between pacing the living room and rocking herself in Aarush's room, calling out his name, imagining him talking to a father he did not know. That woman had come to take Aarush's father from him, and she could not let that happen. They were all in it together, Mr Sharma, Dhruv, Anil William and now his daughter!

It was as if her whole body felt hollowed out by the bright white light of a blast and she was now a shell of her former self, as if she was out of her body floating above herself watching everything happen to someone else.

She sat perfectly still, as if by doing so nobody would see her. Her head was in a daze and had gone to a place that was numb and distant where she was dying crying yearning and full of sadness.

She felt Aarush was trying to escape from his room, so she tried to lock his room, but she felt that he kept wedging his foot in the door. Finally, she opened the door and went in and felt terrified when she saw that his eyes had become great dark holes that were trying to devour her, trying to kill her.

"Aarush, I am your mother, do not hurt me!" she cried.

His face had turned purple, his mouth became an open dark saucer that was letting out noise like an air raid siren, she tried to get away, but he was after her in an instant, so she ran out of the room and into the kitchen, got a knife and brandished it at him.

And that is how Dr. Wilson and Dhruv found Aadrika, brandishing a knife, eyes looking crazy, face swollen and blotchy as she let out an ugly blood curdling scream that was so loud that it reached Khushboo's ears in the car and frightened her.

Dr Wilson's eyes were full of compassion, and he spoke firmly and patiently as he held out his hand and walked towards her.

"Aadrika, what are you doing with that knife? Give it to me now and come with me."

"Where are you taking me?" Aadrika asked, narrowing her eyes suspiciously.

"To a hospital where you will be looked after."

"What about Aarush? Who is going to look after him, doctor?" she whispered. "But he is trying to kill me so maybe it is better I go with you."

"Yes, it is and don't worry we will look after him too..."

As the doctor led her out of the flat, she looked back, blew a kiss and waved and was then led to an ambulance that was standing outside the flat.

Dhruv stayed back to talk to the doctor then, after shaking hands with him, walked towards his car, running his hand through his hair in perplexity. He opened the door and as soon as he got in said.

"Right let's take you to that restaurant we spoke about."

"No Dhruv, I don't want to eat anything, I want to go home." Khushboo cried, still in complete and total shock.

"Khushboo, you need to eat something, you have been through a terrible ordeal." His fingers cradled her head as his thumbs stroked her cheeks till, she was calm

"Not like this you are not!" Dhruv said firmly. "Anyway, I need to explain my part in all this. Oh, I don't think either of should drive, we'll walk, the restaurant is not far from here, and the fresh air will do us good too."

They walked in silence, and Khushboo's wiped her teary and burning eyes with the back of her hand.

As soon as they reached the restaurant, they were shown to their seats and seeing Khushboo's pallor, Dhruv asked the waiter to get them coffee A.S.A.P and as soon as it had arrived and Khushboo had taken a sip, Dhruv asked

"Now, Khushboo what were you doing in Aadrika's flat?"

Khushboo explained how she had come to see her client's tenant, who he had requested to find accommodation for as she was being evicted. He had felt sorry for her, being a single mum with a son, and then being scammed by a friend she trusted.

"And that man, Dhruv, she said was no other than my father, Anil."

"Anil is your father?" Dhruv asked in surprise.

"Yes, but how do you fit in all this?"

"Khushboo, I am not proud of my part in all of this but the least I can do is be honest. We knew each other at the care home and when we left were married and had a son... But we separated and Aadrika took my son from me, and would not let me see him, and finally, she told me to get out of the house!" Dhruv ran his fingers through his hair.

He told her everything leaving nothing out even his plan with Anil "So, according to plan, I was at the airport, and we got along so well that she even invited me to live at her flat till I found somewhere, but my plan was to be close to my son."

Dhruv had insisted she eat so she had ordered Caesar salad for herself whilst Dhruv ordered a steak, which when it came, smelled good beefy and rich. "We'll order chips separately; I was not sure you would like some."

And when she nodded, pointed to the waiter and asked him to add them to their order. During the course of the dinner, Dhruv explained that Aadrika had no son called Aarush. Dr. Wilson, the man who had approached him at their previous date. He had told him that his son had been born stillborn, but Aadrika had not accepted the fact, so, the hospital had called in a psychiatrist.

"I had always thought her to be naïve and mentally fragile because she was so sensitive, but never did I think that she could deceive everyone into believing that she had a son who was alive and well! I mean, I did not realise that one could spend your whole life looking at people you loved in a tilted way, as if you knew there was something in them you did not like but were trying to ignore or were deliberately blurring your vision to; until something like this happens and just looking at that person is terrifying!"

"I know exactly how you feel, for I would never have expected anything like this from my father. I mean my father has erred on so many levels that he seems to have layers and layers of immoral acts. Deceit betrayal, infidelity! And I apologise on his behalf in his part in all this, but has Aadrika been violent before?"

"No that is what is so bizarre, when I spoke to the doctor just now, he said it may be the result of the stress of losing everything, your father scamming her, being evicted, sexually harassed at work, and the lockdown that finally tipped her over the edge. And keeping up the charade of having a non-existent son could not have been easy, at least not with me there every day asking when I could see my son. And I am guilty in this, if only I had left her alone."

Although Khushboo was shocked at his behaviour, he was being honest with her, and for that she respected him.

Dhruv took out a packet of cigarettes, lit it with his lighter than sat taking quick shallow puffs.

"But I am going to make it up to her in whichever way I can, starting with that employer of hers who has been harassing her at work"

"You are not the only one in overlooking something or not acting on time. I neglected to act on time for a client of mine with the result that it ended with her husband killing her, and he did that in front of me." Seeing Dhruv's puzzled expression, she explained what had happened to Olga.

"But in my case, aside from the satisfaction that he is safely behind bars, there is nothing I can do but live with the fact that I albeit unintentionally, caused another's death. Oh, Dhruv you would have liked her, she was so sweet and naïve!" She wiped her eyes with the back of her hand.

Chapter 89

"But why didn't you tell me you were married, Dhruv?" Khushboo asked.

A piece of chip was poised on her fork and was an inch from her lips but most of the salad was untouched on her plate.

"I was going to, Khushboo, meeting you has been the best thing that has happened to me and only after meeting you once, I feel I am a changed man, I was a cad before." He smiled wryly "And I was going to tell you today anyway."

"Dhruv, you said you knew Anil, my father? Do you know he swindled us too, he re-mortgaged our house, did not pay the mortgage for the last three months surrendered his insurance policy, cleared out his account and transferred all the money to India! And left me to deal with the mess." She said wryly.

Dhruv took her hand that was lying on the table and brought it to his lips.

"I am so sorry, I was not aware that he was planning to do that to his family too, I would never have encouraged him to con his own family. I have not had one so consider family to be priceless!"

Khushboo sighed, withdrew her hand and wiped her lips with her napkin. They sat in silence for a while, the smoke coiling lazily between them. Dhruv took another puff from his cigarette then flicked the ash on the tray.

"I better ring up the doctor to find out how she is." Dhruv took out his mobile from his jeans pocket whilst Khushboo went to freshen up before she went home. When she returned to their table, he was putting the mobile back in his pocket, a frown between his eyes.

"Is everything alright Dhruv? How is she?" Khushboo asked as she sat on hr chair.

"She is fine, well she is not really, they had to tell her that there is no Aarush, that he was born stillborn and as she could not face the truth, has retreated into a trance."

"Did they have to tell her? But at least she is in the right place now and will get the right treatment."

"Where she should have been given a long time ago, when my son was born, so she could have got the right treatment then! Anyway, let me drop you home, you must still be in shock after the way she attacked you."

"Yes, it was a shock and the last thing I expected! Dhruv, but you do not have to drop me I have the car so will drive, anyway, my house is not far from here."

"Khushboo, I insist, it was because of me she attacked you, so yes, I do feel responsible."

Khushboo did not have the energy to argue so agreed and as the streets were deserted, and Khushboo's house was nearby, they arrived in 10 minutes. But instead of leaving her at the door, Dhruv insisted that he wait to see her safely in.

Sameera opened the door and gave a cry when she saw the state her daughter was in for although Khushboo had freshened up, she could not hide her torn clothes that showed through her jacket.

"Khushboo what has happened to you?"

Seeing the worried look on her face, Dhruv quickly introduced himself. "Khushboo is fine now, but she was attacked by my ex."

"Thank you for saving my daughter, yes she has told me about you. Come in, I insist."

"Yes, come in Dhruv Mum we could do with a cup of tea, and I will quickly go change." She ran up to her room, washed her face with cold water, brushed her hair and changed into leggings and a loose beige top.

As she went downstairs, she heard the voices of her mother and Ekta, and as soon as she entered, her mother got up and hugged her. She wondered if Dhruv had told her mother about her father's relationship with his wife, Aadrika and when she looked at Dhruv he shook his head then turned to her mother

. "Thank you for the cup of tea, I think Khushboo needs it more than I do." He rose to leave when Khushboo insisted he stay. "I want to tell mother everything and want you to be here."

As Dhruv sat down again, Khushboo curled on the sofa and with a steaming mug of tea in her hands, explained the situation, leaving nothing out. When Dhruv saw the shocked look on Sameera's face, he tried to explain.

"I need to make amends for my part in all this!" Dhruv looked vulnerable and ashamed... "it was as if it was not enough that Aadrika was dealing with racism and sexual harassment at work, now I find out that she was neglected by the health system too! Not only are ethnic people getting Covid 19, but they are also being ignored by the mental health and social services!"

"Yes, but there is something we can do, Dhruv we can file a case against William, Aadrika's boss and if you want, the doctors too, there are policies in place to protect people."

"William, maybe, but everything else happened a long time ago, I think it is the care home that are mainly responsible, that is where we were first discriminated against. And I should have seen something was wrong for Aadrika kept talking of how the atmosphere there frightened her, so much so that she still had nightmares about it. She put down her nightmares to the death of George Floyd that had sparked of the subject of racism and how it affected people and I agreed with her."

At first, Sameera and Ekta had been wary of Dhruv in his leather jacket and boots, ponytail and the stud in his ear, and the silence at first had lain heavy between them.

However, he had soon charmed them and although Sameera would not have picked someone like him for her daughter, she could see that he made her happy and although he was married, he had been honest about everything, and when he said he would not abandon his wife when she was ill, both Ekta and Sameera thought it to be a noble gesture.

Epilogue

Every year a rally was held marking the anniversary of the death of George Floyd and as she had the previous year, Khushboo was making sure she showed her support by attending it this year too... But she couldn't help wondering if a protest really changed anything, for racism, especially in cricket, was still flourishing, or maybe a protest was only meant to be symbolic? But they did help in raising awareness and concerns around the issue of racism, its traumatic impact on its victims.in addition, they united people in their fight against any form of discrimination.

Unfortunately, although most people were aware that it existed, they pretended they lived in a society in which, if they followed its rules, they would be content. They believed if they closed their eyes, injustice and unfairness in the world would not exist.

However, by holding rallies and protests, and by keeping the name of George Floyd and how he had died alive in the minds of people, helped raise awareness that discrimination and injustice did exist.

As she drove to the place where the rally was to be held, Khushboo thought of the previous year. Although she dealt with cases of racism and domestic violence in her line of work, it felt as if it was only in the previous year that Khushboo had realized how deep-seated racism really was and its impact and the trauma it left in its wake.

The year had also exposed her father's deception, for he had scammed them of their money them gone to India, leaving Khushboo to deal with the debts he left behind Although the thought that he was having an affair had crossed her mind, it had not occurred to her that he had a mistress, Aadrika, living in London. Khushboo frowned as she recalled Aadrika's maniac behaviour and cringed when she thought that her father's treatment of her had facilitated it!

One day, Aadarsh, called on them and told them that Covind-19 had been spreading so fast in India that her father had contracted it but unfortunately had not recovered. Her mother had been devastated, for despite the dishonest manner he had left them, she still loved him.

The only good things that happened in the last year was the marriage of Ekta and Reyansh and her relationship with Dhruv. The chemistry between them was still strong and although they enjoyed each other's company, neither spoke of the future, However, Dhruv had been forthright with her and that he did not want to divorce Aadrika when she was ill and that he would try and fulfil his duty as a husband., even it only meant visiting so she did not feel abandoned. On the other hand, he had assured Khushboo that he would not get back with Aadrika as they were now separated by something too great and vast ever to be crossed! Khushboo had smiled, for the more she had got to know Dhruv, the more she understood and respected him, and they spent many happy evenings at her house

One evening, they had been relaxing in her house after his weekly visit to the hospital, when she asked him about Aadrika.

"I spoke to the doctor, Khushboo and he told me that everyone's journey through grief is different, and that Aadrika had not got over the death of Darpan when she had to deal with the loss of her son".

Dhruv had tears in his eyes and looked so vulnerable, her heart had gone out to him as she realised that he too must be grieving for his son.

Thereafter, she was careful she gave him space to work through his grief, so meanwhile, Khushboo had decided to sell their house and move to a smaller house with her Mum. But Ekta after finding out about Anil, had insisted that Sameera live with them, soon after she heard the news that her sister and Khushboo's close friend, Aishya, in trying to uncover the truth of what was happening in Afghanistan, had been caught in crossfire and consequently died. She had always thought of Sameera as a sister, so, it was but natural she would her keep her close so they could grieve together.

Khushboo, too, had been heart-broken, for she had been looking forward to her return as, together, both she and Ekta had finally convinced Aiysha to leave her job as a political journalist and her assignment is Afghanistan was to be her last.

She had become sensitive to the pain of others, realising that Ekta had Reyansh for support, she had Dhruv, and after seeing Aadrika and the trauma of facing grief alone she was worried about how her mother would cope, but when she saw how sincerely Ekta and Reyansh loved and looked after her, she was relieved and grateful…

Darkness had come slowly till the faint light of the receding sun had coated buildings roads, parks, and even the people who had collected for the rally were being merged into a shaded Gray of the dusk.

As she parked the car and walked over to their meeting place, Khushboo spotted Dhruv and smiled fondly for, he was dressed in his characteristic attire, a white shirt over black jeans, leather jacket and motorcycle boots, with his hair tied back in a ponytail and stud in his ear...

When Khushboo had mentioned to Isabella the effect that sexual harassment had on Aadrika, she had been horrified and personally made up a case against William for sexual harassment at work, and she had been so determined that she had won the case.

William's wife, Mary, too had come to Reyansh's organisation for help to escape from her violent husband, and her testimony had not only been helpful in winning the case, but she also had, at last found the courage to leave William, Emma too, a colleague of Aadrika's, had testified to his conduct with her.

Khushboo often wondered why things had ended so tragically for Olga, and had no doubt it was due to her, and she felt so deeply about it that she had nightmares about that day. The experiences of the previous year, death of her father and Aiysha, combined with the guilt she felt about Olga, had seasoned her. She now understood what Dhruv was going through, for, alongside their chemistry, they had 'guilt' in common. She was guilty for her part of Olga's murder however, unintentional whilst Dhruv felt guilty about his conduct with Aadrika, which, he felt was partly to blame for driving her to the brink of insanity.

As Khushboo walked towards Dhruv, she stood for a while, her cream trench coat pulled in tightly at the waist, her hair tied back in a ponytail that swung jauntily, wondering what road she had taken that had led her here? A path which she had journeyed on and where, along the way she had been the victim of betrayal, deceit, loss, seen madness and pain in minds that had been shattered because of racism and discrimination.

But having experienced the aftermath of infidelity and betrayal, Khushboo did not want to bury the experiences and lessons she had learnt. However, she now believed that either inside the home or outside, there were areas that were kept clear by men or those in power to accommodate enclosures; that they kept close and empty, waiting for occupants who were of marginal groups so they could be confined in them.

Therefore, to get justice for the victims, Khushboo thought the people should be willing to raise their voice, and be strong to challenge those in power, people who built tall gates made of steel to subdue those very voices.

But, as soon as the powerful felt the voices were becoming louder and clearer, the taller the gate became. This ensured that the lives and minds of the victims remain suspended in uncertainty, and when the victims felt they were not being heard, in despair, would wrap their grief around them like a layer of cling film.

The end

www.ingramcontent.com/pod-product-compliance
Lightning Source LLC
Chambersburg PA
CBHW060858120626
46553CB00001B/125